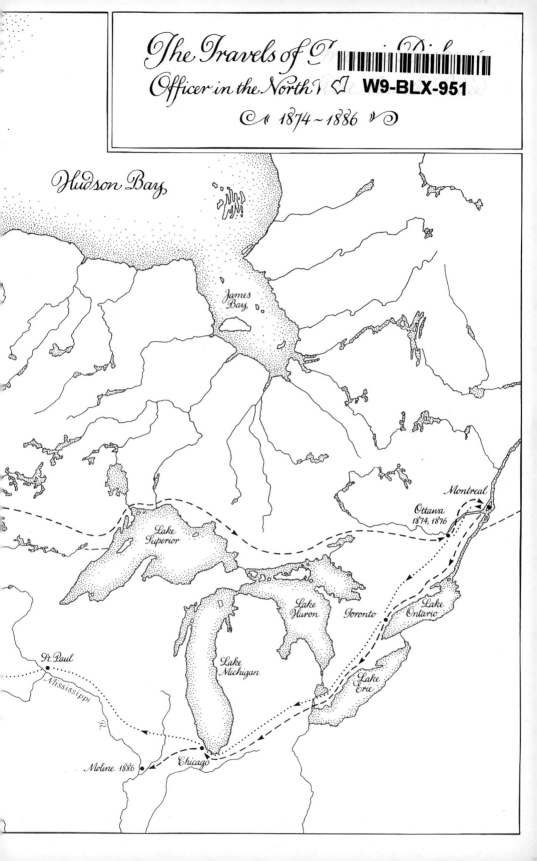

The Travels of [...] Officer in the North W[est] 1874~1886

Hudson Bay

James Bay

Montreal

Ottawa
1874, 1876

Lake
Superior

Lake
Huron

Toronto

Lake
Ontario

Lake
Michigan

Lake
Erie

St. Paul

Mississippi

Moline 1886

Chicago

Dickens of the Mounted
from David
Christmas 1993

Dickens of the Mounted

The Astounding Long-Lost Letters of
Inspector F. Dickens NWMP
1874 – 1886

Edited by Eric Nicol

M&S

Canadian Cataloguing in Publication Data

Dickens, Francis, 1844–1886
Dickens of the Mounted

Includes bibliographical references.
ISBN 0-7710-6807-7

1. Dickens, Francis, 1844–1886 – Correspondence.
2. Royal Canadian Mounted Police – History – Anecdotes.   3. Northwest, Canadian – History – 1870–1905 – Anecdotes.*   4. Royal Canadian Mounted Police – Biography.*   5. Police – Prairie Provinces – Correspondence.   I. Nicol, Eric, 1919–   . II. Title.

FC3216.3.D52A4   1989   971.2′02′0924   C89-094122-X
F1060.9.D52A4   1989

Design by Linda Gustafson
Calligraphy and cartography by Jack McMaster
Printed and bound in Canada by Gagné Ltée

A Douglas Gibson Book

McClelland & Stewart Inc.
The Canadian Publishers
481 University Avenue
Toronto, Ontario   M5G 2E9

For all those other unsung Mounties
who did their best

FROM
The Canadian Encyclopedia

Dickens, Francis Jeffrey, NWMP inspector (b at London, Eng 15 Jan 1844; d at Moline, Ill 11 June 1886), third son of Charles Dickens. In 1864, after numerous unsuccessful career starts, Dickens joined the Bengal Mounted Police in India. He returned to England in 1871 and eventually obtained a commission in the NWMP in 1874. His unspectacular career was marked by recklessness, laziness and heavy drinking. He retired in 1886 and died shortly thereafter. Dickens can be blamed for worsening relations between the Blackfoot and the NWMP and for the growing antipathy of the officer cadre toward Englishmen.

David Evans

CONTENTS

~

Francis Jeffrey Dickens, the fifth child of the eminent novelist Charles Dickens, made his entrance in a letter dated January 9, 1844, that his father wrote to his friend Clarkson Stanfield: "p.p.s. We expect, every hour, to have a Baby born here. If anything happens while I am putting this in the envelope, I'll write the sex in large text, outside."[1]

In fact Charles Dickens's third son did not make his appearance till January 15, at the family home at 1 Devonshire Terrace, London. The baby had been eagerly awaited by his father as a merciful end to Mrs. Dickens's distressful pregnancy. Preoccupied with the midwifery of a contract with a new publisher, Charles was heard to observe that he had already made sufficient contribution to England's population. After the event he wrote to a friend: "Kate is all right again, and so, they tell me, is the Baby. But I decline (on principle) to look at the latter object."

The mock disdain soon yielded to enthusiasm for the newborn postscript. "A prodigious blade," he wrote, "and more full of queer tricks than any of his predecessors have been at his time of life." This favourable review of his work was to be almost the last that "Master Frank" was to receive from his father, or indeed from anybody else that mattered.

1. *The Letters of Charles Dickens*, ed. W. Dexter, Nonesuch Series, London, 1938, vol. 1, p. 560.

Two years later Charles Dickens was wryly remarking to his friend John Forster: "Frankey is smaller than ever." The child was one of those neonates whose birth weight is a false indicator of eventual size, and whose lively personality in the cradle may, according to some authorities, be attenuated by toilet-training.

Charles named his new son Francis Jeffrey, after the distinguished Scottish lawyer, author, and critic, co-founder of *The Edinburgh Review* and stalwart admirer of Dickens's work. Lord Jeffrey had godfathered Dickens's tour of Scotland in 1841. He therefore qualified as a literary figure worthy of having one of the sons named after him, an accolade also represented by Alfred D'Orsay Tennyson Dickens (Alley), Edward Bulwer Lytton Dickens (Plorn), Henry Fielding Dickens (Harry), Sydney Smith Haldimand Dickens (Ocean Spectre), Walter Landor Dickens (Young Skull), Charles Jr. Dickens (Charlie), and Chickenstalker – as the father dubbed Frank. Mrs. Chickenstalker is a minor character in Dickens's *The Chimes*, which came out in the year of Frank's birth, 1844. The nickname was not intended to be pejorative, since all of the Dickens children, and the family dog (Timber Doodle), were subject to the wild whims of the writer whose love affair with words amounted to a magnificent obsession.

The one name that Francis was *never* called, apparently, was Francis. Chickenstalker . . . Spim . . . Frankey . . . Frank – such was the progression, though often the child was merely part of the joint farewell concluding a letter from abroad: ". . . my love to the darlings." Some of Frank's later problems – physical and otherwise – may have stemmed from his being whisked from the cradle at the age of six months as the entire Dickens ménage rumbled off to Italy for an extended holiday. (Some Dickens biographers, such as Hastings and Main, have postulated a nutritional link between the baby's being suddenly plunged into pasta and the later afflictions of deafness and stuttering.) More certain is that the Palazzo Peschiere in Genoa provided Frank with a stable infant environment only briefly before that scenery too was

lofted and new sets were dropped into place: Lausanne . . .
Paris . . . Brighton . . . and finally London's Devonshire
Terrace.

Frank had barely adapted to his new room at Tavistock
House before his father dispatched him and his brother
Wally – who also had deaf spells, but improved after being
sent to an aurist – into a private school in Boulogne. This
marked the beginning of an ill-fated series of efforts by Dickens *père* to detach himself from Dickens *fils* with the rationale
that distant educative fields are greener, and less stony in
their academic standards. Yet Dickens did not neglect his
parental duties between terms. As he explained to the Reverend M. Gibson, headmaster of the Villa du Camp de Droites
in Boulogne:

> In returning the two boys I beg to say that I have exer-
> cised Frank in English reading, every morning for some
> weeks past – generally with a good effect on his tendency
> to stutter. I think it would be advantageous to him if he
> could continue this.
>
> As he wants a little strengthening, will you be so kind
> as to give directions for his having a tumbler of bottled
> porter with his dinner every alternate day. And if you
> approve? I wish them both to learn to dance.[2]

Thus Frank was introduced early to alcohol, for its fortify-
ing value – possibly a paternal error. When the boy was
barely into his teens his father also made the mistake of
overestimating the feasibility of Frank's expressed desire to
study medicine, and sent him to Germany, then the centre
of much medical knowledge, to learn the language. The
sojourn was brief. How a youngster with a bad stutter could
realistically be expected to master such a daunting tongue
is a mystery to anyone lacking Charles Dickens's buoyant
optimism. Indeed, the father wanted Frank to learn both
German and Italian during his school-days, as preparation for

2. *The Letters of Charles Dickens*, vol. 1, p. 584.

his finding a place in the diplomatic service, though he did concede to the Reverend Mr. Gibson that Frank "does not seem to me to have the self reliance and self helpfulness of the other boys." He also sent the headmaster a prescription for a medicine to alleviate Frank's deafness, which did in fact go into remission for a while.

Despite his tendency to walk in his sleep, it became apparent that Frank was not cut out for the foreign service. When he was seventeen, his father entered the young man at the bar and took him into the editorial room of his weekly magazine, *All the Year Round*, having descried "a natural literary taste". The taste proved fleeting. The father clutched at a last straw: Frank's recurrent wish that he might lead a life of adventure on some frontier, where the demand for strong, silent men favoured someone with a stutter. On December 2, 1863, Dickens senior wrote a supportive letter to the Hon. Cecil Beadon, head of the Indian Civil Service, to buttress Frank's application for employment in East India:

> ... He is just twenty years of age, well bred and well educated, quick and clever. My friend Lord Russell gave me a nomination for him to the Foreign Office, and he went up for competitive examination and did extremely well, but came out second. In the hope that a young Englishman of his name may be likely to do some little credit to any chance you may kindly give him, I urge my request on his behalf. . . . [3]

A young Englishman of his name, with other names dropped like rose petals in his path, could hardly fail. Frank went to India and served as an officer of the Bengal Mounted Police for six years, till his father died in 1870. At that point he returned home to participate in the division of the estate. Having suffered sunstroke in India – we know that he was fair-skinned and ginger-bearded, in some respects a shorter

3. *The Letters of Charles Dickens*, vol. 3, p. 371.

version of his famous father – Frank had found a systemic palliative in alcohol. The combination of his inheritance with England's wealth of public houses resulted in three years of bibulous oblivion that taxed the patience of his family. It was his aunt Georgina Hogarth, his mother's younger sister and co-executor of his father's estate, who recognized that the best place for Frank was several thousand miles away from the temptations of London. She organized his nomination for officer in Canada's newly established North-West Mounted Police.

Modelled on the Royal Irish Constabulary, the NWMP was the Canadian government's response to the growing need to police the western Territories, which had been made nervous not only by the Red River uprising of 1869–70 but also by the incursions of American whiskey smugglers into what is now southern Alberta. Having observed the bloody confrontations of the military and the Indians in the West of the United States, Ottawa sought to make differences with the Canadian aborigines a police rather than a military matter. Sir John A. Macdonald's government therefore passed the Act of Creation in May 1873, and in August the first contingent of 150 recruits made the harrowing trek to Fort Garry, where it wintered till another 150 men joined it in the spring.

The new force, armed with carbines, pistols, sabres, and a few field pieces, was headed by a commissioner (the first being Lt.-Col. George Arthur French, commander of the Permanent Force gunnery school at Kingston), with subordinate officer ranks of assistant commissioner, superintendent, inspector, and sub-inspector, the last being the rank assigned to Frank Dickens. The Other Ranks were staff-sergeant, sergeant, corporal, and constable.

Frank departed for Canada in 1874, to begin his last and most hectic career, as a member of the force that would one day become the Royal Canadian Mounted Police or, more familiarly, the Mounties. If Frank ever wrote home to his family, after taking up his duties with the NWMP, none of the letters survive.[4] The letters he wrote to members of the Butts family during the twelve years of his service in the NWMP were discovered only recently, in the course of a routine search through a somewhat inchoate collection of personal papers bequeathed to the University of British Columbia, with which I have had the privilege to be associated for many years. Mrs. Emily Thompson (née Butts) apparently brought Frank's letters with her when she and her husband emigrated to Canada in 1908, and it was her daughter Amelia Sedgwick who willed the material to the university's library just prior to her death in 1926, after the double tragedy of her drowning in the Vancouver city reservoir.

Until his letters surfaced, history's assessment of Frank Dickens – where it noticed him at all – has been generally unflattering. "His superiors consistently rated him as being lazy, alcoholic and unfit to be an officer in the NWMP," says the *Dictionary of Canadian Biography*,[5] adding "Frank Dickens made a definite, if negative, impact on the Canadian west. He was partly responsible for the serious deterioration in relations between the NWMP and the Blackfoot in the 1880s. His misadventures also contributed to the strong prejudice against English officers that existed in the mounted police in the late 19th century." Another, anonymous, judgment of Inspector Dickens was that "he was not merely a hiccup in the history of the RCMP, he was a real menace."

How do we make such scathing assessments accord with the view of the people – admittedly not many, in that great unpopulated land that Voltaire discommended as "a few acres of snow" – people who found Frank Dickens to be a quiet, sensitive man who could be witty and warm when relaxing in conversation with a friend? Perhaps the Butts Letters (as I have taken the liberty of calling them) can help to answer that question, as well as inviting scholarly research, by wiser

4. Reports the Dickens House in London: ". . . we have no correspondence here from, to or about him. . . ."
5. Vol. XI, 1982, pp. 261–2.

heads than mine, into the nuclear family as represented by that of the unimaginably prolific Charles Dickens.

One thing on which all who knew him agreed: Frank was a shy and solitary person, the type rarely esteemed by the military or even by the constabulary. Nobody, or almost nobody, loves the type commonly described as "a loner". When we read the news report about a psychopath who has gone berserk and massacred people to whom he is not even related by marriage, we invariably witness the media interviewing neighbours who describe the killer as "very quiet, kept to himself". Yet, to his credit, Frank Dickens never attempted to assassinate Sir John A. Macdonald, though, as we shall see, he had considerable incentive to do so.

The truth may be that this physically disadvantaged young son of one of the titans of English literature did the best he could as a short, round peg in a painfully square hole. To shift metaphors: he was not a truly black sheep of the Dickens family, but with his equally unlucky brothers made up a grey flock. They all frustrated their sire's strenuous endeavours to find each a place in the sun, the sun whose rays were fatefully fixed on the incomparable Boz. It is so that the reader may judge for herself or himself that Frank Dickens's letters are presented herewith.

Nearly all of the preserved letters are addressed to the Black Mare Inn, a public house not far from Frank's temporary residence in Fulham. The early letters he wrote to Minerva, wife of the inn's owner, Ezra Butts, apparently finding in this couple a willingness to accept him as he was – a compassion not too strained in the owner of a bar in which Frank dissipated much of the legacy bestowed on him by his long-suffering father. Also, Mrs. Butts, an amateur potter, seems to have encouraged his friendship as a link, however ale-stained, with the creative genius of *le grand Charles*.

For their generous assistance in the retrieval of relevant documents and records of Dickens's service in the NWMP, the editor wishes to thank Mr. Charles Forbes, Colbeck Librarian, Special Collections, University of British Columbia; Mr. George Brandak, Manuscript Curator, Library, University of British Columbia; Mr. Basil Stuart-Stubbs, Director, School of Library, Archival and Information Studies, University of British Columbia; Professor Donald Smith of the University of Calgary; Professor John Jennings of Trent University; Mr. Bryce Jacques of the State and Military Records, National Archives of Canada; and Monica Dickens (Stratton) of London. The editing of the letters has also been enhanced by the close attentions to the text of Mr. Douglas Gibson and of my wife, Mary Razzell.

Eric Nicol
Vancouver
April 1, 1989

Part One
1874 ~ 1877

～

Ottawa,[1] *Canada.*
October 12th, 1874.

My dear Minerva,

It was not the best of times, it was not the worst of times, it was Ottawa. And still is, I regret to say, having sat here in my hotel room waiting for my marching orders, and for some-one to bring me a drink – one need feeding on the other, while the Ottawa valley's maples also turn crimson for want of the life-giving sap. In Canada the bar service succumbs on Sunday, and the resurrection takes longer than I consider to be Christian.

As promised (threatened?) before I left England, I am, as you see, writing the first of my accounts of Adventure in the Wild West, though still in the Barely Domesticated East. I undertake this in the hope of one day amassing enough thrill-ing tales of perilous predicaments among the painted savages (I believe they call them "dance-hall girls") to ambush a London publisher. We have ample evidence that, next to my father's books, no writing is more eagerly consumed in the Old Country (as it is called here, reminding me that I am on a voyage from an antique land) than that of the British

---

1. Probably the Russell Hotel, FD's preferred lodging when confined to the capital, on the site of the present Château Laurier.

traveller who has braved this land that God created in a moment of excessive enthusiasm for sheer size, and who has blazed a trail through the trackless forest in the service of our noble Queen, God bless her and all who sail in her!

Please consider this letter to be by way of preamble to those to follow, recounting my heart-stopping deeds as an officer in the North-West Mounted Police, all the letters being much safer in your hands than if I have to decide, in the emergency of being pursued by howling northern hottentots, whether to jettison my rifle or my manuscript.

My crossing the Atlantic – which when crossed can turn quite ugly – yielded little in the way of the printable. The first day out of Liverpool scuttled my fancy about catching the ocean in a summer mood, as well as soundly refuting the advice of an erstwhile friend who before I embarked told me: "The cure for seasickness is to drink a pint of ale immediately upon boarding the ship and remain at the bar till the captain swears to you on the Bible that the ship has docked." My diary for the Columbian horror:

> Thur. Ill. Fri. Ill. Sat. Very ill. Sun. Less ill. Ate dry biscuit. Mon. Very, very ill. Tues. (Blank) Wed. (Blank) Thur. Died today. No regrets. Fri. The ghost was brought tea by cabin steward. Cursed him for delaying decent burial at sea. Sat. Engulfed by St. Lawrence River, with whom I share green hue. Sun. Quebec City. Tottered on deck for first time since leaving Liverpool. Have to admire General Wolfe's persistence. Mon. More river. Tue. Montreal. Landed. Would have kissed ground but too weak to kneel.

And thence here by train (yes, they have trains here, though they can't decide whether to run them as "railways", as God intended, or "railroads", as the Yankees call their version) to Ottawa, the new nation's capital, where everyone is learning the pleasures of spending the taxpaying citizens' money but hasn't the foggiest how to enjoy his own. The shops (or "stores") are barbarous, and the pavements are in fact – as Pa never tired of explaining – unpaved, consisting of raised wooden platforms of planks with gaps down which one may, I have found, drop coins, keys, or even a small flask to everlasting perdition.

You are already familiar with the circumstances of my coming to this protracted land, but let me record them here: I have come to Canada to serve as an officer in the North-West Mounted Police. Romantic, what? I obtained the nomination with the gratuitous assistance of my Aunt Georgina,[2] who had clipped a news item from *The Times* reporting the formation in Canada of a mounted police force to protect the western aborigines from American whisky traders who have found that there is more than one way to skin a buffalo. When, instead of the cash I had asked for to tide me over till Pa's next posthumous royalty cheque, I found this clipping in the envelope under my brandy decanter, I at once sought out the lady who was kindly keeping me informed of events in the New World.

"You do understand, Aunt Georgy, that in hiring me to thwart these 'whisky traders' the Canadian mounted police would be setting the fox to guard the chicken house?"

"Perhaps we can kill two birds with one stone," says she, dipping her pen into the red ink as she worked on the family accounts. "You have a choice, Frankey: either lead a sober life with the Canadian mounted police or get as drunk as you please in the debtor's gaol."

I might have given the choice more thought had I not wished to avoid mimicking the career of my grandfather, who spent so much of his life in accommodation styled to the taste of his creditors. More pertinently, and as I doubtless

2. Catherine Dickens's younger sister, who moved into the household at age fifteen and remained to manage it after the novelist's separation from Kate and his death. This unconventional ménage, which scandalized many of Charles Dickens's contemporaries, says something about his giving precedence to utility over sentiment in his own affairs.

told you when maudlin in my cups, my youthful ambition was to become a gentleman farmer in some semi-tropical paradise, and *The Times* report indicated that the Canadian government would reward service with the deed to enough land to start another country.

Frankly, I would have preferred the Cape, having always had a fondness for elephants. But even if I had not lost my Bengal appointment by overstaying my leave in England, I had no real desire to return to India, where there are already far too many people for me to expect to retire with a lordly estate.

"Very well, Aunt Georgy," I says, pretty cool. "I put my future in your hands, if you'll put five quid in mine."

It has long been my belief that if Pa had married Georgina Hogarth instead of her sister he would have had fewer children and lived long enough to finish *Edwin Drood*. The woman has a natural flair for the Richelieuvian, as witness her successful application on my behalf to Lord Dufferin, the Governor General of this gargantuan wasteland and once a friend (as who wasn't?) of my dear, departed father. His lordship earned his spurs for arduous duty as lord-in-waiting to the Queen. We all have our reasons for choosing exile, and the Viceroy conveyed mine to Prime Minister Mackenzie, with his imprimatur.[3]

I feel no guilt about having obtained this posting thanks to special pleading. I have tried, all my life, not to trade on my father's name, but when my relatives do it for me – and particularly when the relative is Aunt Georgina – I accept the result as an act of G–d. Besides, I intend to give the Canadian government value for its money. I shall astound my family by being a d––n good policeman, with a better service record

3.   Georgina Hogarth told friends how relieved she was to have "got this place" for Frank. She was able to borrow money from FD's brothers and sisters to pay for his passage to Canada – a rare instance of family unity.

than my brother Edward.[4] A new man, for the New World. Indeed I am impatient to set off towards my rendezvous with Destiny, having to wait for the Minister of Justice to confirm my appointment. I believe that he attends a vacancy in the Force. I try not to dwell on what circumstance would create a vacancy in a mounted police only a year old.[5] It is not likely that an officer will have retired so soon. That leaves me prey to picturing some poor devil staked out on an anthill, and I wait for his painful expiration to be officially confirmed so that I may take his place.

Anyway, and not to put too fine a point on it, Canada it is! Dare I hope that when I have a more permanent postal address I may hear from you? While I am no stranger to *being* a stranger, alone in a land of bizarre custom, and indeed welcome the challenge, I shall also welcome word from you that you are receiving mine and (need I say?) find my narrative engrossing beyond belief.

My affectionate best wishes to you and Ezra.
Frank.

⚬

Toronto, Ontario.
Oct. 21st, 1874.

My dear Minerva,

Finally! I have received my marching orders. The march (on rails) has brought me to Toronto, whence I entrain shortly to points south,[6] west, and north in order to attain a place

4. FD's younger brother went to Australia with his father's hope "he may take better to the Bush than to Books."
5. The NWMP became a reality with the administering of the first enlistment oath on November 3, 1873.
6. Via Northern Pacific.

called Winnipeg.[7] I am not proceeding at once, however, as I await the arrival of some of my luggage, including a warm overcoat, that I left in Montreal because I could not be sure that Ottawa would not abandon me at the altar. I have had to telegraph for immediate transmission hither of my effects, though I have kept with me both my father's gold watch and chain – a trinket with which I expect to bedazzle Canadian redskin and whiteskin alike – and the little earthen vase spun by your hands (my sole thirtieth-birthday present). It will be my daily delight to fill your vase with wildflowers, wherever I may be stationed. I cannot hope for the lilac and honeysuckle of England, but I'm sure that the Canadian prairie yields wild grasses that I may gaze upon and remember our *fêtes champêtres*. . . .

I look forward to travel by American train, whose wheels I understand are round, since I have learned why the locals call theirs "the Grand Drunk Railway". It is plain that among other gaps in their education, Canadians have not yet learned how to drink. I speak of tradesmen such as porters, waiters, shop clerks – not readily accepting their lot in life but ever waiting for Opportunity to knock on their door, loudly enough to waken them from their drunken stupor. All ranks are well provided for, in terms of rendering themselves insensible, by this town of Toronto which, the desk clerk assures me, boasts a population of 69,000 served by no fewer than 610 taverns, wine shops, and other founts of spirituous beverage.

Last evening, made desperate by staring out of my window at the grey lake whose cold, white lips lap a shore that visibly shrinks at each touch, I sought out one of the 610 temples of tippling, and there met an indigene – a very large, florid gentleman in the "dry goods business", whatever that may be. Like so many of his countrymen, he imposed his acquaintance upon me as a distortion of hospitality, and his attentions

7. Where a party under Sub-Inspector Frichette was waiting for FD, before proceeding to Fort Pelly, a Hudson's Bay Company post northwest of Winnipeg.

were made tolerable only by his paying for the drinks. After asking me my name, his first question was "You're not Catholic, Mr. Dickens?"

"Indeed I'm not, sir," I said.

"Good! Then you must be a good Protestant. Come with me, and I'll show you a bit of fun."

The ruddy giant – he said his name was Thompson – then took me rather forcefully by the arm, out to the planked street and past the main station which sensibly faces the lake and turns its back on the squalid little town. He led me down to the waterfront, to a wharf on which roistered a score or so of other forced émigrés from local bars. They were building little cairns of rocks, all the while bawling songs in which the Pope seemed to figure, and occasionally peering into the darkness of the lake.

"What's up?" I asked my host.

"The *jig's* up!" crowed Thompson, whose accent was becoming more blatantly Irish in his excitement. "That's what, Mr. Dickens. Grab a rock."

Rather than appear stand-offishly English, I picked up a stone the size of a cricket ball and, feeling rather foolish, said, "Now what?"

"Now *that*, me boyo!" He pointed to the lanterns of an approaching lake steamer, from which, across the rippled black waters, came the strains of an Irish ballad sung by revellers to whom the melody mattered less than the volume of sound. "The annual midnight cruise o' the Knights o' Stinkin' Columbus!" he bellowed. "Hold your fire, boys, till you see the whites o' their lily livers!"

This order was cheerfully ignored, as the Orangemen did not wait for the ship to nudge the dock before they began pelting the cruise passengers. The papists responded with a will, hurling at us anything movable on deck – bottles (of which they had ample), picnic remains, deck chairs, our own stones – all in a cursing, hooting hubbub that yet had something of a civic rite, like observing the Queen's Birthday.

Someone on board threw me a life-belt. Not being in the

water at the time, I had no real need for the ring, nor for my serving as the pin in this rather Torontonian version of deck-quoits. Losing consciousness as well as interest, I must have subsided to the ground. When I recovered my senses, Thompson stood over me, grinning.

"Welcome to Canada, Mr. Dickens!" he blared, with a front tooth or two fewer than earlier in the evening. "That'll remind those b————ds that Toronto is an Orange town." I know that he was not referring to the distinctive colour of the brick in this parish.

All of which explains why today, when my headache moderates to mere agony, I plan not to talk to strangers, restricting my sightseeing to King Street, which the desk clerk tells me is Toronto's Pall Mall and most fashionable promenade. If anyone asks me my religion, I am a devout Druid.

October 22nd, 1874.

My bags are found! I would rush to one of the multitude of churches in which Toronto abounds, and there give thanks for this deliverance from the evil of lost luggage, but I know that another deity has been at work. The desk clerk, noting my name for the first time, asked me if I was "any relation to the great English novelist Charles Dickens". When I admitted to being a son of same, the clerk at once pounded his tocsin to summon a platoon of porters whom he sent scurrying to all corners of the Dominion to search out my tea chests.

And now I have them. Not the first time, of course, that my father's name has worked wonders for me. It not only opens doors for me, it shines the knobs, unrolls the red carpet and carries me, blushing, across the threshold. G–d, how I hate it! But I have long since learned to bow to it. When Pa obtained for me the nomination that bought me gold braid in the Bengal Mounted, that was when I handed in my resignation as the captain of my soul. Those born to the pale glow of parentally-reflected glory are doomed forever to travel to the ends of the earth, as have I and my brothers,[8] torn between the advantages of riding on our father's coattails and hoping that at last these will be stretched to snapping point, and what we do will be, as the street artist's sign says, ALL MY OWN WORK.

In a few hours (6 p.m.) I entrain for Hamilton and eventually St. Paul, Minnesota. It may strike you as odd – my having to travel south into the United States in order to travel west into the Canadian Northwest Territories – but the direct route west[9] is, I'm told, decidedly primitive, across the Great Lakes, whose temperament in winter would cause even Ulysses to cling whimpering to his anchor, then endless miles between rivers by portage – that abominable Canadian custom of carrying one's boat on one's back. With all due respect to the Force's pioneers, who took the direct route exactly a year ago, better late than never! Despite my rather devious route, I look forward to the relative comfort of the railway carriage and to having my first glimpse of the America that Pa exploited so mercilessly, on his reading tours. Wish me "bon voyage", my friends, and, prithee, write to me at NWMP, Winnipeg, Canada.

Your venal voyageur,
Frank.

8.   Alfred, like Edward, went to Australia. Sydney ("Ocean Spectre") joined the Navy and perished at sea. FD's older brother Walter went to India and died there.
9.   Taken by the original NWMP Divisions "A", "B", and "C", the infamous Dawson route from Prince Arthur's Landing (later Port Arthur) to Lower Fort Garry, twenty miles north of Winnipeg, October/November 1873.

❧

St. Paul, Minnesota.
October 25th, 1874.

My dear Minerva,

H—l and D—n! That is my epistle from St. Paul. Forgive me the profanity, my dear, but my introduction to the United States has convinced me that the Americans are still fighting what Canadians call the War of 1812. Having lost that particular extension of the Napoleonic Wars, the Yankees have now replaced their soldiers with railway conductors, one of whom recognized me at once as the English foe and put me into a "boxcar" (a goods van) with six other male passengers considered to be enemies of the Republic. My protest that I was an officer fell on deaf ears. Such is the murderous prevalence of equal rights in this country that all ranks were cast together into a barely mobile replica of the Black Hole. My bed: straw on the floor. This I expected to burst into flames at any moment from the heat radiating from a charcoal stove that Americans seem to consider to be faulty unless its cast-iron plates glow red and the stove pipe sways and hisses like a Bombay beggar's cobra.

One of my straw mates has been a recruit also on his way to Winnipeg. As his superior officer I felt obliged to set an example of the stiff upper lip in the face of hardship. My upper lip, I find, stiffens much better if it is wrapped around the rim of a glass. I therefore shared my emergency ration of rum with Constable Flynn, having persuaded him that the medicinal draught was the only protection against "the deadly swine fever that plagues the American Mid-west". When Constable Flynn dozed off from the heat and the nostrum, I was able to finish the bottle with a loose upper lip, cursing and kicking the sides of our careering kiln.

But worse awaited. My first view of the state of Illinois, a place where I should like to spend more time in the future, came with our train's lurching to a stop in a Chicago stock-yard. Constable Flynn awoke and, upon stumbling out of our van, saw that he was surrounded by thousands of penned and panicked pigs, squealing and emitting a horrific stench.

"Migawd, the swine fever!" he screeched, and, clapping a kerchief over his mouth, staggered back down the track towards Toronto. I was obliged to tackle him, like a Rugby footballer, but he fought me like a madman, screaming "We're all gonna die!" and rolling us both into a foul mud puddle where we grappled like hippos in rut. Our exertions brought a pair of railway policemen running. They stood us upright, soaked and reeking, one of them demanding:

"Who in h–ll are you clowns?"

I drew myself up to my full height – which unfortunately never takes long – and replied: "Sir, we are North-West Mounted Police."

The impudent b––––rds then broke into guffaws, and as they traipsed off I heard one of them snigger to the other: "God save the Queen!" I wanted to whip Constable Flynn with his own tongue, but had to admit to myself my fault in having mentioned swine fever in a country so rich in pigs, and indeed where so many of the wild boar are bipeds. In fact, once we had both sobered up and were once more rattling westward, I sought out the constable in his straw and apologized for misleading him.

"Swine fever," I assured him, "is infectious only if one's body becomes too warm."

After that I had not only a comrade in arms but an ally who kept that d––n stove from baking us. Indeed, I began almost to enjoy our iron horse's puffing progress through verdant Illinois into the green woods of Wisconsin. I was still many miles from Winnipeg, but clearly the West is not to be won in a day.

This bucolic mood was shattered by my arrival here in St. Paul, in whose rail station I sit writing this missive using my bag as an escritoire (please excuse pencil). This is the end of the line! I must transfer to a place called Fargo (ominous name), Dakota Territory, and proceed back northward to Canadian territory by stage-coach. *Stage-coach*! This is no mere trot in a Hansom cab from Charing Cross to the Strand. It is a journey of hundreds of miles, in a conveyance that would be an affront to a load of fence posts. I am very tempted to do what Constable Flynn did the moment our train pulled into St Paul – desert. Before he swung out of our ambulant hovel, grinning hugely, he informed me that it was common practice for ambitious Ontario lads like himself to sign up for the NWMP as a means of getting free transport to the vicinity of the Mississippi.

"Southward, ho, for me, Dickie," yelled Flynn, waving an obscene farewell. "Bags of greenbacks to be won on the paddle-wheelers if you're handy with the cards." He then departed from Her Majesty's gendarmerie with the final words "You're a sap!"

Why did I not follow him? For one thing, I am loyal to the Service, and for another I always lose at cards, even when I cheat. It follows that I should be lucky in love, but I have proved that it is possible to suffer the slings and arrows in all parts of the body. I know that I tempt the Fates by remaining too long in the U.S.A. The lawlessness of the American West does not attract me, and the people are too volatile for my taste. They carry the law in their holster, leaving no room for a bottle.

I shall therefore be on the fateful stage-coach when it leaves tomorrow morning. I wish I had been issued my uniform. If our coach is ambushed by Indians, I may die looking like a civilian – a blot on my service record.

Your fearless (within reason) friend,
Frank.

〜

Pembina.
October 29th, 1874.

Dear Minerva,

Please don't ask me where this place is. They tell me that it lies on the border between the United States and Canada, and I am too weak to dispute it. What matters is that I occupy a cot in the scant accommodation of the staging post. Ill. Again. I have what the people here heartlessly dismiss as "Tecumseh's Revenge". It was partly my own fault for ordering, before we left Fargo, a breakfast different from that being wolfed down by the other passengers: baked beans. Baked beans! Just before being confined in a coach whose windows are closed against wintry blasts!

Too late, alas, I learn that I should have resigned myself to the baked beans du pays, instead of the lake trout. I should have seen in the trout's baleful eye, as it lay on my plate, the intent to take someone with it to the Happy Hunting Ground.

The stage-coach driver refused to stop, despite my shouted pleas. This is still Sioux country, I was informed by the baked-beans coterie. One elderly travelling companion took a perverse delight in informing me that no one was sure where Chief Sitting Bull was at the moment, but that there was general agreement that he has not been gracious about being herded into a reservation and is, indeed, in a rather filthy mood. Since the fabled warrior commands what has been called "the finest light cavalry in the world", the odds against our stage-coach's outrunning a charge of this very light brigade were as long as my face.

"But lookee here, yer English," says my toothless informant. "Sittin' Bull likes the redcoats. Too bad yer wearin' black." He clacks his tongue on his gums in glee. "Where's yer uniform? Throw up on it?" He hoots with laughter.

I did not find his hilarity infectious, as the coach driver, a
real Jehu, was adhering to one speed only: fast and furious,
the main direction of the coach being up and down. My sole
desire was to get out of that hurtling wagon long enough to
void my misery. If the Sioux had chosen that moment to
pierce my body full of arrows, I would have given them my
blessing, a benison as heartfelt as anything St Sebastian could
muster.

I wish that I could say that, having my head out the window
so frequently, I saw something of the country. But one does
not absorb a great deal of the passing scene when one's eyes
are closed and it is the mouth that is open. One of the other
passengers, a gaunt American whose lofty hat held both a
Derringer and a photo of his mother, made no effort to
conceal his contempt for my distress, till he learned that I was
travelling to join the North-West Mounted Police. Then he
became very solicitous, and during one of our stops for a
change of horses he produced from his carpetbag a sample of
a provision that he hoped to sell, in quantity, to the NWMP –
a chunk of bully beef preserved in a tin labelled "PRIME CUT".

"Sir," quoth this cadaverous pitchman, disregarding the
fact that I was leaning weakly against a wheel while others
bolted down more beans, "you must try this superlative
product. Not only is the meat a succulent beef lovingly
detached from selected steers, but the container guarantees –
absolute warranty, sir! – that it may be kept in a chuckwagon
for months, nay years, and when opened will be as fresh,
tasty, *and* nutritious as the day Bossy gave her life for king
and country."

"*Queen* and country," I croaked.

"Oh, pardon me, sir, I didn't know he'd died. My condolences." He whipped out a tin cutter and decapitated the
tin. "Do try some of this Prime Cut bully beef, sir. It will
settle your stomach and give wings to your spirit." He held
out to me on his knife a wedge of purpled flesh liberally
mottled with yellow fat. . . . That is all I remember of the
ride, till dropped on this cot, where for two days I have

feverishly recalled my father's telling us children about his
wild rides in a post-chaise and four when he was an apprentice
reporter for the *Morning Chronicle*, covering political meetings
all over the country, jotting notes on the palm of his hand as
his carriage pitched about, and several times being upset into
ditches many miles from London, yet always getting back in
time for publication. What frightens me now, about my
father's story, is that it was probably true.

I hope to be on the next stage-coach north, on a diet of
dry bread and brandy. To be continued . . .

∾

Winnipeg, Manitoba.
November 19th.

Although I am not certified dead, an officer here at Fort Garry
called me "the late Sub-Inspector Dickens" because I was
unavoidably detained in Toronto and Pembina. It seems that
Division "E" left without me, for Fort Pelly. I missed them
by only two days. That didn't signify the end of the world
to me, given the distance involved and the hazards of the
American menu. But nothing would do but that I should try
to catch them up, in company with a few other new recruits
and Paymaster Dalrymple Clark, who from the start eyed me
as extra expense.

The Paymaster was well aware that, because the main body
of mounts had trotted off without me, the horse provided for
Sub-Inspector Dickens had to be specially *hired* . . . you may
gasp, if you wish . . . by His Honour the Agent for the Minister of Justice, said horse being delivered *personally* to the
Lower Fort (a fastness about which I shall complain later),
by a gentleman who needed to be reimbursed, as well as
provender to feed the said horse and, incidentally, Sub-

Inspector Dickens.[10] Thus I hit the wintry trail with the maximum of overcharge and the minimum of underl—en. I cannot describe to you the horror of setting forth into the Unknown divest of a properly-fitted uniform. There simply was not time enough for me to be measured by a tailor whom I had reason to trust.

Shortly after our tiny entourage rumbled out of Fort Garry we ran into extremely cold weather, the temperature plummeting with an abruptness that literally took my breath away. The ground was shrouded by snow that will – I am told gleefully by Canadian comrades – lie there for the next five months. I am also told that the aborigines have a hundred different words for snow. I have only one – unprintable. Worse awaited me, however, than frozen landscape.

A few days out, as our party topped a snowy rise, a chilling spectacle stopped us in our tracks. Straggling towards us came a full division of Mounted Police, at least 50 men, some riding slumped and sagging, others trudging in the snow beside ponies whose heads drooped with exhaustion. Bringing up the rear, a few span of oxen. The ragged column was headed by an officer who, alone of the troopers, sat ramrod straight in the saddle and stared straight ahead. At me. As we closed, he held up a hand to halt his sorry brigade. Because his uniform was much the worse for wear, I could not at once determine his rank. But assuming that I was the senior officer in my own party, I drew my horse up beside him and said:

"May I be of assistance?"

A pair of blue eyes blazed at me from under a fur cap that seemed to be the remains of an animal that had died of exposure.

"Who the devil are you, sir?" His voice rasped like a stone on the axe blade. As I momentarily pondered the wisdom of taking umbrage at this rude introduction, Paymaster

10. For details of the accounting of this inauspicious debut, see Appendix A. FD arrived in Winnipeg November 1 and departed the next day.

Clark joined me to whisper in my ear: "It's the Commissioner!"

I had, of course, heard of Commissioner George A. French.[11] He is the C.O. of the entire Force. He commanded the cavalcade that had set forth in such splendour in July, who had surmounted unspeakable hardships of terrain and weather to reach Fort Macleod, and had now returned the thousand-odd miles to Swan River[12] to confirm it as the Force's permanent HQ. So what was he doing here, glaring at me? I decided that the course of prudence dictated my answering his question first:

"Sir, I am Sub-Inspector D-d-d-d-d . . ." The anxiety of the moment produced my damn stutter. The "D" of my own name became the insurmountable obstacle it was when I faced the headmaster at school in Boulogne. The harder I tried to detach my tongue from the roof of my mouth – fearing that the haggard heroes shivering behind the Commissioner might freeze to death before I could complete the introduction – the more tenaciously it clung to my palate. Asking the Commissioner just to call me "Frank" seemed, in the circumstances, inappropriate. In any event he intervened.

"You're Dickens," he snapped.

"Thank you, sir. Yes, I am he."

His lips tightened into a thin line as straight as if it had been government-surveyed. "You're late."

"For what?" I intended no impertinence. It was not as though my presence was urgently needed somewhere in order to help suppress a riot or rebellion. What was the hurry? "Did I miss something, sir?" I asked.

11.   Born in Ireland, Royal Artillery officer, organizer of the NWMP, knighted for service.
12.   French was already incensed by what he found at Swan River barracks: an unfinished line of buildings strung along a ridge of granite, the site treeless with maximum exposure to the biting north wind, cracks in the unseasoned wood, and no hay for the animals. Canadian historians have described it simply as a government project.

"You missed the bl—dy boat, sir!" His words emerged as live steam in the chilled air. My pony shied nervously.

"No, sir," I said. "I caught the boat. It was the train I missed. There was a problem with my luggage in Montreal, and –"

"Enough!" The volley caused my pony to rear – its first show of energy since we left Winnipeg – and I slid ignominiously over the tail to land on the snowy trail. Luckily I landed on my feet and was able to remount quickly with what I hoped was a disarming smile, though my spine was vibrating like a struck gong. Reining in hard to control my animal, I shouted to the Commissioner: "I've been ill, sir. Too sick to travel."

At this the Other Ranks turned their slow heads to stare at me with unblinking, bloodshot eyes, muscles twitching in cheeks. I at once regretted my voicing the excuse, valid though it was, and my discomfort was not eased when the Commissioner moved his horse close enough to mine for me to be able to see the hairs in his nostrils withering in the flame of cold fury.

"*Sick?*" he said. "Too sick to travel? Sir, in this force you keep moving when you're well, you keep moving when you're sick, and you keep moving when you're d——d well dead! Do you understand?"

"Yes, sir." I had gleaned the message. As had everyone else within earshot, which included most of western Manitoba. Mentally I faulted Commissioner French for loudly dressing down a fellow officer in front of the men. One of the first rules I was taught, in the Bengal Mounted Police, was that, to preserve the respect of the men, any such wigging should be done in private. Granted, in this situation (the middle of bald prairie), privacy was at a premium unless we withdrew over the horizon. But as I looked the Commissioner in the eye, disapproval must have glinted in mine, as his face flushed redder than ever and he blared:

"You will turn your party around, sir, and accompany my column back to Winnipeg!"

With that, he whirled his horse away, and his tattered troop hauled itself back into motion. As the men rode past me, in all variety of gear, I saw that they were too trail-weary and wan even to enjoy the spectacle of my humiliation. They were simply grim spectres, driving hard towards relief from misery.

My party swung in behind the Commissioner's column, and I was promptly consternated by the pace at which he led us back the way I had just come. Was the man mad? His entire troop, gaunt though it was, seemed to smell the barn, or more likely the taverns of Winnipeg, riding like demented demons. Although relatively fresh, my horse soon fell to the rear. I've never felt more like a camp follower, as the temperature suddenly dropped further and we were whipped by gusts of snow that turned the entire procession into white ghosts, horsemen of the apocalypse, with mine the palest horse of Death despite my frantic effort to keep her dusted.

The column slowed only when the oxen struck patches of ice, and wheels spun in vain. During one such pause I noticed a trooper shivering in the remnants of summer uniform, obviously unprepared for this early onslaught of winter after the long march from the Rockies. He wasn't even wearing his gloves. I took off my cape and put it around the constable's shoulders, only to hear a bellow from up forward, a voice I had already learned to recognize even when blinded by snow.

"Put that g–dd–mn cape back on, Dickens! That man is twice as hardy as you are. You'll be of no use to Canada as a bl––dy ice bag!"

I hurriedly retrieved my cape. The constable nodded gratefully, and I slipped him my gloves. He at once stuffed the gloves down the front of his britches, as if to ward off frostbite from an appendage more precious to him than his fingers. It gave me an odd feeling, but I was too busy being unnoticed by French to brood about it.

That frigid ride to Winnipeg gave me an insight into Napoleon's retreat from Russia, without the compensation of having visited Moscow.

To the Commissioner's credit, he drove us the 120 miles in 30 hours, without losing a man or an ox. In fact he had completed the herculean march to Fort Macleod and back with not one loss of human life or limb, more than nineteen hundred miles and constantly at risk from attack by Indians, whisky traders, hunger, thirst, flood, and – his men have told me – the world's most uncomfortable type of boredom. He was of course greeted by the town as a hero, which he was. All the more difficult for me, however, having never got off the mark. I ache to join Hannibal in his conquest of the Alps, but it seems that one of the elephants is standing on my foot.

No word from you yet, my friends. I hope that this chronicle of frustration has not dimmed me in your esteem.

With affectionate wishes,
Frank.

~

Winnipeg, Manitoba.
Nov. 22nd, 1874.

My dear Minerva,

I have had my first taste of battle. Unfortunately, the conflict was between me and the Minister of Justice. The Minister has demanded an explanation[13] for my tardiness in reporting to dear, departed Sub-Inspector Frichette.[14] I know what is bothering him: the extra expense for transport. Horse and hay. I shall not inflict the details upon you, since the gruesome accounting may make you faint unto swooning. Just let me say that the Canadian government gives new and fresh meaning to the term "petty cash". It comes from having

13. For the relevant correspondence, see Appendix B.
14. *Sic.* Sub-Inspector Frichette commanded the "E" Division group which FD was supposed to join in Winnipeg, but which left without him.

administration by Scotsmen. Penny wise and pound foolish: that is their modus operandi. Their greatest joy is to discover in their books an unapproved expense incurred by an Englishman.

Anyway, I believe that I gave a good account of myself in my reply to the Minister's laying on the claymore. I passed it to the Commissioner, who confided to me that he would append a note finding my explanation for lateness satisfactory and I would not need to stand in the corner with a dunce cap on my head. After the debacle of the Swan River barracks – for which the Canadian government paid a wasted $30,000 – he is even more incensed with Ottawa than I am. This may be the strongest bond between us. It is the common enemy that creates comradeship, and it makes it much easier for us to get along with the Indians when we know that our real foe lurks in the Justice Department.

To compound my already mixed feelings, I have received a separate report from the Minister of Justice confirming my appointment, November 4th, as a Sub-Inspector, NWMP, approved by the Governor General in Council. With my name crossing his desk so often, perhaps the Minister suspects that I am trying to take advantage of that name. "Because his father is Charles Dickens" – I hear him muttering – "he thinks he can take liberties. Well, we'll soon put a stop to *that* nonsense!" G–d, it is hard to be a Somebody, when you're already a Somebody's son.

These glancing blows delivered by Fate I salve in the taverns of the town. If I am to be Winnipegged for the winter, I believe it to be my duty to reconnoitre thoroughly the whisky traders who take advantage of us simple policemen by giving us firewater in exchange for valuable coins of the realm. To do so I must excuse myself temporarily from the Stone Fort – a very senior bastion, by Canadian standards, formerly occupied by the military and still redolent of old colonels – and travel the few but perilous miles (one's horse can trip over an inebriate lying in the road) to the village whose shacks house 4000 lively souls. I am told that "Winnipeg" comes from an Indian word meaning "murky water", and see no reason to doubt it.

To the Lord, the Red River Settlement must appear as so many rectangular leeches whose mouths are clamped firmly to the river from which each draws sustenance. With their haying at the back end and their houses at the river end, these four miles of log abodes constitute our Metropolis. The closed ranks of thatch-roof homes also front on the seasonal bridge that the river becomes when frozen in winter. On the nether shore St. Boniface, the demure milieu of the Métis (the "mixed-bloods" who combine Indian and French blood with a dash of Scotch in alarming proportions), becomes more accessible – already the ice is thick enough for the first dog trains to be yelping their way to Winnipeg – so that here Canada's Confederation is bonded according to temperature.

These settlers are, however, no ordinary rurals. Not your stock Farmer Brown is the Winnipegger, who tends to come from unspeakable places like the Orkney Islands, or mainland Scotland, or Ontario. Until recently almost all of the oldest residents, the Métis, hunted the buffalo that still roam a few hundred miles to the west, and for the "winterers" who made hunting their mainstay of livelihood, Winnipeg was traditionally the spot where they cashed in their trophies and spent the sudden wealth with an abandon that, while hardly provident, made for some very well-catered celebrations. This grand tradition lingers on. People after my own heart, these friendly Manitobans. Too much so, as I found out to my chagrin.

You see, Minnie, winter is the high season for social affairs in Winnipeg, with dances, weddings, and funerals. I gather that couples hold off getting married till winter (except in an emergency), so that everyone can give his full and prolonged attention to the Red River Jig, and the dying of the elderly *en saison* is equally appreciated, as an occasion for a funeral cortege, relieved by refreshments, that is worthy of Frederick the Great.

As an acceptable alternative to the Hell's Gates saloon I have attended two weddings and one funeral in the past week. It was at one of the wedding celebrations that I discovered the sad truth that I lack the physical stamina for a career in the Canadian West. I am indeed convinced that it was in order to escape the demands of the likes of Winnipeg's dance *fêtes* that Alexander Mackenzie became the first white man to traverse this country to the Pacific Ocean.

The wedding in question was that of a couple whom I had never met but of whom I became immediately fond when a fellow officer, inviting me to join him as a guest, described the quantity of roast beef, buffalo tongue, plum puddings, and spirituous beverages that was being conscripted for the nuptial feast. Why the host was calling up reinforcements from the Stone Fort did not concern me till it was too late. With the return of the wedding party from the church, and the salutatory volley of guns, I was swept into the first house. (The expansive festivities required two houses, one for the taking on of food and drink, the other for working these off in the heat of the jig.) There was a brief delay while the ladies exchanged their wedding finery for something more compatible with muscular exertion, and the two fiddlers tuned their fiddles as though these being flat made a particle of difference to the outcome of the battle.

Then, the fray was on! I at once lost my comrade, the burly arms that bore him away belonging to a Britannia with red hair. All of the attractive ladies had partners, either permanent or quickly requisitioned, leaving only the very old or the very young to forage among us wallflowers. I was singled out by a freckle-faced daughter of the house – aged, I guessed nervously, about eleven – who boldly invited me to escort her into the melee. I hesitated but momentarily. I had the choice between child-wrestling or embracing the seated elderly lady – the bride's grandmother, I assumed – whose knees were jittering as she waggled her eyebrows at me.

I chose wrongly. The girl child had much more energy, and

to spare, than the old lady, who, given the pace of the dance, could reasonably have been expected to expire before dawn. The pinafored dumpling whose hand gripped mine like a vice was clearly determined to do as much damage as possible before she was sent to bed. Nothing in my life – including the dance lessons that my father made me take at the Boulogne boarding school – prepared me for the Scottish Reel as it was unleashed that night. Not only did the reeling make the whirling Dervish look like an experiment in inertia, but there was no respite for the perspiring reelers and jiggers. When the fiddlers became incandescent from friction, the players merely gave way to the reserve team, which maintained the relentless rhythm as though the enduring troth that had been pledged depended on polka without pause.

Once or twice I escaped to the house of refreshment to lubricate my protesting joints, but each time I was dragged back by the junior hurricane. Moreover, as evening moved into morning, the girl seemed to grow before my bulging eyes, like Alice in Wonderland, except that I was the one who had found the bottle labelled DRINK ME. This mystery was solved when the old lady tottered into me, cawing:

"Why're ye dancin' on yer knees, mon?"

I knew then, though dimly, that I must be only moments away from jigging on my chin – socially unacceptable on a crowded floor. I crawled out the front door and was briefly revived by the blast of cold night air. The respite was quickly curtailed as I was bowled over by the bride's mother and the groom's father, who appeared to be trying to perform the Russian squat dance on hoar frost. They sought to enlist me as a fellow Cossack, but I fled towards the river in an icy glissando accompanied by a wolf howl that I traced to my own throat. . . .

That concluded the wedding party, as I recalled it. It was the Commissioner who, two days later, in his office, dourly filled in for me the details of the latter period of my tribute to Hymen.

"It was enterprising of you, Dickens," he growled, as I

stood at attention, gazing at the disapproving portrait of our dear Queen hanging behind his desk, "to try to demonstrate to most of the populace the Force's prowess with the dog sled. However, I doubt that we achieve that goal when it is the officer who is between the traces, hauling a sled full of barking dogs, through a crowd of thigh-slapping civilians. Would you agree, sir?"

"Yes, sir." I now understood why I woke up the next day smelling like a kennel. "I can only say, sir, that I am very fond of dogs, and I allowed the exuberance of the occasion to affect the approved method of harnessing them to the sled."

"I'm glad to hear that, Dickens," scowled the Commissioner, closing the interview with some discouraging predictions about my future if I continued to indulge my fondness for the bottle.

Perhaps I should have added that it appals me to see the dogs straining at sled-loads that would defeat a yoke of bullocks. Instead I took my leave, vowing to limit my weddings to one a week.

> Your older if not wiser friend,
> Frank.

~

> *Dufferin, Manitoba.*
> *December 10th.*

Dear Minerva,

Since I wrote to you last month my only correspondent has been the Minister of Justice, in Ottawa. He has billed me $200 for the special transport that conveyed me from Winnipeg to Winnipeg! Of all the infernal cheek! This because Commissioner French was in such a foul mood about the Swan River barracks fiasco that he reported me as late, like a headmaster jumping on a schoolboy because the master bought a pair of shoes that crimp his carbuncle. Needless to say, I am resisting payment.[15] I have spent a good deal of my leisure time lately composing a reasoned, temperate reply to the Minister, editing out all references to illegitimacy in his immediate family.

I mean, d––n it, two hundred dollars represents more than a month's pay. How am I to afford the necessities of life, when the barman refuses to extend me more credit? I have had sobriety forced upon me in the middle of a Canadian winter, when the blood has greatest need of alcohol to prevent it from freezing in the veins. Someone maniacally determined to look on the bright side might say that my having to keep moving to avoid refrigeration is salutary. Rubbish! I am battling to retrieve my two hundred.

I am also mourning the loss of temptation resulting from "D" Troop's being moved from Winnipeg, with its few but precious amenities, here to Dufferin. This climatically petrifying post is positioned precisely on the planet to be the only place in the world where a person warms to the prospect of being sent to H––l. It squats on the border, 80 miles SW of Winnipeg, opposite Fort Pembina, of unblessed memory.

The High Command has designated Dufferin as "temporary headquarters" of the Mounted Police. This means that we enjoy the hardship while being spared the glory. Our comrades out west garner the attention of the hero-worshippers, while we here at HQ attract the attention only of the "cooties", as they call the more permanent residents of our barracks. The Canadian louse differs from other varieties of the species that I have met: it has a tiny hump on its back, wherein the insect stores enough of our blood to sustain it while the Troop is away on duty. Its fellow vermin, the Canadian flea, can leap for amazing distances, as though aware

15.   From start to end of his career in the Force, FD showed skill and determination in defending against Ottawa's attacks on his pay.

that it inhabits a land so broad that a normal jump would fail to keep pace with the advance of civilisation.

Mention of the ubiquitous fleas brings me to my uniform. I have drawn, that is, received, all my uniform, and am trying to make it fit. It is not easy to find a good tailor in a town of 3700 living in a huddle of shacks. The scarlet Norfolk jacket[16] is totally unbecoming to a person of my stature. Doubtless I shall look more impressive in the saddle, but in the mirror I resemble a Mandalayan sunset observed over a pair of corded stumps. The Force's theory is that the red coat will intimidate the Indians and deprive them of the excuse of shooting me in mistake for a buffalo. Touching faith indeed, given the fate of the British redcoats who marched shoulder to shoulder into the withering fire of the American revolutionaries. I should be grateful, I suppose, that the flaming jacket does not have a bull's-eye stitched on the back, as a convenience to the outlaw.

To complete the ensemble, I wear a blue cape and white gloves. The red, white, and blue – long may I wave!

The regulation NWMP headgear suggests that the Canadian government hopes to subdue the West by making the entire population, native or otherwise, helpless with laughter. I thought I had seen the last of the pillbox hat, in Asia, but here it is, small as life, strapped to my chin to heighten my resemblance to the organ-grinder's monkey.[17] It is the one style of military haberdashery that combines maximum exposure to sunstroke with minimum protection from frostbite, while being too shallow and of too mean a circumference to shelter a flask. As for the cork pith helmet that I shall be wearing for special ceremonies, the potential menace is a brass spike atop the helmet, something feared by every drinking officer who forgets that he has left his hat in his chair.

16. Later shortened, though not at FD's request.
17. The forage cap was the forerunner of today's broad-brimmed "Smokey the Bear" hat. The Stetson did not become officially part of dress uniform till January 1, 1901.

My fur cap and coat and winter socks are reasonable enough, but I balk at the moccasins. Cosy they may be, even on horseback. From my experience in the Bengal Mounted, however, I judge it to be basic to civil deterrence that an officer wears boots. Do the Cossacks wear moccasins? Jackboots are essential to the threat of police brutality. Or, if the Powers That Be expect that the moccasins will enable me to flit soundlessly down deer paths in pursuit of unsuspecting miscreants, they flatter my footwork. A person afflicted with a speech impediment must depend heavily on the other end of his body to express his will. I intend to have nothing to do with my moccasins, unless obliged to eat them.

My u-----clothing is optional. I am advised to own at least three one-piece suits of heavy-duty woollens, worn simultaneously. When I remove them – to bathe, for instance – depends on how early spring comes to the Canadian prairies.

"You'll know it's time to change your skivvies, sir," the stores sergeant told me, "when you rip 'em and they bleed."

I must accustom myself to this hyperbolic kind of frontier humour, with which Canadians imperil proper deference to rank. My father would have approved of their Rabelaisian democracy, *en principe*, as a born *farceur* who would have seen familiarity breeding contempt to be the least of his procreant worries.

Of deeper concern to me is the weaponry issued to all ranks. I have no qualms about the short Snider-Enfield carbine, so long as I am not called upon to fire it. I am an indifferent marksman, and have been shocked to see some of our recruits here using Scotch whisky bottles for target practice. Have they no respect? My dearest wish for *my* rifle is that it may remain safely domiciled in its saddle bucket, except of course when being cleaned by my batman. And long may my Deane and Adams revolver live in its holster! Debate is raging in the Force, I learn, as to whether the revolver should be worn on the left side, butt forward, or on the right side, butt facing aft. (Unless one is left-handed, of course, in which case the options are reversed.) I have no preference, not being possessed by the ambition to be a "quick-draw artist". The American West appears to be infatuated with this skill, but much of the function of the NWMP is to impress upon both the Indians and the whisky runners the fact that we are the *last* to draw a weapon. For us, right makes might, and I hope with all my heart that we are not wrong.

Oddly enough, it seems to be working. If we can continue to avoid the violent confrontation with the Indians practised by our noisy neighbours, it will be a feather in our cap (though I shall be happy to eschew the full headdress). Perhaps I shall find my future in this land, after all. An Englishman in the Royal Engineers has told me, on oath, that some parts of Canada are actually habitable, all year round. He mentioned the west coast. That may be my Garden of Eden. For I am resolved to find something to like in this country. Pa came to America full of expectation of finding the New Jerusalem of the world's oppressed, and went home to complain that the country was too big, too dirty, and too uncivil.[18] He never forgave the Mississippi River for not being a Thames with happy darkies dancing in the bulrushes. But I have the advantage of having lived with the Ganges, and am prepared to admire any Canadian river, however graceless, so long as it does not have bloated bodies floating downstream – goats, cows, people. I have yet to observe one vulture hovering over the Canadian landscape, and I take this as a good omen.

With many good wishes, your friend,
Frank.

PS   I forgot to mention my lance. Very similar to that wielded by our troops in India, crimped pennant and all, but reserved, thank Heaven, for ceremonials. The plan is that we shall drill with them in clear view of the Indians, who will be sobered

---

18.   Charles Dickens's *American Notes*.

at once, seeing that we may dispatch them to H––l as shish kabobs. The press sometimes refers to us as "Lancers of the North-West Mounted Police", an unsettling designation as I have a great deal of difficulty holding the reins and the lance at the same time. One or the other I must grip with my teeth, at what has proved to be a risk to troopers riding near me.

In Bengal, rather than tent-pegging[19] (let alone pig-sticking), my main use for my bannered pike was to determine wind direction. I am really rather good at reading a lance, and count on my profiting from this skill once we move out of Manitoba, where the wind is such that it once plucked the lance from my grasp and hurled it, like a spear, into the side of the necessary house (fortunately unoccupied at the time).

PPS   I have also been issued a horse, which of course facilitates riding outdoors.

PPPS   Our "D" Troop comprises five officers (the other four being veterans of the Great March West last summer, with all that this means for me as sole "tenderfoot" or "greenhorn"), 55 non-commissioned officers and men, 77 horses, and 184 cattle. The cattle are unranked. They may be slaughtered in any order, so long as we keep the complement up. They and we are housed in noticeably similar buildings abandoned by the Boundary Commission, those doughty pioneers who remorselessly tracked the 49th parallel westward. The quarters are more comfortable than those of the ill-fated "E" Troop, whom we left behind at the spanking new Swan River Barracks, in that we don't wake up under a blanket of snow bestowed by holes in the roof.

Perhaps I should have signed on as a Boundary Commis-

---

19.   Indian cavalry sport in which the rider, at full gallop, tries to transfix with his lance a wooden peg stuck in the ground.

sionaire! It must be satisfying work, to drive a sturdy, square post into the ground every few miles, and mark it "U.S. Territory" on one side, "British Possession" on the other, knowing that north of the post reigns law and order and the Union Jack, while south of it anarchy rules, the domain of gunslingers, disorderly beverage rooms, and dancehall girls whose virtue is no longer in question. If surveying were not a trade, I would be nothing loath to turn in my riding crop for a quadrant, taking the measure of the giant stars that make the prairie night sky one of the wonders of the universe. I should, of course, expect someone else to dig the post holes. As you'll remember, I have rather small, writer's hands, inherited from my pater. Manual strength, or rather the lack of it, may be my undoing in a Force that expects every man this day to do his duty, which may include milking a cow.

With no chance of our venturing west till spring, I have been assigned to drilling the new recruits. Handling men is not my forte. If anything, Minnie, I am worse at it than at handling women. Nature deprived me and other stockily-built officers of the stature essential to command immediate respect in both sexes. No doubt because Commissioner French had the opportunity to observe my proficiency as a horseman, I am supervising foot drill. Perilous. In this frigid weather, a man needs something warm between his legs. On the other hand, the drill square is within the walls of the post, so that I am close enough to the buildings to be able to race to a stove ere I lose any part of my person to frostbite.

You may find this incredible, but I swear that this is the drill regulation: drilling may not be suspended unless the temperature falls below -30 degrees[20] Fahrenheit *and* a wind is blowing. Here a wind is *always* blowing, in winter. It is one of life's few certitudes. Thus I spend much of my time leaning like a Hebridean pine in front of a group of fur-bearing mammals with frost on their whiskers and hate in their eyes. They dread my giving an order, because my speech

20.   -34.4° Centigrade. This regulation has since been modified.

impediment can delay a command such as "Stand at ease" just long enough for their feet to freeze to the ground. I have seen men topple to the ground in India, from heat prostration, but they didn't shatter. Here I drill them in dread that because of my unquestioning obedience to a thermometer, something – an ear, a leg – will crack off a recruit, and I shall be billed for it.

Most of my duties as an officer are supervisory, thank G–d, but on occasion I have been required to stand in for a sick NCO (Non-Commissioned Officer) and instruct the men in revolver-loading drill. For this manoeuvre I must remove my gloves, to show the recruit how to insert the bullet into the chamber. This movement may sound simple, but first I must place my rifle between my knees (numb), butt to the ground (slippery), to hold it while I use my hands (cold as the Ghost of Christmas Present) to load the revolver. The position offers several opportunities for a self-inflicted wound that I cannot even discuss in polite company. You understand why I include the NCO's health in my prayers.

In these Arctic conditions I am grateful for my beard, which provides a windbreak for my face. I would be even more benefited by a full beaver, as a comforter for my chest, but dress regulations appear to reserve the longer beard for the higher officer.[21] Indeed, I feel fortunate to supplement my Sub-Inspector's moustache with what is recognized by the cognoscenti as the Charles Dickens beard. I have a distaste for trading on my father's likeness, but when it is a matter of survival, I am happy to concede the resemblance. I only wish that I could dispense with the chin-strap on my cap, as this creates the lamentable illusion of securing a set of false whiskers. I unquestionably command more respect with my hat off. Whether I am enhanced by removing other clothes is something known only to a select few, all of them tailors.

21.   FD errs. The order book stated: "All individuals of the police force can please themselves as to wearing whiskers, moustaches or beards, but those who prefer to shave must do so daily."

Here, as in India, although I never deliberately draw attention to myself as Charles Dickens's son, the connexion is quickly made, especially by the English officers and men, some of whom, like me, have served in Bengal. I don't blame them for being somewhat in awe at first. When one's father lies in Westminster Abbey, it affects how people treat one, though one lies on a wood cot in Dufferin, Manitoba. When they weary of the interminable card games, some officers in the mess look at me as though they would like me to tell them a story. The winter evenings are so long, my stutter would undoubtedly help to pass the time. Since I have no facility whatever in spinning yarns, however, I don't try to compete with the further adventures of Mr. Pickwick. I have no desire to become known as Dickens the Lesser, a second-generation scribbler. My only hope is as a man of action, whose deeds will speak louder, and more fluently, than words. When at last my story appears, it will be as factual history,[22] borrowing nothing from the imagination and owing even less to the grand author who saw his fictional characters as his family, and treated his family as fictional characters.

What particularly pips me is when a brother officer, emboldened by imbibing, asks me: "What was your father *really* like?" The only question that galls me more – usually asked by a Canadian – is "What *is* your father really like?"

"He's dead," I reply. But this rarely satisfies their curiosity. I must elaborate, with a catechism that I know by rote and that I can repeat without a single stutter: "My father was a very loving man. He loved me, my brothers and sisters, my mother and her sister, his father and mother, his mistresses and friends, the poor and the downtrodden. All of humanity he loved. My father gave us a wonderful home which he made over into a house – in London, in Paris, in Genoa. Wherever he was, I could be sure that my father was thinking of me,

22. When asked if he would consider publication of a book based on his experiences with the police, FD replied that if he did, he would title the book *Thirty Years Without Beer*.

because he always included me in the farewell paragraph
of his letters to my mother . . . 'the prodigious Chickenstalker' . . . 'the phenomenon'. . . . My father was a man of
amazing energy and genius. I wish I had known him."

A letter from you, my dear, will hasten the end of this
winter in my soul.

Your Frank.

∼

Dufferin, Manitoba.
January 15th, 1875.

Dear Minerva,

Still no word from you. It is so very frustrating to be unable
to ascertain – by communication with a mutual friend, say –
whether you are receiving my letters, have moved to another
address, or – G–d forbid – have been seriously ill. I pray that
what has happened merely reflects the normal workings of
the Canadian postal system. As the Queen's mail must be
routed from here through the U.S.A., my letters to you may
have been intercepted by fanatical Fenians seeking revenge
for the Battle of the Boyne, and who may be aware that
Commissioner French was born in Ireland. No doubt there
is a less sinister explanation, which I must find the patience
to wait upon.

Certainly nothing has interfered with my correspondence
from the Minister of Justice. After considering my carefully-
reasoned objection to his charging me $200 for that ridiculous
turn-around trip, he has reduced the bill by seven dollars.
Seven dollars! This is like telling a man who is about to be
hanged, drawn, and quartered that he may keep his nose.
And there is no appeal, no higher court to which I may have
recourse. I have committed my life to a Force whose motto

is "Maintien [*sic*] le Droit"[23] (Uphold Justice), yet in the very first test of Justice I find myself upheld by the heels.

In being financially persecuted I have a kindred spirit in Sub-Constable Flynn, who has turned up here after his desertion and a short-lived career as a Mississippi card shark that proved to be a flounder. The excuse given to the Commissioner was that he had been robbed by American bandits and forced to wash dishes to earn his fare from the Dakota Territory. He could have told the Commissioner that he was captured by gypsies who made him string their violins – he would have been pardoned, because this "outfit" is so desperately short of men.

I was pleased to see Flynn again, even though I don't like him. When one is lost among strangers, even an old enemy offers the compensation of being a familiar face. On our first encounter on the drill square I asked him: "How's the swine fever, constable?"

"Much better, sir," says Flynn, grinning, "since I give up mixin' with Yanks."

I sometimes take Flynn with me when I am inspecting barracks, one of the commoner duties with which I am entrusted. In truth, I inspect the barracks so regularly that my rank of Sub-Inspector has taken on the connotation of looking under bunks. Flynn looks under the bunks for me; that is, instead of me. This frees me to concentrate on inspecting higher surfaces, such as the men. I try to be compassionate about the appearance of the Other Ranks, especially if it is evident that a man has been drinking to the extent that he sways while standing at attention, or subsides to the floor before I can inspect him. I am not totally abstemious myself, and most of the men know it. Despite my issuing warnings instead of putting a man on charge for intoxication that would cost him $3 (first offence) or $6 (second offence), I am as often as not rewarded with an insult, usually in the

---

23. The fractured French was soon corrected to the present motto: *Maintiens le Droit.*

form of a request that I perform a sexually impracticable act. In the Bengal police any native trooper who tried thus to intrude on an officer's reproductive system would have been soundly flogged, at the very least. With Canada's Mounted Police Force, however, I have only the option of reporting the offender for an insulting remark ($5), or for starting an argument ($10). Why starting an argument should be twice as costly as an insulting remark is a moot point. Since a constable earns only 75 cents a day, however, I do my best to interpret his starting an argument as constructive criticism, so long as he refrains from spitting on my boots. *That* is disputatious.

What is beyond argument for all ranks is that Dufferin[24] is not Winnipeg. It is a grubby little dump, a pimple on the behind of creation, to which my "D" Troop has been relegated[25] because the C.O., Commissioner French, refuses to stop badgering the government for squandering a fortune on the Swan River HQ that was built as a gazebo for mountain goats. His protracted bellows have now been picked up by the Opposition in the House of Commons, as evidence that the government organized the Mounted Police for the purpose of rescuing a group of building contractors from the need to do honest work and charge fair prices. There may be something to this belief, since I find that for a young country, Canada has a precocious appetite for politics and the spoils thereof. I am willing to fight against the odds with heathen savages and whisky traders, but I am frankly terrified by Canadian self-government. In India we had nothing comparable, by way of unpredictable hazard, except the occasional man-eating tiger, or rogue elephant on the rampage.

You will not have missed the irony of my being marooned in a border bazaar named after the dignitary who obtained

24.   Now Emerson, Manitoba. The fort was used as a staging-area by the NWMP.
25.   FD was apparently under the illusion that other NWMP posts were more comfortable.

for me this situation. To my knowledge, Lord Dufferin has no plans to holiday in Dufferin, Manitoba. A pity, as I should have sought the honour of escorting the Viceroy on a tour of the desolation, pointing out the contrast between this station and his beloved Simla, on the balmy slopes of Mount Jakko, where he built his Viceregal Lodge among the wild strawberries and cherries, apricots, and heady bougainvillea.

"Would milord care to see the Manitoba version of the rope trick, in which we stretch a rope between our abode and the outhouse so that we may answer the call of nature without becoming hopelessly lost in a blizzard? As for flora, where in India would milord see such a host of golden p——sholes in the snow?"

However, Lord Dufferin has chosen to remain in absentia, rather than grace his namesake town with a baptism of sleet. Tonight I shall drink his health, which he sustains, I am told, with the excellent wines of Montreal. And I shall raise a silent toast to you, Mrs. Butts, from whom each day I hope to hear.

Your faithful friend,
Frank.

∾

Dufferin, Manitoba.
March 31st, 1875.

Ezra Butts, Esq.
The Black Mare Inn, Shepherd's Hill, Surrey, England

Dear Butts,

I have received your letter of February 19th. I am shocked to learn that Minerva has, as you put it, "chosen a life of shame far from the marriage bed." We have both, I think, recognized that she is what is called "a free spirit", a personality that often goes hand in hand with artistic talent, but I still have difficulty in believing that she has run away with another man, particularly since she left behind my collected letters to her, which you say you found in an empty ginger-beer container. If you have read the letters you know that our correspondence – Mrs. Butts' and mine – attests to the innocence of our entente. I wrote to her biographically, and she never wrote to me at all.

At this moment I am too discomposed by your news to consider reasonably your suggestion that I continue the correspondence, addressing my letters to you instead of Minerva. I expect to leave shortly with my fellow troopers for the Far West and a life that may be too full of action and adventure for the composition of belles lettres.

I am, sir, your obedient servant,
Francis J. Dickens
(Sub-Inspector).

～

Dufferin, Manitoba.
May 2nd, 1875.

Dear Ezra,

The departure of "D" Troop has been delayed, giving me
the opportunity to acknowledge your letter of April 2nd, in
which you inform me that you have very kindly asked your
purveyor of spirituous beverages to order for me, via New
York City, a crate of Scotch whisky. I doubt that delivery can
be accomplished without a major miracle, such as the Lord's
dividing the Red River to enable the chosen brew to cross
into Canada. But I am sustained by faith, the only whisky
available here on the border being an American corn whisky
that they call "Bourbon", presumably because, as was said of
the French monarchs, it has learned nothing and it forgets
nothing.

I am saddened to hear from you that Mrs. Butts has written
to you to ask that you send her my letters, along with her
leather potter's apron. I agree with you in your opinion that
your wife's lover wants my letters for purely commercial
purposes, to profit from my being the son of Charles Dickens.
You are quite correct in refusing to convey my letters to her.
I want *no* publication till my story has been told and I can be
sure that it has enough merit to entertain and inform readers,
though my name were Francis Jeffrey Duckfeathers.

I am, yours gratefully,
Frank Dickens.

❧

Swan River Barracks, Manitoba.
Sept. 25th, 1875.

Dear Ezra,

Your letter of July 18th has found its way to me here at Swan
River Barracks, which you won't find on your map but are
many miles northwest of Winnipeg and even the most elementary forms of Temptation. All the more reason for me to
appreciate your diligence in keeping me informed of political
and social events in England. I had no idea that the first
roller-skating rink has opened in London, or that the city's
main sewerage system is completed – no connexion, I presume, between these two exercises?

Also very timely was your money order for £50, to defray
the expense of packing and mailing to you a buffalo hide, to
be displayed on the wall of your inn. Because of bungling by
the quartermaster, I am threatened with unexpected expenditure,[26] and have taken the liberty of cashing your money
order though I cannot promise you immediate delivery of the
buffalo hide. I should point out to you that the head of a
buffalo – which you think will add decorative appeal to your
hostelry, mounted above the bar – is sizeable and therefore
awkward to parcel. More pertinent, however, is the fact that
I have not yet seen a buffalo, the vast herds having been
pushed westward by the spread of what this Dominion amus-
ingly calls civilisation. I take it from your letter that you
desire a buffalo that I have killed myself, either with a rifle
or, as you say flatteringly, "with your bare hands". I have

26. FD ordered, without authorization, saddles and slickers from
England for himself and fellow officers. Ottawa wanted to charge him
customs duty, but after a long siege agreed to allow him free entry –
with a stern warning not to try it again.

every expectation of meeting a buffalo in the very near future, and yours will be the first hide I send oversea.

Our Troop will be grateful to move on from this brutal post, which could be attractive to only a vengeful Zeus looking for a wide selection of rock to which to chain the overly assertive Prometheus. The men have had to spend the hot season – and I know that this will surprise you, but it does become very hot indeed here, hot enough, to answer your question, "to melt all that snow" – preparing a parade square by removing the mammoth boulders with which the misbegotten site is strewn. This back-breaking work involves using fire and water from the nearby Snake River to split the rocks, on late-summer days when the temperature alone hereabouts is enough to sunder granite.[27]

Hellish, penal drudgery it is, and I hate to watch the men doing it. After all, they are not convicts, or slaves. One or two of the other officers are so insensitive as to sit on a chair in the shade of the fort's wall, to supervise the work. I make a point of moving about, making sure that the men have enough water for themselves as well as for the rocks. I must walk the fine line between displaying sympathy and encouraging the familiarity that can be fatal to discipline. Dealing with Canadians, I deem it prudent to err on the side of humanity. The days are coming when my life will depend on the response of my men to a critical situation. I wish to reduce as much as possible the length of time one of my constables will take to decide whether my life is worth saving. If he ponders for more than a week, I have obviously failed to lay the groundwork for handling an emergency.

I am therefore content that (I'm told) some of the men – behind my back – call me "Dickie". Better a Dickie than a Chickenstalker!

27.   In his *Reminiscences of the Great North-West*, Sam Steele recalls the plutonian scene on the Snake River, so named because masses of garter snakes basked in the sun "and some of them were even found in the barrack-rooms." (p. 96)

The parade square was, unfortunately, made level in time for the inspection by Major-General E. Selby Smyth, head of the Canadian militia.[28] I am ever wary of Smiths that spell themselves Smyth. And hail from Hibernia. My apprehension proved to be warranted. One of those blue-eyed ramrods, General Smyth made little effort to conceal his disgust at the status of our post. He found a lamentable imbalance of spit and polish – too much spitting, not enough polishing. Over the winter our wardrobe had become somewhat various, prompting the General to scold us for losing visual distinction between officers and men. He favours swords for the officers, because they "make a significant impression on the Indian mind". He has clearly been influenced by the U.S. Cavalry, whom the American Indians call Long Knives. I look forward with muted enthusiasm to being encumbered by a long knife as well as the pennon lance, the carbine, the revolver, and the riding crop. If I make any deeper impression on the Indian mind, I shall be unable to move at all.

The General was also critical of our equitation, unfortunately singling me out as an example of the failure of man and horse to move as one, or even two. "I see at least three objects in conflicting trajectory," he told me. I am not surprised. Although I have spent most of my professional life in the company of horses, I am not really fond of the animals. I welcome the benefit of the mount's making me look taller, but I have never considered the horse to be this man's best friend, or even anything more than a casual acquaintance.

We are told that a horse can smell fear in its rider. I refuse to be afraid of this admirable creature, but the animal does seem to be able to sense that, when I am sitting on its back, the course of wisdom is to remain immobile. My forte as a horseman has always been that of taking the salute, on parade, like the Queen, God bless Her. "A living statue," a superior officer once complimented me. I never need to use my spurs

---

28.   Appointed by the government to tour all Mounted Police posts and report to Ottawa on the efficiency of the Force.

on a horse. It stays quite still without bullying. A mutual understanding – that is what I try to establish with a horse that has some breeding. The horse understands that I shall not employ it to chase other animals – the fox, for example – because I consider it vulgar. Nor will my horse be asked to join a posse (very popular with the Americans but distinctly *déclassé*). I refuse to gallop, canter under protest, trot only when necessary, and walk my horse only when both of us are convinced that to do so offers advantages over remaining stationary.

"Most of your men don't even know how to *saddle* a horse," General Selby Smyth informed me. "They approach the horse from the wrong side."

This would have flummoxed me even if I had not had a small libation, in advance, to celebrate the General's visit. I know that it can be risky to approach a horse from the rear, but the other sides seem equal. So I asked him, man to man, "Which, sir, is the right side?"

The General stared at me hard, suspecting facetiousness that I had not intended. "The *correct* side, Inspector, is the side *opposite*. *Your* men go to the near side and toss on the saddle complete with carbine, wallets, girths, and straps, trusting to God that it will all land upright and in the correct order. That, sir, is ineptitude born of sheer laziness. I assume, sir, that you dress *yourself* one article at a time. You owe your horse the same toilet."

I kept my mouth shut. Frankly, I thought my lads did rather well in the mounted drill for the General's scrutiny. None hung on to his horse's neck – a proclivity of new recruits – and everyone kept in line, though the line was parabolic. Yet the General's comment to me was: "Some of your horses look lame." He then proceeded to inspect the animals and found that several had hoof disease. "It's caused by insects," he told me accusingly, as though I were responsible for the teeming bugs of western Canada. "Your men will need to wash every hoof with carbolic soap. When they get out on the trail, a thousand miles from nowhere, having a senior officer is a luxury, but having a healthy horse is a bl--dy must. Do I make myself clear, Inspector?"

Pellucid, I thought. But I saluted and thanked him for sharing with me a few of the judgments of his eventual report[29] to the government. As the General's party left our post, I said a prayer, not for him but for myself: "Dear God, let me begone westward before those d--n swords get here!"

Your western correspondent,
Frank.

PS   There is some talk at HQ of organizing the Force's best horsemen into something to be called The Musical Ride.[30] This is taking the form of a sort of equine Roger de Coverley, and I fear that I may have been responsible for starting the madness. One day at Dufferin my horse was startled into a gallop by a somewhat embarrassing noise and I inadvertently rode with my eyes closed right through a line of lancers without hitting anyone, then reined my horse around, lost control, and went pell-mell through them again. Some fool saw the intersection as clever, when put to music. Now there is no telling what this aberration may do to the character and reputation of Britain's cavalry, especially if the Indians see us doing it. In my view, the Mounted Police should learn to walk before we try to waltz. Luckily, my hearing problem excuses me from extraneous exercises dependent on band music, unless the trumpeter and I are sharing the same horse.

PPS   Thank you for your kind opinion of these aide-mém-oires. You represent the honest, English readership (rather

29.   Smyth's report was to rate FD as an officer of "no promise", being "physically weak in constitution, his habits not affording a good example" – probably a reference to his drinking problem.
30.   The Musical Ride was first taught to the Mounties in 1876, by Sergeant-Major Robert Belcher, ex-9th Lancers.

than the snobby intellectual) that I hope to woo with my book one day. Despite the dismal experience of my brief association with my father's magazine,[31] I am not convinced that I am entirely without literary talent. God keep you!

〜

Swan River Barracks, Manitoba.
July 13th, 1876.

Dear Ezra,

I have not written to you for some time because our post has been under siege from a plague of locusts. Our hay and other crops have been devastated by these Canadian grasshoppers which will eat everything, even the paint off the walls. I can't imagine why the Lord is thus punishing our land, but it must be a sin mortal enough to make Satan gasp. Chief Constable Sam Steele,[32] a veteran of the Great Trek to Fort Whoop-up and the Far West who has joined us here, tells me that the grasshopper gets bigger as one moves westward. He once tried to throw a saddle on one, he says, but the brute mired him in tobacco juice, then leaped the corral fence. Having seen what these creatures can do to my underg–––––ts hung on a line, I have no reason to doubt the constable's account.

I find Steele intimidating because he was once a Permanent Force man, and an instructor in gunnery to boot. It has been my experience, as a police officer, that erstwhile militia who have cut their teeth on a brass mortar never regain respect for those of us common mortals who have never touched off a field piece. When I see Sam Steele measuring me with those flinty eyes, the term "flash in the pan" takes

31.   In 1861, when FD was 17, Charles Dickens took his son on staff of his magazine *All the Year Round*.
32.   Later Colonel S. B. Steele, C.B., M.V.O., and the most articulate Mountie of them all.

on a personal connotation. Looking at Sam, a very model of a modern mounted policeman, I sometimes wonder if I am really cut out for this line of work.

Commissioner French, I regret to say, is resigning from the Force he organized two years ago. Although we are by no means messmates, he seems to have forgotten the strained circumstances of our first meeting. I think that we now respect each other, I him for his splendid record as leader of the NWMP, he me for my efforts to exorcise the demon rum. Yes, Ezra, as my former publican you will be astonished to learn that I am now, if not totally dry, at least, like parts of dear old India, arid for much of the year. I can honestly credit this moderation less to strength of will than to absence of opportunity – the key to virtue in all things. We are a long way from the border.

To honour the Commissioner on his retirement, our post presented him with a gold watch and chain, a gift inspired by my father's timepiece, which the Commissioner has admired on our rare formal occasions, when I needed it in order to know when I might leave. The Commissioner is leaving – the Force, that is – out of disgust. What the savages and the murderous whisky traders and the stark conditions of climate and country failed to do, Ottawa did. It broke his spirit, by sheer financial bungling. I feel close to him, in his defeat, because I too have bled from wounds inflicted by the honed pens of the government's berserk bookkeepers. I went to the Commissioner in his office to bid him goodbye, as a comrade in umbrage.

"I want you to know, sir, that I respect what you are doing." I held out my hand.

He did not take it at once. I could see that he was fighting off the surge of emotion. He was actually biting his lip. At last he took my hand with a grip that made me wince, and he said:

"Thank you, Dickens. It is officers like you who make me feel better about quitting the Force."

Fort Carlton, NWT.
August 21st, 1876.

Rather suddenly, I find myself at this post far to the west on
the North Saskatchewan River. It is an old Hudson's Bay
Company trading post, which of course means that it is much
more comfortable than a modern NWMP post built by the
government. Indeed, Swan Song Barracks have been abandoned, as our HQ, and now become a roadside shrine at
which the Canadian taxpayer may pause to make an excretory
offering.

Our Troop left in too great haste for me to alert you that
I am at last heading west, to our new HQ: Fort Macleod. Forward, ho! In July we heard that Lt.-Col. James Macleod, the
hero of the first great trek, had been appointed as the new
Commissioner. Almost at once (August 6th)[33] he appeared
at 6 a.m. at our gate with his adjutant bearing an order for
the entire headquarters staff and most of "D" Troop to be
ready in three hours to march 1150 miles! Three hours! I was
so distracted that I filled both my water bottles with water.

Col. Macleod must have noted my difficulty in coping with
the early hour, since he assigned the overseeing of the horse
shoeing and harnessing to Sgt.-Major Steele, and told me
to make sure that the barracks were "left in good order".
Whenever our Dickens family moved house – which was
often – in Europe, my mother always told the servants to
wash the windows, so that the next residents would not think
us slovenly. But my men were dashing about so headlong
that I couldn't find a volunteer for any kind of last-minute
housekeeping, and in the end I simply thumb-tacked a note
of apology to the door of the officers' mess and locked up.

Miraculously, Macleod and Steele between them gener-
ated enough energy in our men to have the whole outfit
moving out of the barracks square at 9 o'clock. And what a
thrilling sight we were, that sunlit August morn! By G–d,

33. Actually, August 8, 1876.

Ezra, there are few moments in a man's life when he feels truly alive, when the shiver runs up his spine to confirm that every part of his being is focussed on a future that lies somewhere beyond the horizon, the same tingle that Hannibal must have felt when he urged his elephants into the Alps, that our own King Henry must have known leading his bowmen through Normandy's hills to their rendezvous with fate at Agincourt.

Leading us out of the post was our band, the first of the Force, and suddenly the most harrowing aspect of headquarters life – overhearing band practice – was made worthwhile. The band's instruments had been delivered by dog team from Winnipeg, yet in four short months they had achieved what, to my admittedly inexpert ear, sounded like angels, trumpet-tongued. Proudest of all strode forth our seventeen-year-old bugler Bagley, his cheeks puffed like old Aeolus himself, as if bound to blow us to the Rocky Mountains by sheer horn power.

"Have you ever seen the like, Sergeant?" I asked Steele as we passed through the gate.

"Yes, sir, I have." He smiled grimly, and I knew that he was thinking of the Great Trek of '74, which departed from Dufferin with all the splendour of challenging the Unknown. Even the troops' horses were of different colours,[34] I'm told, so that a man had merely to look at the rear of the horse in front to know that he was riding with the wrong troop.

I have always insisted on having a black horse, since this is the one and only colour for a British mounted policeman. The black steed and the scarlet tunic complement one another perfectly. *Le rouge et le noir*, life astride death. How-

---

34.   To start the long march to Whoop-up, "A" Troop rode dark bays, "B" Troop dark browns, "C" Troop light chestnuts, "D" Troop greys, "E" Troop blacks, and "F" Troop light greys.

ever, the Ethiop thoroughbred has fallen into disfavour,[35] with the result that I embarked on my voyage aboard a "broncho", a type of plebeian western range horse that is nondescript in appearance but durable in service, and for this memorable occasion had had his wiry fur brushed, his bridle shined, and his tail pulled.

Unfortunately, as we plunged westward into adventure there were few to witness our gallant departure. A gaggle of troopers who were remaining behind to hold the fort, a smattering of halfbreeds. No matter. I think my father would have been proud of me, for once, to see me leading forth my Troop. I could not have felt more sublime were I riding Copenhagen, the Iron Duke's charger. Gallant Copenhagen! I still remember the day that Pa woke me and my brothers at three in the morning so that we could go to his offices of *Household Words* and watch the Duke of Wellington's funeral procession moving along Fleet Street to St Paul's.[36] It was seeing that moving homage that first made me want to be a military hero, if that could be arranged for someone lacking both the physical and mental qualifications. And now I was on my way to showing my father that the sword, if not mightier than the pen, may be almost as effective in impaling the Prince of Darkness.

On your side of the Atlantic all roads lead to Rome, but in these parts all trails lead to Batoche, the spot where the ferry crosses the South Saskatchewan River. This infernally powerful stream is as wide as the Thames at Westminster, although somewhat cleaner. One evening when we were camped near Batoche village, I made a point of paying my respects to the ferry. I strolled along the rutted cart-track in

35. When the main force was en route from Montana to Dufferin, June 1873, the overnight camp was hit by a violent thunderstorm. A lightning bolt stampeded the horses, the western breed reacting better than the climatically unseasoned animals brought by boxcar from Toronto. Some of the latter were panicked for scores of miles, back across the border, before being recaptured.
36. November 1852. FD was eight years old.

the magical, late-summer dusk, the light lingering as though reluctant to leave the undulant course of the placid stream, around whose bend of poplar-shaded banks sat, snugged to shore, the rare water spider.

The ferry is not a racy sloop, to be sure. Its defiance of the current is made considerably less audacious by its dependence on the steel cable[37] strung from shore to shore, a filament along which the water spider tows itself to and fro, as though stubbornly working on a one-strand web. As I watched from a rise above the river, the ferry sidled across the flow once, fetching back to my shore a small party of men who, after an animated discussion, broke up with most of them heading for the village. One, however, came striding to where I lay sprawled in the grass admiring Progress in Canadian fluvial transport.

How the man could have spotted me so quickly in the tricky slant of sunset, I cannot guess. But in no time at all he was standing over me, as I scrambled to my feet, brushing straw off my britches. He had a mien that inspired deference in the beholder: of sturdy, even barrel-chested, build, in his fringed hide jacket, handsomely decorated with needlework floral designs in the Métis style; long black hair curling down his pillared neck in a natural ruff of courtly vestment; and a face nut-brown yet unwrinkled, in which blazed two eyes that would have daunted the panther, however famished.

The man's demeanour was both resolute and faintly cavalier, an embodiment of how I imagined D'Artagnan would have looked – without, of course, the silk hose, and with a rifle in place of a rapier. He was clearly a Métis, but a Métis such as I had not met on his own turf.

37. The cable was to play a major role in the Battle of Batoche, nine years later. When the sternwheeler *Northcote*, recruited by General Middleton as a dreadnought, tried to escape Dumont's sharpshooters, the Métis dropped the cable to try to snare the craft, knocking off her funnels and sending her floundering backwards downstream – the first and last naval engagement on the Canadian prairies.

"Good evening, sir," I said.

The man nodded, and murmured, "Ne bouges pas." He then swiftly unslung his rifle and raised it so that it pointed straight at my head. My viscera balled into a knot. I watched his forefinger squeeze the trigger – the thought that I presumed to be my last was: yes, he is following the drill prescribed by the musketry manual. I closed my eyes and braced myself for the impact. The bullet winged past my ear. I opened my eyes to find my assailant striding past me, into the undergrowth beside the path along the river bluff. I was still rooted to the spot when fifty yards away he stooped to pick up the "cottontail" he had shot. Silently gliding back to me in his moccasins he held out the small rabbit, and displayed with a flourish the fact that the single bullet had hit it cleanly in the eye.

I didn't know whether to admire the man's marksmanship or complain that he had imperilled my left ear, which needed all the outer shell it could deploy. Before I could decide on an attitude, we were joined on the path by an elderly villager on his way home from a day's fishing that had, on the evidence, proved barren.

"B'jour, José," rumbled the mighty Métis. "Tiens." And he handed the rabbit to the codger, who was plainly grateful to receive the makings of a dinner and a pair of fur mitts.

"Merci, Gabriel, merci!" The old man ambled off, cradling his prize. I, however, felt a fresh tremor of anxiety. "Gabriel." There could be only one Gabriel in this place – Gabriel Dumont. A name to be conjured with, gingerly, as it had been around our campfire the night before. Even Sam Steele had spoken the name with something approaching reverence. Not only was the nearest crossing-point upriver named Gabriel's Crossing after him, but the most awesome legend belonged to this prodigious Nimrod, and perennial leader ("captain") of the buffalo hunt.

Dumont was of particular interest to the Justice Ministry at this time, with a warrant out for his arrest (prudently ignored by law officers) for having assaulted a member of the band of buffalo hunters to whom he was chief of staff. The pummelled hunter had violated "the law of the plains", the unwritten statute stating that the hunting band waits together till the propitious moment for attack on the herd. One hunter trying to steal a march on the others could stampede several thousand buffalo, thus ruining the hunt for the rest. The discipline of the Force, I gathered, was as nothing to the discipline of the buffalo hunt, which could take a man's horse, leaving him helpless.

For having enforced this ancient law of the plains (too sensible entirely to have been legislated by the Dominion Government in Ottawa), Dumont had received an admonitory lecture from my old Nemesis, Major-General Sir E. Selby Smyth, G.O.C. Militia. Yes, the same generalissimo who questioned my knowing which side of the horse is mountable. I felt such an immediate bond with Dumont that I could not restrain myself from blurting out to him:

"Major-General Sir E. Selby Smyth!" – and I held my nose in a universally-understood gesture.

Dumont roared with laughter. "B'en sur!" he said, and he held *his* nose. And there we stood, in an enchanted moment of communion, two soul-mates, each holding his nose in a twilight whose aroma was beyond reproach.

Dumont left me with an impressively firm handshake and the four-square eye-to-eye look of rebels on opposite sides of the law. As he walked away from me I realized that it was not D'Artagnan that he reminded me of, but my father – leaving me with the purposeful stride of a man going to attend to something more important. . . .

Much as I delighted in the brief encounter with that Canadian rarity – an intelligent man with a robust talent for rollicking, who (they said) would take a gamble or a dare as readily as other men take a breath – I was disquieted by the easy aura of authority and command that emanated from his person, the blending of all that is best and bravest of the red man and the Frenchman. Better for us of the Force were this river's Charon an old boatman whose only purpose is to ferry us souls to whatever Hades lies on the nether shore from the sleepy environs of Batoche.

After an uneventful crossing, marked only by the offensive jokes of some of my comrades about the ferry-less rivers that lay to the West, and tasteless speculation about my swimming abilities while grasping my horse's tail, we reached Fort Carlton on August the 18th, at sunset. It had been quite the most inoffensive journey I had made since leaving England. This, I'm told, is the best season (August-September) for the northern part of the eastern Territories, the countryside burnished gold with grasses and birch and poplar, and plenty of game for the cook's pot clustered around the little ponds known here as "sloughs", pronounced "slews" for reasons that lie beyond logic. For the first time I have had the impression that Canada may, after all, be habitable. By someone, that is, besides ducks, aborigines, buffalo, and English remittance men. The North Saskatchewan River is an amiable, meandering course, and I am amazed by the number and variety of waterfowl that find fulfilment in wading.

The single, terrifying peril of our progress on the trail was one that I had been warned about: the northern mosquito. "She measures six inches," a Winnipeg barman told me, "and that's *between the eyes*." I thought that he was exaggerating for humorous effect. But no. In the hierarchy of airborne monsters, the winged dragon of China must yield place to the Canadian north's mosquito. Perhaps I should be grateful that the creature does not have claws, to bear its prey off like Sinbad's giant roc. What these Harpies lack in prehensile swoop, however, they more than make up for in numbers and their capacity to suck their victim's body dry of blood before he can raise his rifle. In order to sleep, each night I must wrap myself inside blankets till swathed like an Egyptian mummy. Even so, I, whose hearing is such that I can be unaware of a train whistle while standing beside the engine, am kept awake by the hideous, high-pitched whine of the brute's approach, then the yet more awful sound of its proboscis sawing a hole in my tent's canvas, and finally the deadly silence that means that it is perched on my shroud, preparing the *coup de grâce*.

Normally I shun crowds, as you know, but a large, outdoor assembly of humans is made attractive when it diverts at least some of the bugs away from me. I was therefore thrilled by the spectacle that greeted our eyes as we rode into Fort Carlton: circled about the fort stood hundreds of conical tents, "lodges" which housed the 2000 redskins assembled for the signing of the Treaties. The ceremonies had begun the day before, but the dust still hung in the yellow twilight air, kicked up by the scores of bareback-riding bucks putting on a show for the white commissioners. Our arrival swelled the number of the Force escort to 82 men, so that I needed to appear to be a match for only 20 Indians.

To my alarm, our arrival produced pandemonium in the Indian camp because our band suddenly let fly with a martial air. The women grabbed their children and fled into their tepees. A group of braves gathered and came towards us, their painted faces grim. Our band stopped playing, bumpily. My hand hovered over my carbine. The leader of the natives' welcoming committee, to my horror, singled me out for attention as the nearest officer, and stood close to snarl something of which I understood nought except that he was not merely passing the time of day. Our interpreter then galloped up to my aid, and, having had the snarl repeated, told me:

"They are impressed by our drum, sir. They're willing to trade us a horse for the drum."

A crisis. In my judgment, the drum was the vital organ of our band. Beating a horse would not produce the same morale-boosting cadence. If the Indians had coveted young Bagley's bugle, I might have acceded at once to the trade, and if they had wished to take the fife, I should have gladly given *them* a horse. But I was prepared to fight for our drum, and was about to instruct the interpreter to ask the Indians how they would like to see a tympanum made with *their* skin, when Sgt. Steele moved up to speak quietly to me out of the side of his firm-set mouth.

"It's all right, sir. The Injuns will all be given money after the treaties are signed. They'll be able to buy their own drum."

This message having been conveyed to the welcoming committee, the meeting broke up. We proceeded past the treaty commissioners' tent, a marquee set upon a hill, to give our side the advantage of speaking from on high, and cantered triumphantly into the Hudson's Bay Company's stout enclave, to fall into our bunks with a prayer of thanks to the fur trade.

The next morning, the plain before the tent was the scene of the most extraordinary spectacle I have witnessed since I left India: the redskins, clearly in festive mood because the commissioners had provided the food for the party, put on a show worthy of the crowned heads of Europe. Advancing in a huge semicircle, amid a bedlam of womenfolk, children, and dogs, they wildly fired rifles into the air, yelling and pounding tomtoms, while hundreds of their horsemen put on a dazzling display of riding, racing in serpentine array, their bodies daubed and feathered to make each buck appear to be a fabulous creature, half bird, half horse, yet moving as a single demoniac power.

I shall never again be able to regard an English steeplechase with any degree of respect. Sitting astride my pony, with no function other than to look magisterial, I still found my jaw dropping in astonishment. I am baffled by how an Indian riding bareback can wheel on a penny – "buffalo hunters", they call these mounts. I wished I had blinkered my own horse's eyes, lest it see that saddle and stirrups and spurs are superfluous if the rider is truly capable.

Mercifully, things quietened down when the Cree chiefs – the principal chiefs being Mistahwahsis and Ahtukukoop, whose proud bearing was a tribute to having a multi-syllabic name – and their councillors approached the seated group of commissioners for what is called the Dance of the Stem. I was surprised that there was no preliminary jaw-jaw[38] by our people, in the grand tradition of the talking shop back at

38.   FD forgets that his troop missed the first day of the ceremonies.

Westminster, to stultify the opposition into submission. But no, the chiefs got right down to business, producing an enormous ceremonial pipe with a stem long enough to put paid to Pickwick. The chief with the senior wrinkles pointed the stem at the four points of the compass, then handed it to a young warrior who performed a stately dance with it, the whole crowd slowly converging on us the while, and their horsemen tearing past as the mood suited them. We had to depend on our interpreter to assure us that the Dance of the Stem was standard pomp and circumstance, and not – as occurred to me – the prelude to a well-catered massacre. Our Métis interpreter's name was Peter Erasmus, half Cree, half Dane. Recalling that the original Erasmus was noted for his malicious sense of humour, I watched him closely, as he instructed our commissioners on the pipe protocol, and was ready to break for the fort at the first sardonic curl of his lip.[39]

All went smoothly, however. Our commissioners – Lieutenant-Governor Morris of Manitoba and the Territories, resplendent in cocked hat and enough gold braid to garnish the whole British Admiralty; Chief Factor Christie of the Hudson's Bay Company; and the Hon. James McKay, a prominent Scotch Métis and member of the Manitoba government, conceivably chosen because of the imposing aspect of his 28-stone frame – each in turn took the peace pipe and respectfully stroked the stem. I found it hilarious, but resisted the opportunity to die laughing.

With the fondling of the corncob, the friendship of the attendant tribes and the white man was officially sealed. The Indians held off actually signing the treaties, however, since they were having such a good time. As the days passed into a week, it became obvious that the red men would delay the consummation of racial harmony with the whites till the food ran out. Since the food *was* running out, and the commissioners had failed to accelerate matters by showing the Indian

39.   His concern was unwarranted. Peter Erasmus was a loyal veteran of the Palliser expedition into the Rockies in 1857.

chiefs the florid uniforms that each would receive (after signing) from the Great White Mother – a scarlet coat, decorated with gold lace, and a gold-banded topper, plus a silver medal the size of a dinner plate as badge of fealty – Colonel Macleod delegated me to supervise the distribution of food in such a way as to disabuse the Indians of any idea they might have had of all leaving the conference looking like the Hon. James McKay.

"Dole it out, Dickens," said the Commissioner. "But graciously."

I prefer not to think that he chose me in order to impress upon the chiefs the dangers of what can happen to a person who eats too much of the white man's food. But as my men hauled forth the remaining stores of flour, meat, and tea for the approval of Chief Ahtukukoop[40] (Star Child), my handling of the Queen's largesse may have lacked self-assurance because of my suddenly seeing myself as the orphanage master to whom Oliver appealed, "Please, sir, I want some more." These, too, it struck me, were hungry children, and we were perhaps taking advantage of them. I put the thought out of my head.

In any event, it was not my demeanour that was the deciding factor in the chiefs' signing the treaties, but their eagerness to don their uniforms and pocket the $25 cash.[41] The final assembly was addressed by a fiery Cree warrior called Poundmaker (another name that my father would have relished). This Indian has been especially adept in constructing buffalo pounds into which the animals are stampeded and trapped. He certainly had great presence, for a savage. Tall and handsome, dignified in bearing, he gave us the shortest speech of the day – a mercy one would not expect from the

40. The other Cree chief was Mistahwahsis (Big Child).
41. A "gratuity" of $12, followed by a yearly annuity of $5, went to every man, woman, and child attending the treaties-signing. To encourage the Indians to pursue farming, the government promised to pay each band $1000 a year and provide instructors in agriculture.

barbarous – and the most thoughtful. He told the commissioners – through our interpreter, of course – that the Indians understood the need to find a substitute for hunting the diminishing herds of buffalo, as a source of food, but that as farmers they would need much help and advice from the white man. He said he hoped that the Indian children of tomorrow would be treated as fairly as the children of the paleface.

His words bothered me. Surely it is fanciful for us to expect to transform these free-roaming nomads into yeoman farmers, successfully tilling the same patch of soil, this evolvement having to happen a good deal more rapidly than the time it took us – says Mr. Darwin – to come down out of the trees? Please do not be alarmed by this unseemly introspection, Ezra. I promise not to make a habit of being socially aware. God forbid that something in the blood should lead me into writing that reflects a concern for social justice! I must strive for a refreshing callousness, the blithe expression of sauve-qui-peut. I shall – I swear! – plumb the depths of the superficial.

At any rate, Poundmaker's words did not bother our good Governor Morris, who rose under his plumed headdress to deliver a lengthy political bluster about the rosy, if limited, transition period, after which the Indians would be expected to provide for themselves. There was no doubt in my mind as to which of the two men had struck the gong of history that will reverberate through the years. What merry mincemeat my father would have made of *our* man!

If this be treason . . . I apologize to Her Majesty.

Blessing you,
Frank.

❧

Fort Pitt, NWT.
September 15th, 1876.

My dear Ezra,

Your letters of the 3rd and 30th of July have reached me at this H.B.C. post, west of Fort Carlton but another suckling of the Saskatchewan River. The case of ale that you say you ordered for me has not yet arrived; this is possibly just as well, since the main theme of the treaty negotiations here has been the role of the Mounted Police in protecting the Indians from firewater. Having learned to drink in moderation myself, most of the time, I am more saddened than the naturally sober by the failure of the natives to be able to absorb alcohol in any amount whatever, without going berserk. I have it on the highest authority (my aunt Georgina) that it is impossible to tell from my demeanour whether I am drunk or sober. This aplomb, I contend, is something gained by a millennium of English civilisation. It is denied – perhaps because of some physiological factor – to both the Canadian Indian and the Irish, both of which are unduly susceptible to violence when under the influence. These poor redskins have natural resistance to neither potation nor the pox. I wonder that they have survived, even in such reduced numbers as they have mustered for these treaty signings.

The last of these has recently taken place here at Fort Pitt. The same spectacular show by different bands of howling heathens, the same interminable speeches by the Governor, the same trembling of the earth when the Hon. James McKay lumbered into the verbal fray. Chief Sweet Grass lived up to his name, signing readily, but I did not care one bit for the truculent Big Bear. Big Bear has only the temperament of his namesake, being a shortish, rat-faced individual with the perpetually sceptical expression of a Soho pawnbroker. He has been a delinquent in treaty-signing from the beginning, and here he repeatedly stood up to complain to the commissioners about our enforcing the law of hanging for murder. The little b————r is smart enough to recognize that among warring tribes murder is a highly subjective crime. A Cree killing one Blood is a murderer, but a Cree killing 20 Bloods is a warrior. I gathered that Big Bear is not a devotee of the modified warfare in which a brave gains credit by simply touching an enemy and hastening away – a jousting style that makes excellent sense to me.[42]

Several times, while the Governor was trying to waffle his way through a legal distinction blessed by the Great Spirit, I found Big Bear's saturnine gaze fixed upon me, unblinking, as though he could sense that my mind was not altogether at ease with the guide lines of capital punishment as applied to a people for whom slaughter is a form of recreation, as it was for the Highland Scotch a few generations ago. I did not attempt to out-stare him, but gazed with some intensity at my horse's right ear.

With the last signature affixed to Treaty No. 6 – and Big Bear chose not to sign it for some time – Her Majesty's Canadian government has paid out a total of $47,000 (about £10,000) – only $17,000 more than it paid for the construction of the unusable Swan River HQ – to 4982 Indians, in exchange for Territories several times the size of the whole of Great Britain. The Canadians have made a good bargain, in the sense of now having the credentials to run a bazaar in Beirut.

However, as my Troop prepares itself to move on – to the long and perilous safari south-west to Fort Macleod, through the domains of the Blackfoot, and the Blood, and the Peigan, most of whom are temperamental kin to the American Sioux – I am acutely cognizant of another complaint voiced by Major-General Selby Smyth during his inspection of the Force, namely that he had found a significant number of the Indians

42. This "counting coup" system was described by a wag as "taking the gory out of glory".

to have field glasses, traded to them by the Americans, whereas *no* field glasses have yet been issued to us custodians of law and order. This helps to explain why our patrols rarely encounter Indians, and when we do come upon a war party the surprise is ours. I do not look forward with unalloyed enthusiasm to our column's being shadowed by redskins equipped to see and identify us much sooner than our unassisted eyeballs can make out specks on the horizon. It may have suited Admiral Nelson to put the telescope to his blind eye, but at least he had the choice. If we must go into battle against people armed with field glasses and rifles, where is the advantage of being civilised?

> Your good friend,
> Frank.

PS   I offer my condolences on your having lost the ceramic mugs that your wife crafted for your public house in happier days. It's grievous that Minerva would have arranged for a cart to come and haul away your drinking vessels, but I applaud your offering no resistance. If it is any consolation to you, let me tell you that the vase she gave me as a farewell token I am now using as a urinal. Functional art at its best, on winter nights when the commode seems remote.

> F.

~

Fort Walsh, NWT.[43]
October 5th, 1876.

My dear Ezra,

My head is still spinning, like a parlour globe of the world,
after the Troop's march south from Fort Pitt. I am truly
in mid-odyssey now, Ezra! My "D" for Dandy lads met a
formidable adversary in the form of the South Saskatchewan
River. After days of navigating nothing more demanding than
the endless "creeks" of this region, we came up smack against
this snaking stream, running broad and deep, all the way out
of the snowy Rocky Mountains that lie many hundreds of
miles to the west.

It took us *three days* and many anxious moments to get
men, horses, and waggons across the river. We had to build
rafts of emptied packing-boxes, lashed together with cottonwood limbs (cottonwood is a sort of poplar with annual dandruff) found along the bank, and covered with tarpaulin. All
the waggons were dismembered and the parts loaded on to
the rafts, which were paddled by a number of men on each
trip across the river. Commissioner Macleod having charged
me with the responsibility for the safe conduct of the hapless
prairie schooners, I accompanied the first raft across a river
which, the instant we departed from its bank, became a
raging torrent. Before my eyes passed all the lovely bridges
of Europe – Westminster, le Pont Neuf, il Ponte Vecchio.
What a triumph of engineering they are!

I had no time to ruminate on these enlightened means of
crossing a river, however, being kept busy trying to set the
cadence for my men, as they flailed at the icy water with
paddles fashioned from planks of cart. My cursed stutter
ruined any hope of rhythm, and my attempt to keep time

43.   Now Maple Creek, Saskatchewan.

with my hands, like an orchestra conductor, drew so many pained glances that I eventually confined my assistance to silent prayer.

Lest you picture me lolling, like Cleopatra being barged up the Nile, I assure you that I did lend a hand with our landing on the south shore, and lugging the cargo up the bank. At such times I dearly wish I were physically stronger, as being the superior officer of a man who can carry a 200-pound axle on his back farther than I can comfortably walk unencumbered is most mortifying. Frankly, I doubt that I should have joined the Force had I known that the commission involved so much carrying of heavy objects over rough ground. In India I had bearers. This, by contrast, is quite unbearable.

After rafting the inanimate across the river, our next task was to make swimmers of more than 100 horses. Whatever their other virtues, our mounts did not take to the water like the proverbial duck. On the contrary, despite the entreaties of the halfbreed guides remaining on the north shore, the ponies milled about, the neighs definitely not having it. I sat on my horseless saddle, contemplating the lively possibility of my being marooned on one side of the river by a horse on the opposite side. It is a long walk to Fort Macleod, especially if one is pulling a wagon.

Finally, Sgt.-Major Mitchell and Constable Daly volunteered to show the horses how to swim. Mitchell, a large, imposing figure with a stentorian voice, stripped down to his lingerie, mounted his horse, and loudly urged the animal into the river. The horse would have none of it, promptly swinging around and scrambling back up the bank. Mitchell then armed himself with a stout stick as quirt, and with everyone yelling encouragement he tried again to convince his horse that what it faced was nothing more than an unusually large water hazard in the Grand National. Treading water, clinging to the horse's back, the sergeant-major finally managed to convince the beast that salvation lay on the Dickens side of the course.

Behind him, Cst. Daly fared not so well in the strong current. Attempting to ride his horse across, he was dumped as the animal breached and rolled. Both disappeared below the surface, and when they reappeared Daly was hanging on for dear life to his horse's tail. Luckily his horse came up sighted on Mitchell's horse on our south side, and struck out for a familiar face (or opposite end), towing Cst. Daly to safety amid laughter and cheers. Both horses were then walked up and down the shore in plain view of the balky herd remaining, till they too took the plunge, towing their riders Daly-style, and the crossing operation concluded with me convinced that it was a pity that the NWMP was organized too late to give the command to Moses.

However, the good Lord must have approved of Colonel Macleod too, since He rewarded us with a land of milk and honey. The geese were migrating southward, and in such sky-darkening numbers that I was able to fell one without any test of marksmanship beyond knowing how to squeeze the trigger. Besides roast goose and duck, our menu has been rendered gourmet by the addition of bear steak (*côte d'ours Grizzly*). At the edge of a wooded bluff (a hill with a stand of trees, as I may have mentioned) we sighted the mother grizzly with her cub feeding on the carcass of a buffalo, and a huge beast she was, daunting our horses, which shied away from taking us within range. It was one of our halfbreed guides, on his more nimble pony, who got close enough to bring Mama Bear down, though it took a fusillade to finish her off. When I was able to approach the body, with great care, I found that the legends about the huge size, the teeth, the claws, and the great thick fur of the "ursus horribilis" are all true. The guide who brought her down promptly set about "skinning 'er out", at which point I withdrew. I felt sorry for the cub, scampering away as a new orphan, but its mother died in the Queen's service, and tasted delicious.[44]

44. The grizzly's hide later decorated a wall of the Fort Macleod barracks.

Yes, Ezra, I have at last seen a buffalo, or bison. Indeed, a multitude of buffalo, or bison, two days north of Fort Walsh. These animals truly present an incredible sight. When our hunters rode in upon the herd, it broke into a rumbling stampede that made the very ground tremble, yet the buffalo cannot be described as fearsome even when thundering past in thousands. The creature is clearly no relation to the Indian water buffalo, which has the disposition of a Hecate with the toothache. What a field day the tiger would have with these massive, myriad, and strangely docile ruminants! It is plain that they have prospered because the open prairie is their ideal protection from predators – except man on horseback. Now, however, I am told that the herds are barely one tenth of what they were. Certainly the herd instinct, which has served them so well down through Lord only knows how many aeons, makes them their own worst enemy. The hunter needs merely to shoot into the mass of moving flesh to be assured of a hit. I have read that buffalo hunters south of the border kill them in their thousands for sport, while nearby Indian tribes go hungry.

I followed up one of our halfbreeds as he brought down a young bull, and watched as its front legs buckled slowly, the great beast crumpling to the ground like a sigh made visible. I had the chance, standing over the carcass before the butcher went to work, to observe that the buffalo appears to have been born in some bestiary of mythical monsters – the head and shoulders of the Arctic ox, the body and tail of a lion. If the tempers had been reversed, what a Minotaur we would be facing daily! As it is, the buffalo seems to be one of the kine that God placed in the Garden solely to be Adam's dominion. The Apple Tree is noticeable for its absence, but I am grateful to the Creator for the bounteous buffalo, and that our efforts to convert the Indian to agriculture have not come too late to save the buffalo from being driven over the cliff to extinction.

It is hard to believe that the natives would do this to themselves, were it not for the demand for buffalo hides traded for American whisky. The Indians normally use every part of the animal in most ingenious ways: the meat – fresh or as pemmican – for food, the fur and hide for clothing or tepees, the sinews for their bows, or as thread, the internal organs as containers, the bones for utensils, and so forth. However, white men (those wretched Spaniards) gave them the horse, and the Americans have given them the rifle, stacking the odds against the dumb brute that would have a better chance of survival did it not teem in such quantity. I find a moral in this, as a naturally solitary person: there is *no* safety in numbers. When Fate calls for my hide, it will have to take dead aim.

For the nonce, however, fortune has smiled on me and my comrades as, laden with spoils, we completed our journey to Fort Walsh, the air crisp with approaching winter and snow visible on the Cypress Hills to the south as we rode through groves of natty little pine and spruce, and splashed through sparkling brooks, and at last descended from the benchland into the valley of Battle Creek. With the fort in view, we swung onto the well-used Benton Trail[45] – and is there any sight more welcome in the wilderness than the beaten path? Our band striking up a spirited if discordant air, we entered the gate to the cheers of the incumbent "B" Troop, each of us as emotionally requited as Caesar entering Rome with all of Gaul in his saddlebags. Hardship overcome. In the absence of a woman, and there are no unclaimed white women within a thousand miles, this is what puts the curl in a man's whiskers, Ezra. And mine never felt bushier.

I am sorry to hear (your letter of August 26th) that your health has not been of the best since Mrs. Butts left. May I suggest a change of scene? In my experience, one may become quite literally sick of home, if home is an unhappy place.

45. From Fort Benton, Montana, this route north via Fort Assiniboine serviced Fort Walsh.

Perhaps you could bring your daughter Emily to Canada, which Lord knows can make good use of a seasoned publican.

With warmest wishes,
Frank.

∽

Fort Walsh, NWT.
October 10th, 1876.

My dear Ezra,

We ("D" Troop) leave shortly on the last leg of our hegira to Fort Macleod. This will loop us closer to the border than any sane person would want to be. By now you must have read in the English papers about what happened in June, just south[46] of our line of march: the annihilation of Lt.-Colonel George Custer and all his men by the Sioux, in the Battle of the Little Bighorn. According to our information here, the headstrong colonel was so convinced that God is on the side of the U.S. Cavalry that he failed to reconnoitre adequately the strength of the Sioux and Cheyennes who lay in wait among the ravines, warriors thick as the river reeds. Result: two hundred soldiers slaughtered – more troopers, I am uncomfortably aware, than the NWMP has in the field for the whole of the western Territories!

One begins to understand why the Canadian government has sent policemen instead of soldiers to win the West. This country simply cannot afford to be glorious in battle. Discretion is not only the better part of valour, it meets the budget.

The problem for the Force is that the American Indians continue to show a disinclination to accept the national credo

46. FD dramatizes. The Little Bighorn lay several hundred miles southeast of Fort Walsh.

that the only good Indian is a dead Indian. Assistant Commissioner Irvine, the C.O. here at Fort Walsh, received a confidential report from Ottawa that, instead of waiting to accept the retributive wrath of the U.S. Army, the Sioux may be crossing into Canada for sanctuary. If they use these refuges as bases from which to conduct raids on the Americans, the buffalo fat will be in the fire with a vengeance. That, in effect, is why I (and the rest of Troops "D" and "E") have been hastily dispatched to this unruly parish: to contain a violent domestic dispute among the neighbours. It is one of those situations in which the constable trying to restore order is the person who gets done in, after which the rowing couple make up and blame the deceased copper for interfering in a family matter.

According to Irvine, the leader of the restless Sioux is the infamous Chief Sitting Bull. A delightful agnomen, Sitting Bull, if one hears it while lounging beside the cheery hearth of your English inn, but when one is looking at his picture – supplied by American scouts – posted on a mess wall that may be within arrow-shot of the owner of that implacable profile, one's smile becomes very thin indeed. For, what one sees is the classic image of the noble savage. Rousseau would have loved Sitting Bull. Whether Sitting Bull would have loved Rousseau is more debatable. From what *I* see of the chief, the state of innocence has very flinty eyes, an unforgiving nose, lips tight and straight as a bowstring, and a jaw that would put the wind straight up the Serpent Himself. In my view, Chateaubriand[47] was fortunate not to have met Sitting Bull. The encounter would, I think, have given the maestro of nature-loving melancholy a new respect for civilized decadence.

As the local halfbreeds tell it, Sitting Bull is the son of

47. François René Chateaubriand, French writer whose romantic novels swept France in the early 1800s. The viscount visited the U.S. and afterward claimed to have searched for the Northwest Passage, though he never got farther northwest than Niagara Falls.

Jumping Bull, becoming a great hunter of buffalo by age 13, and while still a youngster being wounded in a hand-to-hand fight to the death with an older brave. Hence the permanent limp and the name Sitting Bull. His reputation as a great warrior is coloured by his being seen to be a crafty medicine man, a primal lawyer, and in fact something of a politician. No doubt the chief has some distance to cover before this part of the world views him as a Gladstone with feathers, but the gentleman does show promise.

There seems, thank G–d, to be little chance of my verifying this character study during our imminent move to Fort Macleod. The latest intelligence we have is that some Sioux have abandoned their camp north of the border, after stealing some horses from our Blood Indians, and have returned to the United States for the winter. It says something about the climate and other conditions in Canada, when a tribe of aborigines facing a shoot-on-sight warrant issued by the American government chooses to take that risk rather than share the shivering amenities of the land of the Great Mother.

Yet I have enjoyed my stop at Fort Walsh (named after our Superintendent) and look forward to even more stimulating times at Fort Macleod (named after our Commissioner). Who knows, perhaps one day there will be a Fort Dickens, somewhere in this interminable yet strangely engaging derrière of Creation. I have a vision of what Fort Dickens will look like: a cosy log-cabin community beside an idyllic waterfall, in a grove of cypress that whispers endearments to a semi-tropical breeze playing truant from the balmy Pacific, and built around a trading post where I shall supervise the exchange: worthless trinkets for which the local, peace-loving natives eagerly trade a mountain elixir that not only gladdens the heart but also miraculously reduces deafness, cures stutters, and increases the stature of Englishmen by at least six inches.

To fulfil this ambition I am encouraged by the immediate presence of my Super – Acheson Gosford Irvine. Here is a man who could stare down the Archangel Michael himself.

He has the square-cut countenance of a parade square, the lower portion of which is brindled gorse. The eyes not only look through one, they leave two clean holes through which the wind whistles as cautionary reminder. You see, Irvine was the officer delegated to track down the perpetrators of the Cypress Hills Massacre,[48] trekking overland from Bismarck, Dakota, to Fort Benton, Montana, where he encountered bristling resistance from the locals when he demanded extradition of his prisoners.[49] In a farcical "trial", not only were the defendants acquitted ("because they had no premeditated design to kill") but our man Jim Macleod was arrested by the Montana "law officers" – and I use the term so loosely as to be wanton – and charged with "falsely imprisoning" one of the charming sons of Uncle Sam. Irvine, a bulldog in resolve, rode to Fort Macleod, where other members of the trader gang had been apprehended, then escorted them the *800 miles* to Winnipeg, the nearest place for a proper trial to be held. Eight hundred miles, Ezra! Can you wonder that our Indians were struck agog, to witness such determination to bring the murderers of the redmen to justice? More incredible yet, though he could have taken a comfortable post in the East, Irvine returned here to what he calls "God's Country". To which my *very* muted rejoinder would be, "If this be God's Country, Heaven help the Devil!"

Oh, yes, Superintendent Irvine impresses me every bit as much as he does the Indians. I envy not only his service record but also the handsome desk on which he writes in his room – I have a table – as well as his tasteful window curtains. Granted, these do not rival the tapestry of Versailles, but

48.   In 1873 a party of American wolf-hunters, very drunk, slaughtered 36 Assiniboine of a band that had moved north of the border in pursuit of buffalo. An outraged John A. Macdonald ordered a two-man expedition to track down the murderers, the episode becoming the immediate *raison d'être* for the NWMP.

49.   The 1875 extradition trial was held in Helena, Montana, a boisterous exercise during which the Canadian representatives were threatened with lynching.

they are gaily patterned to shame my own window hangings, which I am tempted to call – were I not loath to shame my father's name (again) – sour drapes.

Please forgive me my verbal trespasses, my friend.

Frank.

〜

Fort Macleod, NWT.
November 4th, 1876.

My dear Ezra,

Tonight I write to you from the very end of the Force's thin red line – Fort Macleod. Beyond this point, westward, lie the Rocky Mountains, whose jagged, snow-mantled peaks do indeed gleam like God's sentinels to the Promised Land. Beyond them lies the domain of panther, timber wolf, and gold prospector, culminating – as a series of crazed Scotchmen discovered – at the salty Pacific. The fort stands rakishly on an island formed by the Old Man's River[50] and an amiable channel called The Slough. The Slough of Despond it certainly is not, however, as the water burbles clear and lively over a river bottom pebbly enough to set the sun's rays dancing a merry hornpipe. I'm told that the trout teem in this pellucid stream in quantity to dilate the pupils of Izaak Walton. No, I do not partake, since it is considered bad form to finesse the trout with a shotgun.

I'm also told that the river sometimes floods in the spring-time, and has a dramatic reunion with The Slough that may, of course, complicate our sleeping arrangements[51] and require my dropping anchor before retiring on my bunk. At the

50. Later called the Oldman River.
51. In fact the fort was moved to safer ground a few years later, the site of the present museum replica of the fort.

moment, however, the river runs thin and wary of the winter closing in. Soon its chuckle will fall silent.

Perhaps, as an innkeeper, you may be curious about the accoutrements of our little walled city – Carcassonne-sur-Vieux. The log lodgings are still a-building, but I must say that, though they lack both the permanence of stone and the elegance of the Bloody Tower, they afford the warm, je-ne-sais-quoi charm of living inside a tree that was; so to speak, a forest made horizontal. Wood looks congenial even when it isn't, and we are permitted to line the walls of our rooms with factory cotton to help reduce the influx of dust, which is the main soil crop of the region. (Here, Ezra, the men have a joke that we don't dust the furniture; the dust *is* the furniture.) We also have wooden plank floors, an exciting improvement over the naked earth of my previous forts.

When I recall how fastidious my father was about redecorating the great houses that he was forever buying or renting – the smell of fresh paint is one of my earliest recollections as a child – I have to smile at how he might respond to being shown his son's abode. I suspect that his comment would be something similar to his acknowledgment of the gift of a cyclopedia from his great friend Forster:[52] "About your beautiful present, conclude that I am like the parrot who was doubly valuable for not speaking, because he thought a great deal more."

However, *I* don't object to my chaste bed of boards and straw. My East Indian training gave me a chance to understudy the Hindu fakir, accommodating himself to his bed of nails. I am still mortifying the flesh. I sometimes wish that I had more flesh to mortify, but am satisified that my chamber, ever so humble though it may be, is more comfortable than the men's barracks, where it is almost impossible for misery to lack company.

Our HQ strength consists of Commissioner Macleod, Asst. Commr. Acheson Irvine, Surgeon John Kittson, and "C" and

52. John Forster, literary and dramatic critic for the *Examiner*.

"D" (mine) Troops under Supt. William Winder and Sub-Inspr. E. Dalrymple Clark (my chief) respectively. Total commissioned officers, 6; NCOs and constables, 103; horses, 105; flies, 10,000. (The flies set a military example, in the barracks and mess rooms, by drilling in squares – right turn, left turn, swing those arms! The late-summer fly is one Canadian form of life that I have found to have an aptitude for smart movement, on or off a horse.)

Sub-Inspr. E. Dalrymple Clark[53] has for some time been Jim Macleod's adjutant. I'm afraid that I present a problem to adjutants. It is part of their job to provide a deflective shield for the C.O. against the importunate, whether croaker or sycophant. I have never tried to toady to the top brass, and though I may have a reputation as a croaker, I make a point of croaking in writing, as befits the heir to the creator of Mr. Dombey. Oddly, this does nothing to ingratiate me with the standard, service-issue adjutant. Instead, he looks upon me as what Canadians (and especially Americans) call "a loner". A loner is regarded as having the esprit de corps of a coyote (a sort of prairie fox), plus personal habits that would not bear scrutiny by recruiters for even the Church of England. This does not disturb me. To the best of my knowledge, our Christian God, too, is *le solitaire*, and not even the Pope has blamed this attribute for the Lord's frequent acts of violence. The crowd of deities upon Olympus were more sociable than either I or God, and I'm sure that you're aware of all the atrocious mischief they got into. However, one does pay a price for wearing a scarlet jacket rather than a long, white robe with a bolt of lightning tucked under one's arm.

Hence the guarded response I received from Adjutant Dalrymple Clark when I made a written request for permis-

---

53 The Force's first paymaster and quartermaster. Like FD, his service did not agree with him, as he developed internal injuries from the long hours in the saddle and died of typhoid fever at Fort Walsh in 1879.

sion to own a dog. I much enjoy going for long walks in this rolling foothill country, Ezra, and a dog provides the companionship that completes the pleasure. To come upon the splendour of a cock pheasant strutting in the tall grass is more of a delight when one can share it with a friend whose tail expresses the ecstasy of bird-watching. And though I may not cast much bread upon the waters, a stick tossed into one of these glacial mineral streams – blue as a Valkyrie's eyes – returneth twicefold when deposited at my feet by a shivering, shaking dog.

"You want a *dog*, Frank?" says Dalrymple Clark, holding my letter and looking across his desk at me as I sat at my own work table. We share the office when this is necessary.

"Please."

"It's very irregular," he says, pursing his lips. "You have a horse. How many of man's best friends do you need?"

"I can't take my horse for a walk – *both* of us walking, that is. People will talk."

He knew what I was referring to. At Fort Walsh one of our constables took to walking out with a heifer on our roster of cattle. When called on the mat he insisted that the relationship was entirely platonic, but the damning fact remained that the heifer began lifting her tail every time a red jacket went past the pasture, and the bull became quite sullen. So I add: "I should prefer a male dog."

"If we let you keep a dog," demurs the Adjutant, "*everyone* will want a dog. We can't have the fort looking like an Indian village, dozens of curs running about barking and defiling the parade square."

"I'll keep him in my room. Take him out on a lead. Be personally responsible for the disposition of his bowel movements."

"You cannot stop a dog from jacking his leg. The first thing he will do is water the Commissioner's buggy wheel. I'm sorry, Frank – request denied."

I am not so easily thwarted. A bow-wow I crave and a bow-wow I shall have. Even Bill Sykes, I reflect, had the pleasure of a dog's company. Not far from the fort lies a lively little town – two thriving general stores and a chummy group of mud-roofed log buildings that are the resort of small, independent fur traders, gamblers, and vendors of smuggled whisky. I am sure that among the many stray canines camped before the butcher's shop there must be one that will consider it a promotion to become a member of Charles Dickens's family.

I can take a little time in selecting my walking companion, as the first freeze has shaken all the golden coins from the aspen – spendthrift Mother Nature, a woman after my own heart – and put all members of animate species into their furs. The Indians say that it will be a mild winter. Fewer berries than usual, and the wild geese are loitering, in passage to more clement climes. I do not trust the native soothsayers, however, and like the chipmunk I have secured my winter stock of nutty ale. Not here at the fort, of course, but in the town. I have a mutual understanding with an importer of spirituous beverages named Yeast Powder Bill. Yes, that is how he wishes to be known. My father's drolly-named characters – the Chuzzlewits, the Bumbles et al. – would feel quite at home with the likes of Yeast Powder Bill, Mormon Mike, Self-Rising William, Red Waggon Jim, and Liver-Eating J (the last so called because, having killed an Indian warrior famed for his courage, he ate the loser's liver in hopes of improving his own character – a moral lesson to those tempted by temperance to keep their liver palatable).

A glass of Yeast Powder Bill's whisky costs 50 cents. Almost a day's pay for a constable. At such an exorbitant price one might justifiably expect a Highland dew blended by angels fallen from the peatiest parts of Heaven. Not so. As an innkeeper you will want to write down the de facto receipe for what they call "The Paralyser", no doubt in honour of John Palliser, an Irishman mad enough to explore this region before there were pubs:

> one quart alcohol
> one pound overripe black chewing-tobacco
> one handful (large hand) red peppers
> one bottle Jamaica ginger (or, failing that, one bottle of
> mare's sweat)
> one quart of black molasses (treacle), poured slowly
> water (to taste)

Mix and boil the ingredients in a cauldron that has been abandoned by a coven of witches because they ran out of Tartar's lips. The concoction is allowed to mature for five minutes, no longer, as after that it begins to eat a hole in the surface of the Earth.

Those who describe this whisky as fit to oil the hinges of Hell's gate are flattering the product. I doubt that Old Horny would tolerate on the premises a flammable substance over which he had no control. Once trapped in a bottle, the whisky is confined with a cork chiselled from the bark of a Mediterranean oak on which mistletoe refused to grow. One removes the cork from the bottle with the teeth, to avoid damaging the trigger finger.

Need I say, my friend, that I rarely partake of the smuggler's "white lightning". Sheer terror has forced upon me a degree of abstinence more severe than that imposed when I was living among the Asians, whose religion forbids the consumption of alcohol. When I expand these notes into a book I intend to make a more exhaustive comparative study of the astringent powers of Allah and Yeast Powder Bill. The title: THIRTY YEARS WITHOUT BEER. The book may well become scripture for sots who seek to combine enforced temperance with travel to exotic lands.

Whisky is responsible for the Force's presence in the West, Ezra, but the Force seems far from grateful. In fact, while selling whisky to Indians is highly illegal, selling liquor of any sort, even to white men, is also illegal. Strictly speaking, in order to drink one needs a form signed by the Lieutenant-Governor stipulating that the liquor will be put to "medicinal use". This law causes a great deal of sickness on the frontier, but, to be utterly frank, it is not always strenuously enforced, and when it is, our unpopularity rises noticeably in these parched lands.

I am happy to relay the splendid news that 2% beer is legal, however, on the surprising grounds that it is impossible to become drunk on such a potation. Legend in the Force has it that our leaders performed an experiment on a "volunteer" who was ordered – poor devil – to drink as much 2% beer as he possibly could, while his superiors watched closely for tell-tale signs of inebriation. I suspect that several gallons could not have had as much effect as one brief encounter with the distilled dynamite created by Yeast Powder Bill.

The constituents of Yeast Powder Bill's whisky, as well as the good things of life – your letters, for example – reach us from south of the dotted line. Mail from Fort Macleod travels 210 miles south to Fort Shaw, Montana, thence to Ogden, Utah, and into the republican caravans of the Union Pacific Railway. This explains the U.S. postage stamps on my envelopes – may the ghost of George the Third forgive me! While we wait for the long-promised Canadian railway that will relieve us of this galling dependency, the news from Fort Walsh is that Canadian soil is now occupied by a colleague of Sitting Bull, who also took part in the Custer massacre: Little Knife, who pleaded with our officers for sanctuary, saying: "We left the American side because we could not sleep. We heard that the Big Woman was very good to her children, and we came to this country to sleep quietly."

Clearly Canada has gained a reputation as a soporific. Having a history of sleepwalking, I pinch myself occasionally to be sure that what I am doing for the Big Woman is in fact a waking activity, not a rather elaborate dream. I wish that I could report to you my having a leading role in some feat of Mounted Police heroism that would testify to my being fully awake. Alas, for me the paths of glory lead but to the trader's store in town, to supervise the inventory of supplies brought to us by ox-waggon from Fort Benton, Montana. I have tried to persuade myself that it is a dramatic spectacle – a bull train of several spans or teams of oxen, with 10 pairs of oxen to each waggon, lumbering inexorably into Fort Macleod, their armed men lunging at me with invoices. . . . But the drama lacks something.

November 18th.

Let me add some exciting news, before mailing this: I have my dog! Half a dog, anyway. My sommelier, Yeast Powder Bill, owns a four-legged guardian of his premises who needs exercise as much as I do. (Mr. Kittson, our post surgeon, gave me my annual medical examination recently. I have rarely heard a man heave so many sighs, while writing down a column of question marks. He concluded the examination by suggesting that I show less devotion to duty riding a chair and do something to regulate my pulse, which at present has the rhythm of an African fertility dance.)

Yeast Powder Bill calls his dog Dog. I have no quarrel with his choice of name, since it is less affected than the names my father gave to the Dickens family dog – Timber Doodle. Also known as Mr. Snittle Timbery. How can one expect a dog to live with dignity when called Mr. Snittle Timbery? No wonder my recollection of the poor animal that was lugged with us everywhere[54] is of a profoundly sad-eyed hound given to sudden fits of howling, as if pleading to be called Rover. Call it revenge, if you wish, that I have therefore decided to

54.   Timber Doodle accompanied the Dickens family on its mass exodus to Italy, July 1844 (when FD was 6 months old), with Charles Dickens, wife Kate, her sister Georgina, and his other children, Charley, Mamey, Katy, and Walter, plus the maid Anne and Kate's domestic staff and Roche the courier, in an outsize coach.

call my half a dog Boz.[55] An Irish setter of sorts – all sorts – Boz is plainly the result of one of Nature's major experiments in cross-breeding, making him the ideal pet for a Métis, or for a white man who believes that the mongrel is more intelligent than the pedigreed lap-poodle, since his brain has had to wrestle with the problem of whether he was bred to hunt ducks, fight terriers, or impersonate a German sausage.

So far as I can judge, Boz has no sense of smell at all. His hearing, however, is superb. This makes us thoroughly companionable, since it is my ears that are largely ornamental, but my nose is keen enough to make my dealings with the unwashed redskins almost unbearable, keen enough, as my colleagues say, to catch the scent of snow. And it was through freshly-fallen snow that we took our first walk together, Boz and I. At first he was uncertain of my motive in taking him away from guard duty in town, hanging back in case a quick retreat was called for when I turned out to be a cat-lover. But as we progressed along the river path, my boots squeaking cheerfully in the crisp snow, Boz moved up beside me, then led the way, p–ssing on small trees to demonstrate *his* good faith. I responded in kind, addressing the same tree he had, and was so engaged when I looked up to see that we were surrounded by a trio of Blackfoot. They sat on their horses and gazed at me impassively. I had not heard their approach, and Boz had failed to scent them, but now that he had them in his sights the old fool began barking at them furiously. This added a good deal to my feeling of vulnerability. In none of my visits to Yeast Powder Bill's spa had I ever heard Boz bark at anyone. His master had vilified him as the worst watch-dog he had ever owned. Yet here, a lonely mile from reinforcements, he was voicing a raucous challenge to the Indian's territory, apparently from some new-found loyalty that could cost me my scalp.

55.   FD's father used the pen-name Boz as author of his early stories for London periodicals. Charles Dickens adopted this "pet name" of a child christened Moses, which became Boses, and finally Boz.

The Indians paid no attention to the scold bounding around their mounts, but continued to stare at me without expression as I finished – with as much dignity as fumbling cold fingers would allow – the restoration. After memorizing my features as those of the white-man-who-plays-with-buttons-in-strange-place, they rode off as silently as they had come. Boz looked very satisfied at routing the foe, but I had no heart for further rambling, and we returned to town on the double.

Before I close, forgive me if I say something about your attributing your illness, at least in part, to the loss of Minerva. Melancholy can be debilitating, I know. Grief is the alchemist that turns our heart to lead. I felt it most strongly when my father died. To receive an inheritance from someone whom you know you have disappointed[56] – that saps the soul. Then there is nothing for it, Ezra, but to abandon the plaguey house and breathe fresh air, though it blow as ice crystals.

I trust, most sincerely, that your health is much improved.

Frank.

∿

Fort Macleod, NWT.
December 12th, 1876.

My dear Ezra,

Our tiny enclave of law and order is presently enjoying a winter phenomenon called the Chinook, which is a sudden and entirely unpredictable warming wind sweeping down from the nearby Rockies. This zephyr is wafted thither from the distant Pacific, and it is said that he whose olfactory sense is finely tuned may smell the brine in the Chinook,

56.   Charles Dickens described FD and his brothers as "limp".

and he whose hearing is acute pick up the faint roar of surf on virgin strands. I've strained for these, but so far without success. What I *have* heard is the story that the scattered settlers in these foothills have a special Chinook waggon equipped with sled runners on the front and wheels on the rear, because during this freak of nature the snow melts faster than the vehicle can move. I rather enjoy the Canadian sense of humour, gargantuan though it is, but doubt that Jane Austen would feel at home here.

Not only have we had (so far) a mild winter that obviates the need for heroic dashes through the snow in pursuit of a demented and murderous wolf hunter, icicles pendant as walrus tusks from my moustache, but the Macleod region is d--nably peaceable. The Blackfoot are fat and friendly, feeding on ample (though I suspect short-lived) supplies of buffalo meat. For the nonce, scalps reside on the pates of the original owners. And among the traders the crimes are so minor as to evoke a sigh from any would-be chronicler of deeds beyond the call of duty. All *my* deeds are well within earshot of duty, so that even an officer with a hearing problem can pick up the routine orders of the day. No less than our redoubtable Sgt. Sam Steele is occupied with nothing more audacious than instructing broncho "busting" – not that I should care to attempt the giddy gyrations whereby he teaches a wild pony the graces of being ridden upon. I want nothing to do with a horse until it has learned to love the saddle the way a lady enjoys her bustle: as a dorsal embellishment.

Colonel Macleod continues to assign to me the dolorous duties of counting beans and checking barracks for the sins of sloth. Sometimes I feel more like an English governess, with a soupçon more facial hair than usual, perhaps, but equally concerned about the ravages of dirty boots on the bed. I am tempted to wonder whether I have been held close to Headquarters, as it is moved like a chess piece across the board of the Canadian plains, because they are grooming me for High Command, or because High Command does not trust me out of its sight.[57]

During a lull in my inactivity, I broached the matter to Colonel Macleod, one evening in the mess, when I deemed him mellowed by a haggis bestowed on him by an admirer. (Yes, we do have a few sheep farmers among the cattlemen in these hills, enough to keep us in disgusting offal such as my commander was ingesting.)

"Jim," says I, "mayn't I have a plum or two of assignment in lieu of the prunes? Let me stretch my pony's legs a little? Bringing in just one whisky trader known to be armed and dangerous – that's all I ask. A crumb of desperate horse thief. Anything but more of those murderous invoices!"

Macleod gave me the corner of his eye by way of amusement. I should tell you, Ezra, that the Colonel is a tall, graceful Scot as rugged as his native Isle of Mull itself. Sam Steele has told me of how, in the course of the Force's first, preposterously difficult portages from Prince Arthur's Landing to Fort Garry, the then Major Macleod set an example for his exhausted men by shouldering a barrel of pork weighing 200 pounds. Two hundred pounds! My G–d, I often have difficulty shouldering my riding whip. Faced with toting a barrel of pork of that weight I should perforce adopt the Hebrew faith, rather hastily, and hope that the boats had no cargo of pickled herring. Do you wonder that I sometimes sense that Jim looks upon me as being something of a regimental mascot? A substitute for the Shetland Pony?

Having digested my question with the remains of his ghastly dinner, Jim says: "Well, now, Frank my lad, I admire y'r spunk. But – let's face up to't – y'r not exactly robust. Granted, y'r not as dependent on the Dutch courage o' the bottle as ye used to be. But I need to be sure y'r not riskin' the lives o' y'r men as well as y'r precious self."

"Send me out alone!" says I, in the full knowledge that such solitary forays are strictly forbidden by regulations.

57.   Probably the latter, given the tenor of his superiors' reports.

Macleod smiles and says: "Y'r godfather would come and haunt me, if ye got ambushed withoot proper company."

"My godfather?"

"Aye. That would be Lord Francis Jeffrey, the great Scottish critic."

"Aye, sir," says I, deflated.

"And a very fine author he was, too. Have ye ever read his review of Wullie Wordsworth's daft poem, 'Th' Excursion'?"

"I fear not." (I regret to say that Macleod is a reader, one of the few vices I have managed to avoid.[58])

Jim's face takes on a look of Gaelic reverence, as he booms, " 'This will never do.' "

Startled, I say: "What won't do?"

"That was the first sentence o' the review,[59] mon! 'This will never do.' How's *that* for shoving a thistle up y'r kilt?"

Later, reviewing the conversation in my mind, I concluded that the main reason why the Commissioner was reluctant to let me risk my neck was that he would be letting down my glorious namesake. However, after citing my personal experience with the pleasure palaces of the world, I managed to pry from him permission to reconnoitre, in casual dress, the town's gambling halls. Roofed with mud – which sets the tone for the tenderfoot's chances – these establishments have incurred my wrath, such as it is, not because gambling is illegal (it isn't) but because they attract highly transient American card-sharks. One of these in particular, Four Finger Pete (so-called because he always orders four fingers of whisky and plays till the glass is empty), deserves my scrutiny. His wife is an American Peigan, a remarkably attractive woman despite the pock marks on a face whose strong features belie her willingly marrying the drifter. A gun or a horse will, I regret to say, buy a white man a wife from her Indian father, and I have heard that Four Finger Pete is not above

58. False modesty. FD, like many *solitaires*, made friends of books.
59. Described by Bartlett's as "Probably the most famous book review ever written."

tossing in his wife to raise the ante in a hotly-contested game of poker.

With regard to the smallpox that has marred his wife's beauty, I can tell you that the scourge was introduced into the West by a white American who left his blanket behind when he disembarked from the steamboat at Fort Benton, Montana. An Indian of the Gros Ventres found the infected blanket and took it home to his village, whose people quickly fell prey to the terrible illness. A raiding party of Blood warriors, on a horse-stealing mission, came upon the desolated village, took the horses and buffalo robes from the dead, and returned to their own camps, where the buffalo had their revenge, many times over, on the unwitting redskins. And so it spread through all the tribes – the Blood, the Peigans, the Blackfoot, the Crees, the Stonies, far into the north – this vicious, silent killer that rode this way aboard a Missouri paddle-wheeler.

I can do nothing about *that* menace, but I may be able to cure Four Finger Pete. I am, as my father used to say, in considerable force. And I trust that you, my dear Ezra, are now in the finest of fettle.

Your friend,
Frank.

Part Two
1877 – 1880

∾

January 1st, 1877.

I delayed sending this till sure that I had no word from you over the Christmas week. I cannot say that Christmas at Fort Macleod has been an utterly joyous occasion, as no other time of the year so sharpens one's awareness of being thousands of miles away from what is, like it or leave it, home. You might think that after all the Yuletides I have spent abroad – many of them in a Hindu land where the goose is sacred and one must wait, carving knife in hand, for it to die of old age – I should be inured to feeling homesick. The Dickens family did put on a good show, however, Pa being present, though in retrospect I have to wonder whether my father was creating grist for his tireless mill – such jollification unbounded! He was never as compulsively ebullient on Guy Fawkes Day, and as for St. Valentine's, I cannot say that our house was ever incandescent with romantic love, particularly after my mother found out about Pa's dalliance with a fair daughter of Thespis.[1]

However, we here at the fort did our best to make our proxy home look festive. I dispatched a constable to forage

1. Actress Ellen Ternan. The affair precipitated Charles Dickens's separation from his wife Kate. FD was fourteen, an age susceptible to the effects of a broken home.

for greenery with which to deck our humble halls. Not surprisingly, he returned with no mistletoe, or boughs of holly,
but did yeoman service in finding and felling a suitable tree
for us. I instructed him to find a conifer of the sort I had seen
as a student in Germany, where such a tree is as germane to
Christmas as Kris Kringle himself. I cannot resist describing
the scene as – forgive me, Father – Charles Dickens might
have written it. . . .

> Yes! The Christmas tree was our own, and what a Christ-
> mas tree it was! Our steaming woodsman spared no
> effort in the tracking and toppling of that tree, I may
> tell you, and from afar we could hear his shouts, so
> lively and so full of the Lord's name, as he dragged the
> formidable evergreen to our gate, falling on the ice,
> getting up, falling down – a scene as jovial as Birnam
> Wood on the move to Dunsinane.
>
> At least twenty feet tall it stood, our noble fir (though
> there were those that said it was cedar, and those who
> would have none of that, that it was pine, and those who
> said "nein" to pine, that it was spruce), too tall for our
> mess hall, so that our constable was exhorted to saw the
> tree in half, the which he did with further crying and
> laughing in the same breath, till at last inside the
> hall the top half stood, proud and pungent on its pitchy
> butt.
>
> What a Christmas feast that tree beamed down upon!
> The groaning board spoke of the loving attentions of
> Inspector Dickens, who looked upon the the succulent
> wild goose and the plump brown turkey, and saw that it
> was good, and he looked upon the ruddy racks of venison,
> boss rib, buffalo tongue, and saw that they too were
> good – though the buffalo tongue had little to say of
> the manger – and Inspector Dickens looked upon the
> effulgent fruits of California, that Eldorado that pro-
> duces gold, frankincense, and myrrh all year round and
> in such generous quantity as to keep battalions of Wise

Men shuttling to promising infants all over North America, and he saw that these too were good, give or take an orange black as an Ethiop's brow.

To elevate spirits already soaring, Inspector Dickens had obtained a permit to serve milk punch – milk punch, no less! – the recipe for which is a secret jealously guarded by generations of cow punchers, who, alone of men and most women, know how to punch a cow to make it yield this Christmas libation that the votaries call "Herod's Brew". The milk punch brought on the speech-making after dinner, in such quantity and volume that the needles fell off the tree with a festive whoosh and the air grew thick with words that whirled about the hall like Dervishes, and the ladies' eyes grew bright as only ladies' eyes can when the milk punch loosens the tongue, till at last one of them, who was Mrs. Shurtliff, wife of the Sub-Inspector, supported by Mrs. Winder, who was the wife of the Superintendent, and Mrs. Armstrong, who represented the forces of good in the village, asked Inspector Dickens to entertain the gathering with a reading from *A Christmas Carol*.

"Ah, madame, I should be honoured to read from that luminous work, but you find me without a copy."

"Oh, I brought mine!" said Mrs. Shurtliff, and much to Inspector Dickens's consummate joy she brought forth the book from her bag.

Could words ever express the profound emotion with which Inspector Dickens, who had been conscientiously checking the quality of the milk punch all evening, rose to read? He of course chose the climactic Christmas dinner scene, because it was near the end, where he could find it, and because Inspector Shurtliff, who was his immediate superior, had kicked him in the shin to encourage his performance. He swayed unsteadily on his game leg, surveyed the eager faces before him, hiccoughed "God bless us, every one!" – and sat down heavily. The applause was far from deafening, but

Inspector Dickens would not have heard it in any event. . . .

Naughty of me, Ezra, I know. However, there are times when I dearly wish that I could cease pandering to my father's popularity, could blurt out that Charles Dickens did not merely woo the Muse, he ravished her. Laid the whip to her. Dragged the unfortunate goddess through every kind of squalor England offers, demanding inspiration in the way that a landlord extorts rent. Now that he's gone, the Muse has crawled back to Olympus, ink-stained and haggard, to warn her sisters never, never to trust a mortal who produces books and babies at the rate a baker makes buns.

For me, this Christmas, the most rewarding moment was my presenting his gift to Boz: a truly mammoth buffalo bone, by courtesy of the Magi – our three Christmas cooks.

Wishing you the good health that makes all else possible,

Frank.

~

Fort Macleod, NWT.
February 12th, 1877.

My dear Ezra,

I am very pleased to learn (your letter of November last) that you are feeling somewhat better for being purged. Purgation is something rarely prescribed by our surgeon, our diet of grains and game not given to lingering long anywhere.

Mr. Kittson was, however, involved in the regrettable upshot of our acquiring the Christmas tree that proved to be the triumph of the season. A few days after the start of the New Year, a delegation of Blackfoot arrived at the post to make a formal complaint to the Commissioner: the constable had inadvertently felled a tree chosen for the burial of the son of a headman of their village.[2] You see, it is the burial custom of the western natives to sew the body of the notable into a robe or blanket and place the deceased on a platform high in a tree, where scavenging animals cannot violate the sepulchre. A charming custom, I think, raising the remains a little closer to God. Whereas, we civilized beings bury our dead in the ground, to accommodate the worms and put the departing soul at more risk from the pull of the nether world. (It can, however, be a rude reminder of one's mortality, to come suddenly upon a tree from whose upper boughs hangs this strange fruit, a ragged shroud.)

Anyway, Jim Macleod deftly passed the grievance committee along to me, as the person responsible for ordering the abduction of the living tomb. I received them in the mess (G–d, they stank, and the stench lingered for days) with an expression – both facial and verbal – of appropriate and indeed genuine regret, trying to explain through my interpreter that the Great White Mother intended no disregard for the burial customs of her loyal subjects in the Far West. My protestations seemed to be failing to mollify them, to judge by their surly frowns and glances over my shoulder. I then spotted the reason: their confounded tree, or what remained of it, was still standing in a corner of the room, with a saucily-rouged Cupid doll hanging from its top bough.

"Ah, the Christ Child!" I exclaimed, and hastily, though reverently, removed the figurine and handed it to the interpreter, saying, "Make sure that this is returned to the sacred relics, and translate what I've just said."

Somewhat appeased, the committee informed me that the tree was intended to be the last resting-place of a young warrior whose leg had been badly broken when the horse he was riding tossed him off a cliff. I gathered that the leg had failed to respond to the treatment by the band's medicine man, and death was imminent. Eager to make amends, I

2. This seems unlikely. FD may be manipulating the facts in this case.

offered the services of Quay-we-den, a Cree shaman who has been sojourning at the post and taking credit for the mild winter.

"Bring the poor lad in," I invited expansively. "Perhaps with the help of our own witch doctor, Mr. Kittson, we can save him from the arboreal grave."

It was an impulsive gesture on my part, and like the majority of my generous impulses it was to prove to have the outgoing nature of the Australian boomerang. For, though the patient was indeed brought to the fort, he was in such obviously parlous condition that Quay-we-den would have nothing to do with him. These medicine men have the same professional attitude as Harley Street: they do not knowingly damage their reputation by taking on hopeless cases. Also, the patient was a Blackfoot, which meant that Quay-we-den's treating him would be akin to President Lincoln receiving surgical attention from General Lee's barber.

"He's a goner." Mr. Kittson looked grim as he covered up the doomed brave. At my urging he had loaded the patient up with laudanum and amputated the gangrenous limb, but to no avail. The patient was mercifully unconscious when, in a matter of hours, he succumbed. I personally led the party that returned the body, wrapped in blankets, to the Indians who had waited stoically outside the fort. They said nothing to me – neither in appreciation nor in disapproval – but bore their dead comrade off on the travois (a triangular rack of poles slanting down behind the horse) on which he had been delivered.

My relief at having discharged my debt to propriety proved short-lived. The very next day the delegation was back. When I met them on the parade ground, their spokesman was formal but blunt.

"We want the leg," he said.

"Ah!" I said. "One moment, please." I took our interpreter aside, to establish the background for this request. Which was that the funeral committee had discovered the absence of one leg when they were about to levitate the body into a substitute tree. Apparently it was unthinkable that the spirit of the departed warrior should have to hop around the Happy Hunting Ground on one leg for eternity. The ritual of burial was intractable about this, as I could judge from the stern glare with which the committee listened to my reply to their request.

"Er, I'm sure the leg is around here somewhere, gentlemen," I said, through the interpreter. "I'll ask Mr. Kittson, our surgeon, where he, um, preserved it. Excuse me."

While the committee waited outside, standing there with the eerie stillness that unnerves me, I hastily sought out Kittson, who was napping on his bed. Shaking him awake, I said: "Where's the leg?"

"What leg?" Kittson squinted at me as though I were quizzing him on anatomy.

"The leg you amputated yesterday. The owner needs it for his last rites."

"Too late." Kittson yawned, with an irritating lack of concern for my delicate situation. "It's been burned. The limb was totally rotted, you know that."

"Then find me another leg," I pleaded. "Quickly!"

"Don't be absurd. . . . "

I was already dashing back out to the committee to assure them. "You'll have your leg, gentlemen. It may take a day or two to retrieve it from the Great White Mother's repository of distinguished limbs. I suggest that you return to your village. I shall deliver the hallowed part personally."

Grumbling, they made off, and I hurtled back to Kittson, who was now awake enough to understand the emergency.

"That old whisky smuggler that we had in the lock-up, the one that died last week – we may be able to exhume him and pinch a leg."

"His finest hour!" I cried. "I'll be much, much obliged, Mr. Kittson."

So it was that I was able to remit, with my own hands, a leg that Kittson had, we hoped, rendered unrecognizable. The Indians accepted the goodwill offering with a grudging compliance, and I rode back to the fort flat out, lest the counterfeit be detected. In the event, I had nothing to fear. On the contrary, the next time I encountered one of the Blackfoot involved, he greeted me with enthusiasm. His entire village was basking in renown, the interpreter explained, as the home of a dead warrior who had two left feet. They took this as a lucky sign, a blessing from the Great Spirit – an interpretation which I was only too willing to endorse.

God's blessing on you, too, my friend.

Frank.

PS   Needless to say, I have sworn Kittson to silence about this grisly episode, May I ask you, too, to refrain from recounting the story, at least till I have been transferred to a post some distance from our Christmas pageant.

PPS   On the subject of whisky smugglers, I am compelled, in all fairness to an otherwise unredeemed commerce, to mention the one saving grace in our apprehension of these rogues. It has taken me some weeks to grasp why several of my men have been even more assiduous in their pursuit of the whisky trader during these winter months. It was not till recently, after one of the heavier snowfalls of the season, that on my daily walk in the purlieu of the fort I came upon two of my constables squatting in a snow bank beside the road, eating the snow with a relish that bespoke something more than simple nostalgia for the treats of childhood.

At sight of me, they both jumped unsteadily to their feet, mouths spewing slush.

"Hello, hello, hello, lads," says I, ever eager to strengthen the bond of understanding between officer and other rank. "What winter sport is this?"

Both constables stood mute as hitching posts, their white

moustaches melting into rivulets that ran down their chins. Says I to – so to speak – break the ice:

"Does the snow taste better here than in the fort?"

"Yes, sir," replies the constable with the wetter knees. "It does that."

His companion frowned as if vexed by the disclosure of something whose existence he would have preferred to keep private. I moved to the snow bank for a closer examination of their excavation, and was astonished to see that the snow they were eating was stained amber. I don't mind hinting to you, Ezra, as a man of the world, that men confined to barracks life get up to some pretty queer tricks, but this was something new. After a moment of horror, I noticed that what they were masticating had an aroma not usually associated with yellow snow.

"Would this," says I, "by some freak of coincidence, be the place where yesterday you dumped the whisky confiscated from the American smuggler who now languishes in our oubliette?"

"It would, sir," A pleading light shone from the eyes of the wetter knees. "Beggin' your indulgence, sir, my strict Christian upbringin' binds me to waste not, want not. I would of done the same, sir, if it had been sarsa-hic-sarsaparilla."

"That's right, sir," pipes his colleague in frugality. "Waste not, not what. . . . "

"Very commendable," says I, scooping up a handful of amber snow and tasting it, like a *connoisseur de la gastronomie*, letting the crystals swish around my mouth, speculatively smacking my lips, before swallowing the spumante.

"A presumptuous blend, but – ah, let me confirm that beyond doubt." I took a second, larger, spirituous snow ball and munched it down. It set my teeth on edge, a reminder not only of the deviousness of demon rum but of my need to find deliverance in a dentist's chair.

The two constables now appeared more at ease with their situation, though somewhat concerned lest my degustation consume the entire snow bank. Says I:

"Let us consider this to be a scientific experiment, in the spirit of the age, a study of the effects of ice-water on alcohol, so that we may better understand the primitive drinking customs of the republican hordes south of the border."

"Right, sir!" chorused my laboratory assistants.

By the time we had completed the experiment, we had ingested empiric proof in considerable amount, to sustain the thesis that snow provides an interesting compromise between water and ice, as what might be called a "mixer" for whisky.

I deemed this exercise not to be a violation of Force regulations regarding consumption of alcohol, as the prohibition is against our *drinking* a spirituous beverage, not against our eating it. I was therefore able, with good conscience, to leave the constables to double-check our findings, and I returned light-footed to the fort with lips chapped gladly in the cause of the advancement of human knowledge.

Frank.

∼

Fort Macleod, NWT.
March 1, 1877.

My dear Ezra,

Despite the best efforts of the Scottish missionaries in these lands to eliminate the exception, man is still the only animal that laughs. The Indians here show estimable resistance to such pious attempts to make them as dour as a Calvinist preacher. Although their photos rarely catch them smiling – as why should they, given their exposure to that Evil Eye that can suck the soul out of Laughter itself – in their less self-conscious moments they exhibit a sense of humour that beguiles even as it baffles me.

I asked Jim Macleod, who has gained more knowledge than I of the redman, how he reconciles this Rabelaisian mirth with the European's perception of the savage as a brute that shows his teeth only in rage.

"Fun is part o' their mythology, Frank," he said. "It's no' easy to winkle out o' them, but an old Blackfoot medicine man who owed me a favour confided to me that a vital figure in their tribal myths is the Trickster. He creates and he destroys, dupes and is duped, takes on a variety of animal forms – aye, and yet he's essentially shapeless except for having his guts wrapped around the outside o' his body, along with a country mile o' penis topped by an enormous scrotum."

"Sounds a little like the Hindu god Shiva."

"But a wee bit ruder. If the Indians view us North-West Mounted Police as an unexplained phenomenon o' nature, chances are that the myth will account for us as something that the cosmic Scalawag blew out o' his backside."

This would certainly explain the jeering that I have received from unfriendly groups of natives, usually when my horsemanship let me down. Among the Blackfoot, the animal most often associated with the Trickster is the coyote, who does indeed have the singular presence of a prankster, to say nothing of a derisive tone of voice, mocking the lunar madness. I feel a greater kinship with the coyote than with any other creature of the plains that I have met, including most of the bipeds. Were I to be reincarnated, Hindu style, I think I should enjoy spending my next time on earth as one of these bright-eyed, bushy-tailed dogs that laugh at coming to heel.

After his telling me of the Trickster, Jim took me to his room and showed me a small, nondescript leather bag tasselled with strips of hide. He took out its contents: some bear claws, a couple of rattles, a pipe – a collection of rubbish, to my eyes.

"A Blackfoot medicine bundle," he said, respectfully.

"One o' our lads found it in a lodge whose owner had died alone. That thing means as much to the Indian as the Cross does to a guid, Kirk-goin' Christian."

"Medicine bundle?" I said. "This stuff is supposed to have curative powers?"

"Much more than that. It's the link between the Indian and his guardian spirit. The Indian goes to the hill-top or doon by the river, smokes his pipe, has a vision, and in that vision sees the forms that his guardian spirit assumes in this life. Yon animal parts in the bundle are the Indian's way o' takin' communion."

I returned to my room unsettled in mind. The more I learn about the ways of these native people, the less comfortable I feel about what we Heaven-sent whites are doing to their way of life. It was so much easier when I knew them only as pictures in an English periodical, feathered fiends galloping around the circled waggons of the dauntless, God-fearing pioneers!

I took out my own medicine bundle, from under my bed. The case contains my father's watch and chain, a pipe, and a leather-bound Bible given to me by a young lady before I left England for India. The Bible has a red ribbon marking the place where I forsook Job for Gin. Yes, I have had my visions too, Ezra – mostly blurred and not reassuring. In those visions my guardian spirit has always taken the same form: Pa. My father is no coyote. Sometimes I see him as a big bear, grumpily eviscerating a critic or publisher. At other times he appears as an eagle, soaring so far above me that I wonder that he can discern my slightest movement to escape his circling shadow.

The Indian has a song to evoke the magic of his medicine bundle, but I have none, other than the hallucinatory lays of your inn. "Drink to me only with thine eyes. . . . " And the coyote howls at the moon.

Your off-key friend,
Frank.

~

Fort Macleod, NWT.
April 20th, 1877.

My dear Ezra,

Your Christmas parcel arrived yesterday, only slightly the worse for wear by travel. The socks knitted by your daughter Emily are very welcome indeed, and I shall do as you suggest: wash them till they have shrunk to a size that fits my foot, then never wash them again. Socks are a continuing problem for us officers, who are supposed to set an example for the men by wearing something under our boots besides feet. I regret to say that one of our sub-inspectors combines his moccasins with long black silk stockings – a sort of buskin Métis. In our strenuous effort to distance ourselves from the barefoot bushman we invite not only ridicule but a good deal of darning. Thanks to your daughter's sturdy weave, I shall have the best of both worlds.

In other ways, regrettably, the conjunction of the Old World and the New has been less comfortable for me. In the matter of names, for instance. I believe I mentioned to you that in these parts the name that a man is known by is less familial than functionally descriptive – Red Waggon Jim the trader, for example. Our own chief, Commissioner Macleod, the Indians call "the Bull's Head", and thus Fort Macleod is "the place where the Bull's Head stays". The name is certainly apt, as these appellations usually are. Only in British upper-class society do we find some ass who projects nothing but his front teeth dutifully addressed as "Leonard" – a travesty against the lion species.

The Indians are quick to note any physical oddity of the white man. If one of us happens to be handsome, he becomes "Pretty Young Buck". If red-haired, "Head On Fire". If unusually tall, "Big Tree". And so on. You can imagine my chagrin, therefore, at learning that their name for me is "Little Prairie Chicken". The coincidence of my father's dubbing me "Chickenstalker" during my first years of life carries an unpleasing haunting echo. I know that "Chickenstalker" is the name of one of his lesser comic personae, but am baffled by the sobriquet "Little Prairie Chicken". The prairie chicken of the western plains is a type of grouse whose most distinguishing characteristic is the mating dance – an attribute that I deny. The silly bird attracts a mate by bowing and scraping and drooping its wings, with a vocal accompaniment described as booming. The cock also stamps his feet, in the heat of unrequited love, whirling in circles and trying to make all his parts look twice as large as they are. None of this description fits me, even when I have been drinking.

I broached my quandary about being "Little Prairie Chicken" as a question to Jerry Potts,[3] our halfbreed scout who seems to have a reasonable explanation for everything. He suggested that it is the way I walk that reminds the natives of the wretched fowl.

"You mean I strut?" I said. (A degree of strutting is unavoidable when one is short in the underpinning and forced to keep pace on the drill square.)

"Strut, aye, strut," agreed Jerry, whose Indian name is "Bear Child" – lucky devil. Having been relegated to poultry, there is only one dignitary hereabouts whose name I don't envy – the Assiniboine chief Piapot. Piapot is a trouble-maker, and I think I know why. The names we are given, I believe, have an incalculable influence on our destiny. How could Ethelred have been aught but Unready, or Napoleon

---

3. The famed Métis scout/interpreter, whose personal exploits exceeded those of the Mounties themselves. A former Hudson's Bay Company scout, Potts once led a raid by the Peigans against marauding Crees and Assiniboines, a bloody battle that left more than 400 dead on the field and at the Belly River ford. Hired by the NWMP, the laconic, bow-legged Potts was their most reliable, sometimes uncanny, guide for years, knowing the entire western prairie like the back of his hand.

have failed to succeed? I am Francis Jeffrey.[4] Lord Jeffrey
was a lifelong admirer of Pa's novels. Indeed, Pa proudly told
me that a friend found Jeffrey one day with his head on his
desk, tears rolling down his cheeks. When she asked what
had happened to cause him such devastating grief, he replied:
"I'm a great goose to have given way so, but I couldn't help
it. You'll be sorry to hear that little Nelly, Boz's little Nelly,
is dead."

You see? – my father named me after a self-admitted goose.
As a further pre-natal indignity, a few years before I was
born,[5] my father's triumphant entry into Lord Jeffrey's home
turf, Edinburgh, was prelude to a terrifying tour of the Scottish Highlands. During that awful event, my poor mother
suffered through torrential rains, rock slides, and a coach
crossing of a flooded stream in the course of which the carriage
slipped off the bridge planks and almost plunged the whole
entourage to its doom. I sometimes wonder what effect this
ordeal – combined with the subsequent tour of America –
had on Mama's constitution and mental state as her body
readied the womb for the Francis Jeffrey that addresses you
now. May I not blame my fragile constitution on my mother's
being frightened by Scotland? The hypothesis does not bear
close examination, especially in this land bedevilled by Scots,
but I cling to the thought when unnerved by the need to
ford the Belly or the Old Man's, which can rush in a cold rage
worthy of Glencoe.

4. Although FD seems to chafe at being named after his godfather
(possibly being aware that Lord Jeffrey wrote a favourable review of
The Chimes, the novel in which Mrs. Chickenstalker appears), Charles
Dickens insisted that he named the boy after the Scottish critic at his
wife Kate's suggestion, her father, George Hogarth, being a Scotsman
and a friend of Sir Walter Scott.
5. In fact, June 1841.

Francis Jeffrey awaits your next letter with the impatience of the Picts and Scots.

Your faithful and heartily obliged,
Frank.

~

Fort Macleod, NWT.
April 30th, 1877.

My dear Ezra,

At last we have some glimmerings of spring, in this land of cold, cold, cold that crystallises the very marrow in a man's bones. How I welcome the sun higher in the heavens! Not the least because it also brings forth the prairie dogs, or "gophers" as the Canadians call them, the little johnnies popping their heads up out of their burrows as much as to say to a spouse below: "It's all right, Mother, the beastly winter has gone away." These marmot-like animals are cordially detested by ranchers and farmers alike, their holes wrecking more good horses than any other single hazard, yet they delight me. They show what having chubby cheeks and a short, twitchy tail can do to redeem a rat.

I too am sniffing the slightly balmier air in anticipation of throwing off the dread disease that the locals call "cabin fever". The doers of Evil are once more on the black wing, and I champ the bit to be after them. During the Canadian winter, idleness breeds mischief only if the indolence remains indoors. The Indian hugs the fire in his tepee, and the whisky smuggler drinks his own stock, to keep warm. But with the spring thaw, Old Cootie can venture among us once more without fear of having his horns snap off.

The nearest I have come to real excitement, this past winter, occurred on a day when the Chinook wind had turned the street of the town into a particularly glutinous stretch of mud, through which my pony was picking his way when we came upon the form of an Indian woman, a "squaw" as we call them, lying curled, like a dog against the cold, in that dreadful slime. Something about the squaw's form struck me as familiar, however, and I dismounted – despite, I may say, the indignity committed on my boot by someone's "cayuse" – and I turned the woman so that I could see her face. She was in fact not drunk, but badly beaten, the handsome face that was already pitted by pox now bearing welts and bruises. Yes, it was Four Finger Pete's woman. I had no doubt whatever that he was responsible for the battering taken by the poor woman. She said nothing to me, but her eyes spoke quite eloquently of mistreatment beyond description.

Confound it, Ezra, I was tempted, then and there, to seek out the Yank gambler and give him a thrashing, a taste of his own vile medicine. I would have done so, believe me, had not the woman – sensing my intent? – struggled to her feet, shaking her head to discourage reprisal, and stumbled away.

In your letter of March 8th you ask – almost wistfully, I feel – "Have you killed anyone yet, in the line of duty?" The answer – and I hope that it will not disappoint you too much – is "No." We of the Force are constantly reminded that we are keepers of the peace. As the Commissioner told us on parade recently: "If you have any notches in your gun butt, it had better be because of an assault by a near-sighted beaver."

I fear that the English newspapers that you have read have enlarged on the violent resemblance between our entry into Fort Whoop-up and the fall of the Bastille. In truth, apart from one surprised old codger, there was nobody at home when our first divisions arrived at Fort Whoop-up in '74 – the evil blokes who traded whisky having long since decamped on advice of their scouts – and the place remains little more than a museum, a symbol of the white man's infamy. Our main function now is to remind Yankee intruders that this is British territory, and to impress upon the natives, by example, that those two blessings of civilization – firewater and firearms – must be used only for a purpose approved by the Great Mother, namely shooting the buffalo and toasting the Queen. In these circumstances, and as a reformed drinker, the most trying time for me is when we apprehend a whisky trader's cache and spill the contents of a barrel on to the ungrateful ground. Such is the extent, so far, of my real suffering.

A more delicate problem for the Force, in maintaining the right, is that among the Indians horse-stealing is considered to be a cultural activity. Acquiring a horse without the owner's consent wins the thief much the same status as an English banker. It is not easy to shake the Indian's belief that a horse is a gift from the gods, unless there is someone actually sitting on it. The native's philosophy is that if no one is using an object, it is quite reasonable to take that object and put it into service. Recalling Proudhon's comment that "all property is theft," I feel uneasy having to lay a charge against a person who is merely giving a practical demonstration of my father's canon, which was aimed directly at the propertied. Fagin would have fitted in better than I, when dealing with the social mores of the Canadian aborigine.

Altogether, the dull fact of the matter is that the presence of the Force in Fort Macleod has meant that most of the whisky smugglers have retreated south of the border and become either American politicians or lawful business men. The situation is so tranquil that in March Commissioner Macleod felt free to return east to rejoin his young wife, Mary, whom he married in Winnipeg last autumn. The couple then proceeded to Swan River for the first meeting of the new Council of the North-West Territories. This momentous event consisted of four men sitting around a small table and agreeing on an ordinance to prohibit the killing of buffalo during certain months. Clearly enjoying the company of his new bride more than that of his fellow councillors, Jim Macleod has written to one of our officers here: "The great Council of the mighty Territory met this afternoon for the first time. 'Tis too bad we cannot have your two beauties" (our cannon) "to thunder forth the fact. There are three members, Richardson, Ryan, and myself: the two first do not speak to each other and Ryan does not speak to me! I have proposed a triangular duel to settle the matter. Remember me to all."

If that isn't a contented groom talking, I am no judge of human relations.

As for the conservancy of the buffalo, our men here have been doing their part by adopting, this winter, two yearling buffalo calves. We also have a pair of domesticated deer, one of which has patronized T. C. Powers' general store in the village, dropping in regularly to help itself to the biscuit box behind the counter. The deer play with the Indian children and the one white child at the post, games of "you-chase-me" that look inviting, though I have so far resisted the temptation to join in the fun. The rigours of being an officer! Also, one must have ambiguous feelings about becoming emotionally involved with a food source. An Englishman will, of course, make a pet of almost any animal, anywhere, including places where women are plentiful. In India, we enforcers of the Raj were seen to succumb to the company of monkeys, mynah birds, even an occasional scorpion, being assured that there was little chance of encountering our little chum staring back at us accusingly from the dinner plate. Here in Canada's West, however, the natives have no religious scruples about eating anything, including the rather rudely excerpted heart of an enemy.

I have therefore leaned to an arm's-length treatment of wild beasties befriended by men. This availed me nought, in the Affair of the Baby Buffalo. To begin this debacle, I unwisely went for a solo ride without Boz, who has the virtue of being not only relatively inedible but also noisily jealous if I am approached by any form of life. As I sat aboard my pony in a field of sweet grass – and I should tell you, Ezra, that the grass here grows right up to the horse's belly – breathing in the scented silence of springtime a-borning, the yellow crocuses saucily giving back to the sun as good as they got, I became aware of something rubbing my foot in the stirrup. I looked down to see that I was being vigorously nuzzled by a buffalo calf, obviously only a few weeks old. The young female waif had taken my pony for its mother, regarding me as a minor growth on Mama's back. (The buffalo is not well-sighted at any age, hence its fatal propensity for running over cliffs with the herd. I sometimes wonder whether the animal is the best choice for the NWMP badge.)

Naturally, like Mr. Winkle and the dog, I tried to shoo the calf away. Although I discharged my rifle into the air, the calf backed away for only a few feet, and looked so forlorn, hurt to hear Mama speak to her so sharply, that I relented. I made no further attempt to disillusion the child, but allowed her to trot at our heels all the way back to the post.

To my considerable discomfort, the first person we encountered, as our little ménage ambled through the gate, was Mrs. Shurtliff – she who never tires of asking me when I am going to get married. Seeing me with the young female buffalo, her eyes narrowed with the strain of putting the worst complexion on the scene. Forgive me, Ezra, for lapsing into the humour of the barracks, but you may have heard Australia described as the country where men are men, women are women, and the sheep are nervous. Much the same situation prevails here in western Canada, except that the women are, if anything, even scarcer, and most of the sheep of the mountain variety, hence of limited access.

It follows that a man cannot rely on his colleagues' accepting him as a female buffalo's adoptive mother. He must either (a) eat it, or (b) find it another mother, preferably within minutes of his being seen with the "crittur" (sic). Wherefore my greeting Mrs. Shurtliff with "Good day, ma'am. I've brought home a playmate for the children. I believe that a young female buffalo makes an excellent pet."

Mrs. Shurtliff did not look appeased. Says she: "Take it to the cook, Inspector Dickens. We don't allow our children to play with wild oxen."

"As you wish, ma'am," says I, leading the calf out of her

sight. It struck me as a betrayal, however, to allow the poor little calf to trust me as its maternal parent, then to present it to the butcher. I have never been accused of displaying an excess of compassion, but I have absorbed enough of the Canadian aborigine's synthesis with Nature to feel that such a violation of the mutual dependency of man and beast would affront the Great Spirit. The Great Spirit is not, one presumes, as influential as the Great White Mother, but why risk alienating the local authority?

"Come along, Little Dorrit," says I. "We'll find you another home." I headed our little entourage towards what passes for the town, aware of stares lodged between my shoulder blades, but happily came upon a Red River cart whose driver had halted on the road (such as it is) to tighten a wheel. I manoeuvred the calf beside the cart and said, "Here's your *real* mama!" Then I wheeled my pony hard and galloped hell-bent-for-election back to the fort.

I didn't look back. It's better that way, I find, when it's time to part from one's family. But I did make a point of entering the fort as ostentatiously as possible, for the benefit of anyone who had observed the earlier arrival. There was, of course, no one in sight. Which underlines one of the axioms of life: Nothing guarantees total invisibility so well as an acute desire to be seen.

The corollary being: I must do something soon about establishing a liaison with a human female, lest I continue to be the object of wanton surmise as to what bizarre means I have recourse to in order to escape the terrifying fate that men out on the frontier call "normal".

> May God preserve *you* from all unsought excesses.
> Frank.

PS Here I yield to the temptation to open my heart to you and admit that I am hopelessly smitten with Jim Macleod's wife, Mary. I hasten to add that I worship from afar, indeed *so* far afar that I am well over the horizon of her recognizance. Also in my own defence, milord, I submit that when Jim brought his new bride home here from Winnipeg there was not a man on this station who did not reverberate like a struck gong, when he met this lovely, totally captivating woman. She wears her beauty as naturally as the sun dons the sky each morning. Not one whit a striver for effect, she commands her hair in the fashion of all the West's women: parted severely down the middle, and coiled into a bun that begs to be broken, like new-baked bread. Her eyebrows alone would be enough to move me to join the queue of men willing to die for them, and her lashes are but accessory to eyes blue as a summer's northern lake, forthright and unequivocal in conveying the unspoken message "Yes, I know that you too adore me, for which I thank you with the modesty required of having been fortunate enough to receive a generous physical inheritance, but let us get on with milking that cow!" Such are the eyes of the Miss Drever who outflanked the Métis rebels, at the age of seventeen, to deliver a vital message to Colonel Wolseley.[6]

Mary's mouth – oh, Creator, how Thou wert inspired when You thought of lips! – melds a Cupid's bow with that of the Amazon warrior: every smile an arrow through my heart, each constriction death to my indecorous dreams. For this lady is no Romantic swooner. Mary travelled with her husband to the Treaties-signing at Fort Carlton, and signed as a witness to that historic document, with a hand as firm as it was fair. Do you wonder that, despite the cautionary tale of David's[7] falling head over tea kettle in love with Dora, I am toppled harder than he, and my case is infinitely more hopeless? Jim Macleod is twice the man I am, and he loves his wife dearly, and she him, and both adore their children, to the utter despair of us who long for her. I have held her in my arms

6. During the Red River Rebellion, commander of the Canadian expedition to quell the uprising.
7. Copperfield.

once, at the Christmas party, in the throes of the polka. And must that brief whirl keep me satisfied till someone fits me with a forage cap of marble? I fear so. Although Mary is left alone frequently, when Jim's duties call him across the plains, he leaves her with an unseen presence that daunts every would-be swain.

Ezra, when I think of Mary Macleod (as I do far too often), there is borne in upon me the contrast between her household and that of the other woman I have loved – my mother. Despite the riches of my father's fame, how terribly impoverished he was as a husband! He spent much of his life trying to escape the debtor's prison of an unhappy marriage. (Did you know that *his* first love, too, was a Mary?[8]) At least he taught me to avoid *that* durance vile, though I languish in the gyves of unrequited lust!

F.

∾

Fort Macleod, NWT.
July 3rd, 1877.

My dear Ezra,

This week's post brought no letter from you, which means that I have something to look forward to *next* week. The waggon train from Fort Benton did, however, replenish the fort's supplies of ink and note-paper, both of which were running critically low. As I may have mentioned to you, almost every officer and NCO, as well as several of the constables (we have a couple of graduates from Oxford and Cambridge on strength), are kept busy chronicling the adventures of the Force in hopes of one day being published. Some, like

8. Maria Beadnell, who rejected Charles and conditioned him for a marriage too pragmatic to succeed.

the indestructible Sam Steele, make copious notes, obviously intending to weave these into a continuous narrative that will enthral lovers of vicarious violence. Others, such as I, allow the text to spring full-blown from their brow, hoping thereby to get it to a publisher ahead of the Mountie (for such is our informal sobriquet, for which I must accept responsibility), whose service to rewriting and editing and polishing was over and above the call of duty. Even Bugler Bagley is writing a book. At times the scratch of pens in the barracks is enough to drive a man mad, if he is already made distraught by a fruitless search for an adjective.

So far we have no scandal such as the one Sam witnessed[9] while in the military: an officer ordered several privates to write pages of his novel, then promoted those who had advanced the plot as a rattling good yarn. Commissioner Macleod is aware of the peril.

"Aye, well, for some o' us," he once said in the mess, looking at me *en passant*, "the biggest challenge o' police work is to make an arrestin' paragraph." I was tempted to riposte with some remark about the value of the short sentence, but didn't wish to seem to be criticising my father's writing style. Like our other *auteurs*, I take care to hide my manuscripts so that a comrade in arms will not be tempted to steal a *bon mot*, a crime for which, unfortunately, the sentence is not hanging though the participle may be. I keep my letters locked in a metal case with my father's watch. One or the other must surely make my fortune, don't you think?

Meantime, I chafe at the lack of raw material for my quill. For some perverse reason, the most exciting adventures befall officers who have no literary ambition. Superintendent Jim Walsh is a case in point. Last summer, no sooner had "D" Troop arrived here in Fort Macleod, with former dens of vice such as Fort Whoop-up as tractable as a church picnic, than things heated up at Fort Walsh, with Jim Walsh receiving the benefit of the summer's one and only dicing with Death.

9. Steele, *Reminiscences*, p. 37.

The Sioux, retreating northward from an American army bent on avenging Custer's come-uppance, had planted their lodges in Walsh's bailiwick. In May he took three policemen and two scout-interpreters to sally forth, straight into Sitting Bull's camp of several hundred lodges, containing at least 500 warriors newly convinced that the white man is as mortal as any other hue of fool. It was Walsh's boldness that carried the day. Surrounded by painted braves escorting him down from the hills, into a camp that included at least four chiefs who had attended the festivities at the Little Bighorn, Walsh gave no sign that he was more moved than a village curate visiting a home for old maids.

One chief told him that it was the first time a white man had ever marched into Sitting Bull's camp. What a glorious precedent! I would gladly give a year's pay, and at least half a bottle of good Scotch whisky, to be able to report to History: into the valley of death rode the half-dozen, no cannonade but the pounding of my heart. . . .

How did Walsh get away with such audacity? He showed the Sioux both the stick and the carrot, warning them against using Canadian soil as a base of operations for forays into the United States, and promising them the protection of the Queen's law, plus enough ammo to hunt Canadian buffalo and fill their empty bellies. In a sense, he won the battle by putting his bullets in the other side's rifles. A stratagem not to the taste of a Napoleon or a Ulysses S. Grant, perhaps, but d––n sensible when outnumbered 100 to one.

The Indians' name for Superintendent Walsh, by the way, is "White Forehead". Whether this refers to his receding hairline or an alabaster brow, I know not. But it is a definite improvement on "Little Prairie Chicken" and, overall, my jealousy of Walsh's *éclat* knows no bounds. Not only has he stolen such thunder as was available, but he took Mr. Kittson, our surgeon, into Fort Walsh to tend to the wounds of those privileged to do or die. This left me temporarily as officer i/c medical attention, because I had been incautious enough to embellish my service application with the information that

I had studied medicine (to the extent of my father's having sent me to Germany to learn the language). The record omitted the fact that my father, having perused the reports from Hamburg, decided that letting me loose in a hospital could set British medicine back 500 years.

"No need to repeat the Black Death," he told me, not unkindly.

It thus fell to me to deliver the baby.

I wish I could say that I mean "deliver" in the sense of delivering a letter, or delivering a lecture. But no, I allude to the considerably juicier ministration to a human mother giving birth to a new Canadian. The impromptu summons came from a halfbreed trader who, while driving his waggon past the fort, heard from the wife in the waggon that she was going into labour sooner than expected. Normally the 'breed will ignore the howls of parturition unless they threaten to frighten the horses, but this expectant father stopped at our portal and came running to us for a midwife – an appointment which, both the ladies and most of the men being elsewhere, I won by acclamation.

Now, one of the first, if not only, things I have learned as a votary of the Delphic advice "Know thyself" is that my thought processes are not improved by an emergency situation. Some people shine when projected into a crisis. I tarnish. I try to keep a cool head, but overdo the chilling and my brain freezes. Instead of leaping into action, I sprawl over it.

Thus my first act of deliverance was to grab my sword. Cutting the umbilical cord was, I knew, a primary function of the attending doctor. I could have run to the cookhouse for a smaller blade, but time was of the essence.

"De 'ead's comin' out!" was the shout from the father, who had laid the mother on the ground but was standing back as though apprehensive that the baby might explode in the breech. When I arrived, the infant appeared to be stuck, as though having sensible second thoughts about entering this vale of tears. But the instant that the groaning mother opened her eyes and saw me brandishing my sword she let out a scream of fright, possibly mistaking me for U.S. Cavalry. At the same time the baby popped out. The contractions may have received a boost from my inspiring mortal terror.

I severed the cord cleanly – the first time in three years that my sword has been bloodied. The squaw then took over quickly, in case I intended further cuts, though it was plain that neither parent was of Hebraic background. The father was delighted that the baby was a boy, and a whopper at that. He hefted the bawling child several times, as a trader judges a sack of flour, and cawed, "Ten poun'! Ten poun'!" Had his thumb on the scales, I think, but I was pleased to be part of the landing of an offspring well above the size at which one throws it back.

As that family turned their waggon homeward, I was struck, not for the first time, at how joyfully the poor welcome another mouth to feed. That baby, I'm sure, had a more cordial reception from his mother and father than did I, on making my first entrance in the human comedy. My father made sure that my mother had the best medical attention, but by the time I arrived he knew that each additional child was costing him another 300,000 words, sweated out at his writing desk. The novelty and delight of procreation had been dissipated, and he accepted me dutifully – with what subtle effect on my body and soul only the Lord Siva knows.

What *I* know is, if I ever father a child – and one will suffice nicely, thank you – I hope I shall be able to greet the baby as radiantly as that halfbreed I helped on his way to the checkered rewards of parenthood. First, however, I shall need to meet and marry a lady, something close to impossible at Fort Macleod. All the white women hereabouts are spoken for, and the Force frowns on an officer's marrying an Indian. I watch the waggon trains coming up from Fort Benton, but women appear to know the end of the line when they see it, and none of them cares to try her luck north of the border.

It looks as though the mountain will have to go to Moham-
med, when the mountain – foothill, if you insist – can obtain
leave to forage in the less exclusively male towns of Montana.

September 30th, 1877.

Not one but *two* letters from you! A veritable deluge of news
from home, for which this parched soul is immensely grateful.
You ask if I have seen an Indian scalped. The answer is Yes.
That is, I have beheld a dead Indian who had been scalped –
a body decomposing beside the trail – but I have not, thank
heaven, witnessed the actual taking of the trophy. I may
chuckle at the scalping jokes passed around by my men
("scalping is a hair-raising experience"), but I find it a dismal
custom, though some students of these barbarous rites say
that scalping and cannibalism are in fact a compliment to the
dead, some of whose valour is thus appropriated. If the Indians kill me, but are disinclined to scalp me, this constitutes
a slight on a par with having one's book reviewed by the
magazine's cleaning lady. I therefore still prefer imitation as
the sincerest form of flattery. If I ever see an Indian staring
hungrily at the top of my head, I shall assume that he is
admiring my hat rather than my courage.

By now you will have read about the extravaganza in which
my hat and the rest of my costume played a bit part: the
signing this month of Treaty No. 7. A prosaic title, that, for
a document that cedes to Her Majesty's government all of
what remains of the great plains.[10] The drill was much the
same as for our grand pow-wow to mark the signing of Treaty
No. 6 at Fort Carlton, but on a more splendiferous scale. Our
Fort Macleod Force pranced forth in high style to greet and
escort the Lieutenant-Governor of the Northwest Territor-

10.   Treaty 7 affected much of the region that became the province
of Alberta.

ies, David Laird, whose attire was calculated literally to knock the Indians into a cocked hat. Then, one hundred troopers strong, we marched the 50 miles north to Blackfoot Crossing ("Ridge Under the Water") on the Bow River, the place chosen by the Indians for this momentous congress. We bore the entire panoply of gentle persuasion: the dear old "D" Division band, the brace of trusty field guns that had contributed so much to the ordeal of French's original trek west in '74, and a baggage train of six light waggons. In the soft, golden light of September, we were, I must admit, a sight to behold as we rumbled into that pleasant wooded valley where the Blackfoot already had thousands of tepees set up.

So confident are we now of the effectiveness of our treaty-signing stage production that Mrs. Macleod and several other officers' wives had been brought along as guests, as well as visitors from as far away as Fort Edmonton, plus a separate enclave of traders bibbed and tuckered for the Indians' treaty money, and several official artists madly sketching to capture the historic occasion on canvas – "bless me, the Bow, those transcendent shades of blue!"

As before, the best speeches were made by the Indians. Old Crowfoot, chief of chiefs of the Blackfoot, was in rare form. Said he: "If the police had not come to this country, where would we all be now? Bad men and whisky were killing us so fast that very few of us indeed would have been left today. The police have protected us as the feathers of the bird protect it from the frosts of winter. I am satisfied. I will sign the treaty."

We feathers preened ourselves, as chief after chief rose to say that he was signing the treaty because he trusted the red-coated policemen. None of them looked at *me*, while voicing this high praise, but all gazed admiringly at Commissioner Macleod. Stamix Otoken. Bull's Head. Good old Jim, who took the broadside of bouquets with never a shiver of his oaken timbers.

For my part, I enjoyed watching our genteel ladies in their pretty gowns, holding their parasols. They had come from the "white" camp side of the Bow to this other, where the most distinguished female present was the favourite wife of Old Sun, chief of the North Blackfoot. Mrs. Old Sun basked in the repute of having accompanied a hunting group that was attacked by a war party of Gros Ventres, one of whom swept her up behind him on his horse with the perceived intent of enjoying her charms at a more convenient time. That this was a tactical error became apparent when she at once seized her captor's scalping knife from his belt and stabbed him in the back, promptly casting aside the dead Lochinvar and riding back to Old Sun's camp, where she was invested with the honour of attending future tribal councils.

On balance, and from where I sat, I judged that Mrs. Old Sun had a milder mien than the missionaries' wives present.

After a week of wordy conclave, the treaty was signed by all the chiefs, most of them carefully making a mark that to me looked like a teetering crucifix. Their signatures were witnessed by virtually every white official and his wife, as though by sheer weight of witnessing we might make the rugged crosses indelible, eternal. I was spared being ogled by Big Bear this time, he being of the already-committed Crees, but as we doled out the inevitable flags, uniforms, medals, and $12 to each and every redskin, I noticed a little Blackfoot lad, festively clad in his best skins and beads, staring at his personal Union Jack as though it were the leaf of a strange and possibly poisonous plant. As I have supervised the crossing of so many palms with silver, it would have relieved my sense of Judas had the lad waved the flag, or eaten it, or somehow made use of it, as our band broke into "Rule Britannia". . . .

Commissioner Macleod did not return with us to the fort, but left at once for the Cypress Hills and a ticklish assignation with an American commission seeking to extradite Sitting Bull and his Sioux to U.S. territory.[11] Macleod took with him

11. The American commission consisted of Brig.-General Alfred H. Terry, who was Custer's commander at the Little Bighorn, and U.S. Cavalry officers and government officials, accompanied by two

Inspector Crozier, Staff Sgt. Steele, and 28 other men – the crème de la crème of a Force in which, it seems, I am part of the milky whey. Yes, Ezra, it smarts. I would give a good deal to be chosen as one of those that Jim Macleod knows he can count on in a critical situation. However, for this engagement he considered me to be best suited to escorting the women-folk back to Fort Macleod. Either he doesn't trust me to be with him, or he *does* trust me to be with his wife – alternative cheeks for the same slap in the face. No, I am not writing this between fits of biting my knuckle out of spite. Nor did I, on the ramble back to the fort, attempt to prove that the Commissioner made an error in judgment when he thought his wife would be safer with me than with Crozier. On the moral level it would be unsavoury, and on the practical level, the likelihood Mary Macleod's betraying Bull's Head for Lit-tle Prairie Chicken – well, the Canadians have a saying about the chances of a snowball in H––l.

Compared to the NWMP Commissioner's lady, Caesar's wife could be passion's plaything. While in India I observed how quickly, in that heat, the white colony could become a shim-mering, fly-blown fleshpot, with colonels and memsahibs slipping into one another's chambers with the rapidity of French farce. Many a cocky young subaltern has thought to win a higher commission by showing the higher commission-er's wife some novel uses for handcuffs. But uneasy lies the head on which an avenging mistress may, at any moment, spill the beans. The closest I came to danger from this quarter came on a tiger hunt during which I shared an elephant's howdah as escort to an aging but lickerish English duchess, who tried to add a fillip to the chase by grabbing me about the upper leg and improvising a newel post to which she clung tenaciously as the howdah pitched and I yawed and she urged the beaters to redouble their efforts, cawing, "We have him now, lads, we have him now!"

newspaper correspondents, one from the New York *Herald*, the other from the Chicago *Times*.

Here in Canada, I have been assaulted only by one or two wives of itinerant ministers of the gospel, ladies who seemed bound to give their husbands special support in the laying on of hands. One of them confessed to me that she would love to have Charles Dickens's grandchild. It is one of the burdens one bears, as a bachelor, that these women see one as a fleeting fugitive from the bonds of matrimony.

Thus, one fine day this summer when Boz and I were out for a walk in the vicinity of a church mission, we were overtaken by a small pony bowed under the weight of Mrs. Q, wife of the minister in temporary residence. Behind her trotted a giant Métis lad apparently given the superfluous job of serving as her bodyguard while she was out and about. Mrs. Q reined in with a jerk that racked my jaw as well as her pony's.

"Inspector Dickens!" she exclaimed, her plump, red face beaming at me to remove any doubt that I had, somewhere, been exposed to an introduction. "What a pleasure to see one of our gallant police officers communing with the beauties of nature!" Of which she was not one, though the bobbing of her eyebrows invited me to include her massive bombazine bosom among the foothills that begged to be explored.

I smiled and touched my shotgun barrel to my slouch hat, but she was plainly in no hurry to proceed, demanding, "Do you come this way often, Inspector Dickens?"

"Quite often, ma'am. It's a pleasant path, and affords an occasional shot at a quail, to diversify my dinner."

"Ooh!" she cooed, the eyebrows again semaphoring a message understood by the British Navy and any man else not legally blind. "I must take care to wear something bright!"

Refraining from assuring her that the chances of my mistaking her for any game bird smaller than an ostrich were minuscule, I resaluted and pressed forward, giving Boz a boot in the rear to rupture his fascination with the hulking halfbreed. Such is my naïveté in these matters that I was genuinely astonished, when Boz and I were promenading the same path a few days later, to come upon Mrs. Q's horse tethered to a tree, with no sign of Mrs. Q or her bodyguard. This mystery didn't last long, as I heard a strong contralto gusting the grasses from the direction of a slough, a pond no larger than one of the *bassins* of Versailles, just off the trail.

"*Abide with me!*" The woods reverberated, the aspen leaves rattling, and it was the first time I had seen Boz put his tail between his legs, whimpering. He slunk close to me, his eyes shifty with canine self-loathing. " . . . *Fast falls the eventide. . . .*"

It was indeed later than I'd thought, and I about-turned smartly to retreat – too late.

"Inspector Dickens!" The voice came out of the bush with a resonant authority that made me know how Moses must have felt when the Lord spoke to him from the shrubbery. "Have you been baptised, Inspector Dickens?"

I froze in my tracks. A person does not ignore a summons from a disciple of St John. On the other hand, one of the things that attracted me to Canada was that the water holes were generally free of crocodiles and snakes. Was it possible that worse awaited me? I opened my mouth to shout towards Mrs. Q that yes, indeed, my mother had had me well and truly sprinkled at the font, but Mrs. Q anticipated me:

"There is nothing like total immersion, Inspector Dickens, to cleanse the soul – hallelujah!"

I had but a second or two to choose my fate: either a ritual submersion with Mrs. Q – with God only knew what added touches of purification – or a bolt for safety, at the cost of a woman scorned and all the hellish fury that she can unleash in a small community. Luckily, my convulsive grip on my shotgun found the trigger. A blast of shot rent the air, and I had the presence of mind to shout "Grizzly! With cubs! Run for your life, Mrs. Q! I'll try to hold her off. Run, run!"

There came the sound of apocalyptic displacement of water, like the emergence of Atlantis, or a herd of elephants quitting their river bath. For a large woman, Mrs. Q moved with amazing speed. Before her leviathan bow wash could crash upon the pond's startled bank, she was leaping naked into the saddle of her piebald pony, her clothes clutched to her chest and the pink spuds of her heels clapping the pony's ribs. They took off like a rocket on Guy Fawkes night.

This episode left me more eager than ever to meet Sitting Bull and to shake his hand, as one beleaguered fauna to another. I should like to ask him whether his classic serenity of countenance does not, in some measure, reflect the fact the Indians are polygamous, their wives mere chattel. Given his enormous energy, I'm sure that polygamy would have suited my father very well, and his being restricted by social convention to having but one wife at a time undoubtedly caused him a great deal of grief. As for me, having one wife at all seems quite unlikely, unless I miraculously come upon some maiden nymph that likes to take long walks with a short person. Perhaps, when I hang up my lance at last, I'll return east in search of a wealthy young American widow. I hear that Illinois is full of such dears, their Chicago pork-belly magnate husbands having expired under an avalanche of corporate dividends.

First, however, I must demonstrate to myself that I am a man worth marrying. Perhaps my fourth winter in this country will prove to be my lucky one. I have subdued the demon rum, Ezra, and also kept my powder dry. Let the curtain rise on a scene of action in which I am the principal player! I have understudied long enough. I know the part, stuttered word for word. Overture, maestro, *please*!

> Your fire-breathing friend,
> Frank.

❧

Fort Macleod, NWT.
December 23rd, 1877.

My dear Ezra,

I have your kind letter of October 13th and am truly sorry to hear that the malady that has bedevilled you for so long has been diagnosed as a painful disorder of the reproductive system.[12] Inherited, of course, as you say. Your father, like mine, left you a cross to bear, but yours is much the more difficult to hold upright. I fear that I cannot answer your question as to whether I have found evidence to support the theory that the disease was brought back to Europe by explorers of the New World. My impression, however, is that the climate of Canada is inhospitable to any pestilence that normally involves removing one's clothes. In any event, I wish you a swift and complete recovery.

Truly dreadful weather now keeps me captive here, though not before a visit to a comely fort that I should very much have liked to have had named after Inspector Dickens – Fort Calgary. At the junction of the Bow and the Elbow rivers, both idyllic streams replete with fish and eddying into ponds where the pretty forest of cottonwood and poplar resounds with the crash of trees felled by the beaver – that industrious chap whose toothy mien is a touching reminder of our dear English peerage – Fort Calgary is the post *non pareil.* No, we do not have a Commissioner Calgary. The place was first named Bow Fort, later Fort Brisebois, after one of our most senior supers, who led the troop that established the original post. Fort "Breakwood" did not suit Colonel Macleod, I gather, even in French, and he changed the name to Fort Calgary, after a wee town on the Isle of Mull, in the haughty

---

12. Probably syphilis.

Hebrides, where he was born.[13] Poor Brisebois! To have
enduring fame snatched away because his name smacked of
Quebec! At least Fort Dickens will survive *that* attack. Well
done, Pa, for being born un Anglais with Scotch connections!

I was able to cast my covetous glance at Fort Calgary in
the course of a new duty that the Commissioner found for
me in the fall: tracking down the cattle "rustlers" (thieves)
who plague the ranchers who are now moving into these
foothills in increasing numbers. Most of the rustlers are Indians who have graduated readily from horse-stealing to the
appropriation of a beast of which the evidence may be eaten
with better appetite. Not all the Blackfoot – indeed very
few – walk off with a live pot roast, and the miscreant tends
to be one of the slower-witted braves who have failed to grasp
even the most elementary lessons in agriculture offered by
the government's agents. He sees a steer grazing on the open
prairie and, as with the unattended horse, he says to himself:
"By Jove, the Great Spirit has provided," and he toddles
home with the bounty of kind Providence. My job – assisted
by my Métis guide and interpreter – is to apprehend this
poor, deluded carnivore and try to impress upon him the
essential difference between a buffalo and a bull that is clean-
shaven. One offender, when he realized his *faux pas* too late
to regurgitate the valuables, came to me and offered his horse
as compensation. I had to arrest him. A glum coup. Our
education program continues to be based on a few days in
the post jail, and the message rarely sinks in far enough to
forestall the repeated offence.

Needless to say, I chafe at overseeing what I view as petty
larceny, though the pilfered object weighs half a ton. My only
consolation, as I lead some bewildered Peigan on a plodding
return through the snow to the fort, is that the Commissioner
appears to believe that I establish a better rapport with the
redskin than do those of his other officers who view the
indigene as a savage beyond redemption. Bless me, Ezra, have

13. Macleod died in Calgary – the Canadian one – in 1894.

I inherited something of Pa's sympathy for the oppressed? What a grisly fate: a compassionate policeman! I must strive to overcome this weakness.

In the course of my rounding up the dismal rustler I have ample opportunity to witness, with each day that passes, the slow disappearance of the buffalo, that most phenomenal provider once teeming like whales in a sea of grass. In the past, the buffalo's best friend has been Indian tribal warfare. The NWMP have mitigated, momentarily, this natural control of the human population of the plains, and the Indian consequently has many more rifle shells to spare for the four-legged target. Moreover, the buffalo is a pitifully vulnerable beast, peculiarly Canadian in being very sociable yet somewhat near-sighted, as subject as a cat to fatal curiosity without the compensation of having nine lives.

The buffalo survived for aeons during which the hunters had to pursue them on foot, with spears or bow-and-arrow. Even then, however, the buffalo could be lured to slaughter, being run over something playfully known as "a buffalo jump". The Peigan tell of their ancestors' staging of the communal buffalo jump, for which the tribe gathered in its thousands. As the opening gambit of the trap, a hunter would mimic an injured calf, bleating and limping under his hide, drawing a lead cow to investigate, the other buffalo following her into the gully where groups of hunters whooped and banged to keep the herd moving faster and faster till at last it pitched headlong over the cliff, dozens of animals piling atop one another in what the Blackfoot call pis'kun, meaning "deep blood kettle". What a reward for compassion!

One would think that the buffalo might come to mistrust the judgment of their lead cow. But then I remember the Charge of the Light Brigade, and must concede that even our own dear Queen may lure us to annihilation. Not far from this fort is a buffalo jump called "Head-Smashed-In",[14]

14. Near the Porcupine Hills. The bone beds are 12 metres deep. Now a World Heritage Site.

named after the young Peigan who, wishing to get a worm's-eye view of the thunderous cascade of bawling buffalo, stood under the cliff. A serious error in judgment. I have stood atop that cliff, alone in the whispering graveyard, and gazed down at the charnel pit, almost hearing the triumphant shouts of yesterday's Indians as they descended upon the dead and dying animals, butchering the cows and young bulls for the meat, hauling away the carcases whose bones would later be split open for marrow, and boiled to extract the fat, and whose hides would be tanned for tepees, moccasins, travois (the ultimate indignity: one dead buffalo being used to transport the remains of another). As abattoirs go, the place was no more grisly than what you'll find at Thames-side, but it still made me shudder, the horror of that cloudburst of flesh.

Après le déluge, nous. How successful shall we be, charged with persuading the buffalo hunters that the game is finished, that they must beat their rifles into ploughshares and farm the land that no longer sustains the great herds? Can we, in a single generation, change the hunter and gatherer into agricultural man, something that took your ancestors and mine a good deal more than a long weekend?

The Canadian government seems boundlessly optimistic that this transition can be accelerated, since it is God's will, seconded by Ottawa. I have my doubts. The Indian of the West is an altogether wild creature, not readily transformed by the message from the missionary that his untamed veldt is now part of Eden, and Adam is a gardener. Sometimes – and I hope I don't shock your religious sensibilities, Ezra – I feel that our Christianising these savages is like the falconer's hooding the hawk. How long can we keep the free, murderous spirit perched on our wrist?

To be fair, let me admit that the government is giving us extravagant means by which to mesmerise the raptor. The latest official dress code for NWMP officers includes the following:

> Scarlet cloth dress tunic styled to the 13th Hussars. Collar topped with gold lace. Austrian knot on

sleeves, with gold eyelets. Blue cloth facings, gold braid filligree. Gold crowns on collar.

Full dress trousers, relieved by one-and-three-quarter-inch gold stripe.

New regulation helmet with gilt spike and ornament, gilt chain and rim plating. White hair plume.

Dress sword. Also light cavalry sword, with motto device.

Scarlet cloth patrol jacket, scarlet silk lining, gold braid trim. Austrian knot on sleeves with gold tracing. Embroidered crown on collar.

Undress trousers, scarlet stripe. Bedford cord riding breeches.

Scarlet cloth mess jacket, gold braid trim. Gold cord Austrian knot on sleeve, blue cloth facing with gold eyelets.

White buckskin gloves.

Blue cloth cavalry cloak with scarlet shalloon. Removable cape.

Forage cap with gold band.

Shoulder belt and waist belt, of Russia leather, gilt buckle, tip, and slide.

Blue cloth mess vest, gold braid trim, gilt studs.

Russia leather sword knot with gold acorn.

These items apart, I am virtually naked. When fully and formally dressed from the tip of my gilt spike to the toe of my glittering boot, or with my father's watch chain pendulous from my gold-braided mess vest, I have looked at myself in the glass and remembered the poignant lines

> *"Full many a flower is born to blush unseen,*
> *And waste its sweetness on the desert air."*

I can't be sure how much sweetness I am wasting on the prairie air (Russia leather can be a bit overpowering, when new), but I do feel that I really ought to be in the Emperor Franz Josef's imperial ballroom, swirling in a waltz with some dark Bavarian beauty whose décolletage twirls the waxed ends of my moustache. Instead, I am gorgeously festooned like this solely to impress a grubby lot of redskins who don't even invite me to their dances.

However, it does, of course, work. Chief Rain-in-the-Face doesn't need to know that my sleeves are embossed with rough Austrian knots to discourage me from wiping my nose on my cuff. To the Chief, my frogs are powerful charms against evil spirits. Chief Red Crow gazes at the gilt spike atop my helmet, and the feathers of his own headdress droop – he is outranked. Thanks to the gold riband on my full-dress trousers – and a pox on those infidels that call us "yellow-stripers"! – I look taller than I do trouserless. My shanks still leave much to be desired, as soaring pillars of authority, but the fact remains that we British do know how to deck ourselves out so grandly as to make the barbarian feel that his submitting to us is something of a privilege.

The Americans – not to put too fine a point on it – simply don't understand the value of the spiked helmet. In fact, their cavalry officers look decidedly dowdy. Green-clad American sharpshooters lurking in the undergrowth were very effective against our redcoats after the dumping of tea in Boston harbour (and Americans still make tea the same way, I might add), but to expect such muted garb to be effective in subduing the redskin shows them to be equally green in the winning of empire. They have had to resort to using the sword against their Indians, while ours remains sheathed in its scintillating and imperious scabbard, Excalibur ruling abroad, too dreadful to be drawn except to salute the Lady of the Lake, or the Great Mother whose resplendence is utterly inconceivable.

With equally burnished good wishes,
Frank.

PS   The best Christmas present I've received this year has been the rumour that the HQ (and I) may be moved to

Fort Walsh, to the thick of the action, near the ever-volatile American Sioux. Much as I relish the bucolic atmosphere of Fort Macleod, the area is docile. We may be kept busy dredging the dregs of humanity into the fort's gaol, but there's little exhilaration in ambushing lost souls. Civilisation encroacheth – there's even talk of opening a school in town. A lamentable luxury, surely, for a place that still lacks a first-class gentlemen's tailor!

PPS Even the weather here conspires against heroic exploit – the winter has been so mild that yesterday (Christmas Eve) the men played cricket outside the fort. A clump of Indians watched the game in impassive silence, but claimed victory when one of their dogs caught the ball and ran off with it. Hardly the stuff of sagas.

PPPS   I can only shake my head, sadly, at your news that Minerva has gone to Belgium to study sculpture under someone named Rodin. It is hard for us to imagine why anyone would go to the Continent – the place being full of foreigners – unless he or she has been sent.

∾

Fort Walsh, NWT.
June 10th, 1878.

My dear Ezra,

Please note that change of address. Note it and join me in thanking God for it. Yes, last month the HQ and our Troop were moved here to Fort Walsh, to bolster the Queen's presence in this hotbed of Indian and international intrigue. At last, I dip a toe into the mainstream of history!

Leaving Fort Macleod was not all pleasure. No only is it a place of sweet breeze and lucid waters, but in returning eastward I may never know what lies beyond the magnificent ranges of Rocky Mountains that beckon even as they daunt. I fear that, unlike stout Cortez, I shall never stand upon a peak in British Columbia and gaze upon the Pacific. I am told that the west coast has a balmy climate and at least one town, Victoria, which, if one holds a hand over one eye, creates the illusion of being in Brighton. I seem to have spent much of my life – in Canada and India – supervising the conduct of rivers, which they say can give a person an exaggerated sense of life as flowing in one direction only, and downhill all the way. People who feel the pull of the sea and its tides are closer kin to the moon, which to the plains Indian is merely a timepiece. He worships the sun, that melter of snows and maker of rivers. Salt air, however, must gentle the spirit, as the Force has no presence yet in that misty land beyond the jagged peaks. I must serve as camp follower to Apollo, as you'll understand when, in a future letter, I tell you about the blood-chilling manhood rites of the Sun Dance – an initiation to manhood almost as appalling as that of the English public school.

First, however, let me rhapsodize about Fort Walsh. The fort has been splinted to strengthen its aging bulwarks, since I last saw it, but still lies in the same flat valley of the Cypress Hills, in defiance of every principle of military strongholds from Edinburgh Castle to the Rock of Sigirya.[15] From its aspect it is impossible to tell whether it is designed to keep people out or in. I'm convinced that the Indians take the latter view. Otherwise they would not be camped – hundreds of lodges – all around the fort and the adjoining small town, a situation that strikes incredulity into the American army officers and agents who keep coming here, trying to recover their delinquent Indians. They stare at us as though we are leading charmed lives, which of course we are, the charm

15. A fortress/palace of early Sinhalese kings of Sri Lanka.

depending entirely on the reproductive rate of the buffalo required to feed not only the Canadian tribes but our American guests, who increasingly choose adoption by the Great White Mother over returning to an ancestral land where the popular belief is that the only good Indian is a dead Indian.

This explains the proliferation of tribes encamped around us in these Cypress Hills – Sioux, Assiniboine, Blackfoot, Saulteaux, Sarcees, Crees. Yes, my old chum Big Bear is still stirring things up in his nomadic way. The Crees, I find, are physically less imposing than most of the other tribes, for which they try to compensate by being more crafty. I can sympathize with them. If I were six inches taller I too could be more forthright.

The Commissioner estimates that we have no fewer than 5000 Indians chasing too few buffalo within a radius of 100 miles of Fort Walsh, and we – including our outpost of Wood Mountain – number only 129. In truth, I'm convinced that the natives would be pitching their tepees even closer to our wall were it not for our band practices. Our doughty minstrels, who came with the Troop from Fort Macleod, are audible proof to the savages that the Mounted Police can endure any amount of suffering. But this does not deter the Indians from making forays into the vicinity of the fort and the stores in the valley, as they find the valley ideal for pony races. These are as wild and whooping as any attack on the war-path. It requires a good deal of trust in the Lord, I find, to be wakened in the middle of the night by yells and hooves thundering past the fort, and merely mutter, "I'll put a fiver on the jockey wearing the red stripes and nothing else."

Our men also engage in football games with the braves. These can become quite boisterous. Indeed, I have refused to referee since the game in which one of our lads put the shoulder into an opponent, and the Indian responded by drawing his scalping knife, causing our man to retire hastily to the clubhouse. I restrict my athletics to rambles alone in the hills, though I miss Boz, whom I had to leave behind in Fort Macleod. (He took it better than I did, I regret to say.)

I expect soon to find a replacement, however, as the Indians are doing a creditable job of replacing the buffalo with herds of canine.

June 17th, 1878.

My completing the paragraph above was interrupted by a remarkable incident. Louis Léveillé, our top scout and interpreter, glided into my office – it was tea-time, and I was dozing over this letter – to say to me: "Sir, Sittin' Bull wan' to see you, *vite*."

You may well believe that this intelligence jerked me wide awake. "He wants to see *me*?" I said.

"Alone. I take you to 'eem, if accep'."

Well, who could not accept? Here, surely, was the moment I had been waiting for all these years: a chance to demonstrate my ability to affect the course of events in western Canada. Hastening to pull on my boots and other gear, I asked Léveillé: "Did he say what he wanted to see me about?"

"No sir, 'is messenger say notting. Jus' you come alone."

What else could Sitting Bull want, I thought, as Léveillé and I saddled up, but to ask me to use my good offices to arrange his surrender to the Americans? If it were food he needed, he would have merely sent his scrawniest headmen to the fort to beg. This, I told myself, is certain to be something special by way of envoy, and I cheerfully ate the dust of Léveillé's mount.

It took us but an hour or so of hard riding to reach the Sioux camp, of which Sitting Bull's followers make up a part. The old chief may be Mr. Sioux to the outside world, but among his own people his power is on the wane. He probably now controls no more than a hundred or so families, but his name still stirs flights of butterflies in the belly. And I felt all the more elated that I was entering his camp with only one man, and he an interpreter, to steal my thunder.

I have given up all hope of ever invading an Indian camp without the inevitable hubbub that is set off first by the dogs – which seem to be able to tell friend from foe even before we get within sniffing range – alerting the women at their work at the dinner fires, who in turn summon the biggest men in the camp, who form a gauntlet that one is ill-advised to run, or indeed walk at other than a stately pace totally out of step with one's inner urge to bolt. In these greeting parties there are always one or two muscular braves who insist on demonstrating their familiarity with the white man's ways by shaking hands. Because they often forget to let go, I have been half-dragged off my horse, before now, in these social encounters, and now eschew the shake but redouble the effort I put into the raised-arm salute of peace, though the assembled children seem to find this amusing.

Dismounting at the chief's tent, I was further sobered by the sight of the guard, a smiling personage holding a U.S. cavalry sword.

"Dat's taken from one of Custer's men," Léveillé whispered, and I wished he had waited till he was asked.

The old chief was sitting with a couple of his councillors when Léveillé and I stepped into his tepee. I was surprised to see a man smaller, and certainly scruffier, than I had expected. Only his presence, his poise, gives Sitting Bull the grandeur that makes one feel that *he* is the one standing tall, and the visitor the one squatting *à terre*.

He was holding his coup stick, a ceremonial weapon consisting of an egg-shaped stone lashed to one end of the stick, the thong at the other end being wrapped around his wrist like a sword knot. A formidable progenitor of the policeman's truncheon, it gave me a headache just to look at it, though my reason told me that the chief now uses it mainly as a prop for photographs.

"Inspector Dickens at your service, sir," I said through my interpreter. "You wished to see me?" (I tried to control the excitement in my voice, but my d––n stutter had its way with a couple of the consonants.)

Sitting Bull replied through Léveillé: "We thank you for coming to our lodge. We too are Shaganosh."

Shaganosh. The Indian name for British. I felt the first twitch of dismay. Since taking up residence in Canada as refugees from the Americans bent on avenging Custer, the Sioux, under Sitting Bull's inspired leadership, have been insisting that they are of English blood, and that some of them were actually raised on our sceptred isle. Their Shaganosh father (so goes their familiar avowal) was King George the Third, to whom the Sioux remained loyal during the War of 1812 by moving northward, in proper disdain for republicanism. There is something touching, as well as hilarious, in this portrayal of painted savages, thousands of miles from the Court of St James, claiming descent from the British royal family. If anyone is flattered it must, I think, be George the Third. But I could detect no compliment to me in my being brought miles for this reminder of the genealogical link between Sitting Bull and John Bull. Indeed, I was somewhat offended, saying to the chief:

"Shaganosh or no, I'm afraid that eventually you must return to the United States, where they have, I understand, a quite nice reservation waiting for you."

Sitting Bull nodded stoically, and said: "You too are Shaganosh, Inspector Dickens. I am sure that you will help us to show the Commissioner that Sitting Bull has the right to remain in Canada as a loyal subject of the Great White Mother."

I was honestly bewildered by the chief's presumption that I could have any influence whatever on the policy of the government of Canada in respect of the repatriation of his wayward Sioux. I said, with what I hoped was firmness despite my nervous throat's closing to produce a startling falsetto, "Chief, I grant you that we Shaganosh have been remiss in allowing your ancestral home to become part of the United States, but the Revolution seems to be irreversible." I bit my lip to indicate a degree of remorse. "However, the law is the law, and the law says that you must return to the States."

I nodded briskly to emphasise the incontestability of my case.

The chief's sly smile did not waver an iota. He continued to gaze at me as though we both knew that the Queen's law was something to be got around. Had he been talking to other members of my family? He then took from the hand of a councillor a dog-eared book, which the chief tapped with his coup stick, gently, before handing it to me. I was appalled to see that it was a cheap, American pirated edition of *Oliver Twist*. The book fell open to a page marker.

"He wan' you read it," murmured Léveillé.

"*Must* I?" The coup stick smacked into a leathery hand. I read aloud: " 'If the law supposes that,' said Mr. Bumble . . . 'the law is a ass, a idiot.' "

Sitting Bull nodded, a faint smile creasing that noble visage, and one of the councillors handed me an inked quill. Whispered Léveillé: "I t'ink he wan' you sign it."

I have autographed copies of my father's books before, but never with so little pleasure. I returned the book to the chief's hand, but his other hand made a gesture to indicate that the audience was over. The old fox assumed that I had been bought like a bag of beans.

On the ride back to the fort, I broke the silence only to say to Léveillé, very firmly: "On no account will you tell anyone, repeat, anyone, about this meeting. Is that understood?"

"Oui, Inspector," grinned Léveillé, and he spurred his horse to throw a little more dust in my face.

I beg you, too, Ezra, to keep this encounter confidential, at least till I have been dead for 50 years. Thank you.

Frank.

~

Fort Walsh, NWT.
September 21st, 1878.

My dear Ezra,

With the mix of tribes about us becoming ever more restive, Fort Walsh obviously sits atop a powder keg with an ample supply of short fuses. We therefore attract any number of mischief-makers eager to expedite ignition. American news-paper reporters, for example. Scarcely a month goes by with-out a visit from one of these harbingers of doom, seeking confirmation of the rumour that their Sioux and our Canadian tribes have joined as confederates in a massive uprising against the white man. They smell massacre, and each hopes to be on hand when the Great White Mother is hoist by her own petard.

One of these check-suited, bowler-domed buzzards sought me out. As I was emerging from a trader's store I was waylaid by a florid person whose bumptious manner at once an-nounced his nationality.

"Captain Dickens, I believe," says he, holding out a hand that felt flaccid as only a printed-rag merchant's can.

"Sir?" says I, not troubling to correct his giving me a rank in the U.S. Army. All of us in the Force are now accustomed to being assigned the rank of captain if we are an inspector, major if a superintendent, with the Commissioner going to colonel. These honorary ranks make it easier for the American newspaper reader to imagine where we are standing in the British square, bayonets fixed and waiting for the inevitable decimation by inferior numbers of unarmed natives.

"Andrew Jackson of the New York *Herald*, " says my accos-ter. "May I buy you a drink, Captain?"

"You may if you can find a legal bar."

His weasel face creases into a grin at this. "I can see that you have your father's wonderful sense of humour," says he.

He then flashes open his jacket long enough for me to see a silver flask snugged into its holster. "That's not your Montana Redeye, Captain. That is bona-fide Kentucky Bourbon. I suggest we repair to my waggon for a small libation."

"Sir," says I, "I don't drink when I'm off duty." I hope that this is up to Pa's standard of waggery, and am rewarded with a hoot and a punch on the arm.

"Spoken like a true son of the Great Journalist," says he, and he puts his arm around my shoulder to walk me to his waggon. A very natty little waggon it is, too. On both flanks the canvas bears in Gothic print THE NEW YORK HERALD, a device to ward off evil spirits, unless they wish to become subscribers. My host has obviously hired a guide/driver and brought up the rear of the waggon train from Fort Assiniboine, Montana. When we are seated inside his *voiture* he produces the flask and a couple of silver tumblers, also monogrammed "The New York Herald". It becomes increasingly easy for me to identify my benefactor's employer.

"To the blessed memory of Charles Dickens!" toasts Mr. Jackson, and I swear that his little ferret eyes glisten with green envy as he tosses back the votive offering.

"Hear, hear," says I, sipping cautiously. It is a superior beverage, but there is nothing like sensing that one is being used, for putting a dead worm in one's whisky. I sip and wait for the quid pro quo.

"You know which is my favourite character in Dickens?" asks Mr. Jackson rhetorically. "Mr. Micawber! Now *there* was a really comical character."

"Based on my grandfather," I murmur.

"No fooling?" exclaims Mr. Jackson, clawing forth a notebook. "You don't mind if I make a few jottings?"

"Jot at will. But I'll ask you not to compromise my position – our colonel has ordered us not to speak to the press."

"I'll *bet* he has! You chaps are dead ducks." He is scribbling as though it is only a matter of hours before I meet the fate of Custer's men. "You don't mind if I quote you posthumously?"

"I can't imagine my objecting," says I, reluctantly empty-ing my glass, unnoticed, down a knothole in the floorboards.

Mr. Jackson squints at me and lowers his voice to indicate his respect for confidentiality. "I hear that you recently met up with our Sitting Bull, in person, and he gave you a real hard time."

"It was, indeed, an encounter I'd sooner forget."

"Care to describe it for me?"

"I think not. Some moments are so terrible as to be inde-scribable. Suffice it to say that only two of us came out of his camp alive."

"Only two! Wowee!" Scribble, scribble, scribble. "And according to my sources, a few weeks ago a hunting party of your Blackfoot blundered into Sitting Bull's camp. There was an exchange of gunfire and several of your Blackfoot were killed. Can you confirm this story?"

"Yes," I say, "except one detail. What the Sioux and the Blackfoot exchanged was gifts."

"*Gifts*?" The flask that was about to refill my glass choked dry.

"Yes. As a matter of fact the two camps have become quite chummy. A good deal of partying back and forth, I gather. Rather inspiring example of international brotherhood."

The reportorial pencil is noting none of this. Its holder is staring at me with a mixture of disbelief and resentment. He now raises his voice to its normal tone of stridency. "Look here, Captain, I have it on good authority that Sitting Bull is on the war-path. Now how about cutting out the bull s––t and telling me what happened?"

"Certainly. First of all, Sitting Bull's camp does not have a war-path. He makes use of the same trails as our Canadian Indians. Secondly, the incident you heard about involved not Blackfoot but the Bloods, under their chief Heavy Shield, who is rather a hot-head. He let it be known, from his camp, that he had a low opinion of Sitting Bull."

"Aha! And *then* there was a bloody battle."

"Not quite. Sitting Bull responded to Heavy Shield by inviting him to tea, I understand."

"*Tea?*" Mr. Jackson spits the word into my tumbler, and screws the cap on his flask. "Our Sitting Bull ate crow for some Indian that America never heard of?"

"I think you have a marvellous story, sir, of the way that living in British territory has brought out Sitting Bull's talent as a diplomat. If he continues to exert such a benign influence as an ambassador of goodwill, I don't see how Her Majesty's government can fail to offer him a knighthood."

"*Sir* Sitting Bull?" His astonishment disappears as he feels his leg being pulled. He scrambles out of the waggon, his face a thunder-cloud, and as I follow him he turns to snarl, "Thanks for nothin', Mister Dickens. And if you want to know the truth, I think that what your old man wrote about America stinks." With that he huffs off in search of more profitable sources of misinformation.

A moment of comedy relief, Ezra, but how long can we at Fort Walsh remain comfortable with our head in the tiger's mouth, when other forces conspire to twist the cat's tail?

With best wishes for your health and happiness.
Frank.

~

Fort Walsh, NWT.
September 21st, 1878.

My dear Ezra,

No letter from you lately, and perhaps just as well, since my grip on the pen has been weakened by a mortifying malady known here as the Fort Walsh Polka. I have never found it easy to write while seated in the necessary house, when everything is flowing *except* the deathless prose. This post has proved to be much more prone to this internal dissension than dear old Fort Macleod, possibly because the drinking-water here is less salubrious than that coursing down from the virgin peaks.

I am also recovering from a major expedition to Sounding Lake,[16] during which our Troop had little water to drink aside from what we could scrounge from the dismal alkali ponds. This alkaline water, I'm told, gives the indigene excellent teeth, though his head may turn to lettuce. Fortunately, I took my own supply of liquid, and if it did nothing for my perception, at least I enjoyed a better quality of mirage. Some of the oases were exceptional.

The occasion at Sounding Lake was the confirmation of Treaty 6 with the Crees camped in that area, and the payment of the treaty money. These treaties with the Indians are like the more common kind of marriage: the wedding is a fine and festive affair, but on each anniversary thereafter it becomes increasingly difficult to muster the enthusiasm of the first nuptial night. The Indians treat the annual payment as an excuse to have a large, noisy party that lasts for days, as do the traders who collect like jackals to relieve the celebrants of their cash. For us NWMP, however, charged with the job of crossing the grubby palms with silver, the annual treks to desolate camp-sites such as Sounding Lake mean the world's longest and most uncomfortable pay parade. This is why Commissioner Macleod has recommended to the government that the grand conclave of tribes be broken up into smaller gatherings held at more convenient locations. The Indians will not like this, the traders will not like it, but, alas, marriage was e'er to stale custom prey.

From all accounts, the Americans have a much simpler method of distributing wealth among the natives, namely by piling the boxes of bullion atop a stage-coach and whipping the horses along a route where the Indians may conveniently ambush it, with a wild chase that leaves a trail of dead bodies

16. About 100 miles SW of North Battleford.

and the survivors with a sense of what one might call creative money management. Hardly comparable was our plodding detachment from Fort Walsh, led by Asst. Commissioner Irvine, with Adjutant Dalrymple Clark, Sub-Inspectors Denny and Myself, Staff-Sergeants Steele and Lake, and 15 men of "F" Troop – an imposing body of men, fluffed up, like the rooster, to make us look bigger.

We had to contend with a junior Sahara of sand hills to the Saskatchewan, and another river crossing – where we carefully floated across the waggon-boxes covered with tarpaulin. This was an exercise that once again made me wonder whether Wordsworth would have so fondly admired the river that "glideth at his own sweet will" had William been up to his neck in the river at the time. Thus ours was a weary band that linked up with the escort for Lt.-Governor Laird, and by the time we arrived at the Cree encampment we were aware that inside the lodges there was a mounting mutter of discontent. We had no difficulty spotting the chief responsible for putting the cat among the wood pigeons: my old chum Big Bear. He had refused to sign Treaty 6 at Carlton two years earlier, and he was still adamant that the allowances were not sufficient. This made for a strained atmosphere. We had to post extra guards, who in the event of attack by several thousand Crees would have given us a few extra seconds in which to comb our hair, before it was confiscated.

Big Bear recognized me, of course, from Fort Carlton and subsequent *grandes fêtes*. He continues to stare at me more than my rank or degree of participation in the conference tent would seem to warrant. It is as though he recognizes in me a kindred impatience with the humbug of trying to make highway robbery an element of modern transport. We both know, I suspect, that it would be a more honest meeting if we both stripped naked and sprang into a circle of dirt, there to flail at one another with our bare fists till one was the victor – his primitive culture, or mine.

However, it was his own kind that thwarted Big Bear's hostility, on this occasion. Most of his fellow Indians were only too pleased to take the money and run off with it. Big Bear did not give up easily, though, arguing indefatigably with the Lt.-Governor that he and his fellows (now largely gone to celebrating) were being diddled by the Dominion. He managed to extract from Laird a promise to submit the chief's wishes to Ottawa. He then departed grumpily, vowing to return next year and expect a favourable reply. I thought I had seen the last of Big Bear, for the time being, but he suddenly appeared at my side as I was closing the payment books, and he said:

"I see dark clouds move to take the sky. You see them too." He walked away, with that curious, shambling gait of the Indian that seems ungainly ... till one tries to keep up with the beggar. I'm not sure how I feel about being a fractious chief's confidant. I cannot afford to take his part, yet I am grateful that he has singled me out for attention, without having read any of my father's books, even though that attention is potentially murderous. "Mixed emotions", perhaps, best describes my feeling.

Our detachment's return to Fort Walsh was uneventful, but the distant rumble of thunder that Big Bear made us hear has a southern echo, or else portends a much deadlier storm. The rumours that fly about this post each day concern a major alliance of Canadian and American tribes – Blackfoot, Sioux, Assiniboine, Crees, and Saulteaux – with the Métis, to drive out the white man from the North-West Territories. The name of the ringleader of this phantom insurrection haunts us like an evil refrain: Louis Riel.[17]

M. Riel is the gentleman responsible for the Red River Rebellion, which happened before I arrived on the Canadian scene, and therefore could not be blamed on me. He is the Métis leader, something of a lawyer, a Roman Catholic, a Quebec hero, elected to Parliament (twice), and banished, very gently, by the federal government to the United States,

17. Who was born (Oct. 22, 1844) within one year of FD, and died (Nov. 16, 1885) within one year of FD.

which strikes me as droll, given the American view that theirs is the Promised Land. A bit like Moses in the desert being exiled to an Egyptian seraglio, what?

Small wonder, therefore, that Louis developed mental problems and now drifts from job to job south of the border, trying to persuade Indians and halfbreeds alike that he is their Joan of Arc, chosen of God to expel the English from their homeland. I know that Ottawa wants us to deal with him (if at all) very discreetly. Burning him at the stake would cost the government votes in French Canada. In fact, even a public trial would smack of martyrdom, forcing Ottawa to choose between justice and politics – an excruciating dilemma. Therefore the onus is on Inspector Walsh to keep scouts on Riel's trail, unobtrusively, and to stamp out the brush fires of a rebellious confederacy as quickly as the Gallic firebrand sets them. So far our Indians have taken Walsh's word over Riel's, as to the readiness of the American tribes to join them in a continental uprising.

The Inspector has not yet asked me to accompany him on any of these high-stakes missions, where bluffing is of the essence. I don't have a poker face, and I know it. I wish to God I did have the ability of Walsh and Macleod to look an Indian chief straight in the eye and convince him that the moon is an oversize Camembert. I have lately been studying the life of Napoleon Buonaparte for a clue as to how, despite his lack of stature, he rose from "the little corporal" to emperor. But I remain baffled. His wearing the lofty grenadiers' hat may have helped, but his success with Josephine suggests that he was able to impose his will even with his hat off. My future with the Force may depend on my discovering his secret.

I do hope that your health is much improved.

Frank.

~

Fort Walsh, NWT.
October 21st, 1878.

My dear Ezra,

I am distressed to learn from your letter (September 5th) that its brevity is necessitated by failing health. I most earnestly join you in praying that your new medical treatment of herbs will alleviate your suffering.

When one considers all the ills that flesh is heir to, one must be astounded by a people that deliberately inflicts wounds upon its young men in the name of attaining manhood. I earlier attended, along with Staff Sgt. Steele and a few other observers, the annual Sun Dance of the Assiniboines on the north side of the Cypress Hills. This event was held in the large Medicine Lodge, which is centred by a post that supports the buffalo-hide cover, and was rimmed with a temporary railing of saplings, behind which stood the applicants for warrior status. Each of these had a willow-reed whistle tied into his mouth by a head-band, and none ate or drank till the ceremony – which lasted for days – was over.

The Medicine Man welcomed each candidate – who was accompanied by his female relatives – in the centre of the tent. While the women held the novitiate, the Medicine Man thrust into his breast muscles sharp skewers, which were attached by thongs to the roof post. Then, to deafening whistling and beating of tom-toms and screams from the women, the brave jerked himself about like a gaffed fish till the skewers tore out through his flesh.

Sometimes the procedure was varied by inserting the skewers into shoulder muscles, with the added weight of a buffalo skull tied to the vicious pins ripping out living tissue. Yet not once did a brave utter a cry of pain or show any expression other than impassive resolve. I'm sure that *I* grimaced more than anyone else present, since Steele sidled up to me in the midst of the gory gyrations to murmur: "Maybe you'd better just watch their feet, sir."

An astringent spectacle, the Sun Dance, Ezra, for a person whose manhood was tested by the dance lessons ordered by his father, in an effort to instil confidence in a visibly shrinking violet. I underwent that terpsichorial ordeal at the Boulogne boarding-school, in the arms of Mr. Cassidy, the sports master who doubled in waltz. I remember vividly my anguish when Mr. Cassidy's free hand slid down to clutch my bottom – a manoeuvre that bent me backwards like a bow – and his eyes skewered mine, as I tried to jerk myself away from some unseen, vile tether.

I suppose that Rugby Football is the normal initiation rite for Britain's warriors. The Mud Dance. The rugby coach, the medicine man. The Indians are perhaps a shade more sensible in that they strip almost naked and save wear and tear on their jersey. About the same amount of blood is spilled.

As our party rode away from the still-throbbing Medicine Lodge, the whistling and drumming and women's shrieks reverberating in my head, I reflected on the fact that the few braves who fail the initiation, who show some sign of suffering, are forever denied the status of warrior, and when the braves go on the war-path, must remain in camp with the women and children.

So far, I have much the same service record.

I have, however, not lost faith in the proving of my manhood, as I remember clearly that I bore Mr. Cassidy through "The Vienna Woods", with stoicism, till he tried to kiss me, whereupon I stepped very hard on his foot. The howl he emitted was not unlike that of the Assiniboine Medicine Man evoking the Great Spirit. So, go ahead and test me, O ye gods! I shall not flinch . . . unless it truly *hurts*.

Meantime, at Fort Walsh we have our own ceremonies designed to test the stamina and pain threshold of the men. For reasons that escape me, this post has the reputation of being the most demanding in the area of spit and polish. The mounting of the guard each afternoon at two calls for full dress: buckskin breeches of a whiteness to stun a Vestal Virgin, helmets, gauntlets, and belts buffed with clay from nearby hills till an unwary inspecting officer risks snow blindness. So acute is the competition between the rival barracks that the men have been known to carry their contestant bodily across the dusty square to the parade ground. Shocking.

I can understand that these excesses of deportment are a necessary safeguard against laxity during periods of routine duties, but it is unfortunate that as an officer I must set a good example of meticulous grooming, sometimes without the sine qua non of the British officer's cleaning equipment: a batman. In India I was able to ignore the red dust because there was always a wallah to wipe it off my boots. But the grey dust of western Canada is something I must often contend with myself, when it isn't grey mud, and I fear that this is a war of attrition that I cannot hope to win.

As if not kept busy enough maintaining their service costume, the men put on amateur theatricals that require additional fussing with funny hats and striped bloomers. I stay clear of these productions, except for the odd stint as stage manager, my aptitude for which is probably in the blood and must therefore be closely watched. Our Negro minstrel shows demonstrate to what level a police band can sink unless confined to the parade square. A frequent performer in these burnt-cork operas is Mollie,[18] the ebony laundress for the fort, who boasts that she was "the first white lady" in the Cypress Hills. The claim is not as absurd as it may seem, since many a trooper here, starved of feminine companionship, swears that Mollie gets whiter with every month that passes, and could in time become as fair as Ophelia herself. I suspect that, besides her routine laundering, she takes as much starch out of the men as she puts into their shirts. She has winked at me, once or twice, but I avoid any ministration

18. Confirmed by Turner (*The North-West Mounted Police*), vol. I, p. 418.

that might shrink my reputation as well as my stockings. Although, Heaven knows, one does become lonely here. Where are you, Mary Macleod?

I do, however, attend all the theatricals, front and centre, and applaud diligently regardless of how excruciating the antics on stage may be. Indeed, I am genuinely amazed by the energy of our lads, such as the troupe of thespians that hurried back to the fort after arresting "Four Jack Bob" Everson for assaulting an Indian, in time to present a quite lively production of "Dick Turpin". I am of course often asked if I have a copy of any of my father's many theatrical pieces, and I have to disappoint the inquirer. When I left England for Canada, it never occurred to me to stock up on Pa's comic sketches, as part of my provisioning to impose the will of a Queen who – at home or abroad – is not amused.

The only dramatic scene I have been involved in with our actors occurred when one of them, wearing make-up as Little Red Riding Hood, took a break from rehearsal by strolling into the parade square and encountered a painted brave, with long, braided hair, who happened to be reporting a horse theft to me. As I watched the two gaudy faces staring at one another, I realized how difficult it is to recognize the civilised by cosmetics alone.

January 5th, 1879.

I have delayed posting this letter in the hope of hearing from you. Also, to be completely honest, celebrating Christmas has left me a little short, financially, and the U.S. postage required to send this on its merry way looms larger in the season of wassail. The mess was tastefully decorated for this Christmas. In lieu of the Christ child we had a picture of Superintendent Walsh (titled "Sitting Bull's Boss") facing the entrance, hung with silvery chains and bits from the stables. Decking the walls were gleaming carbines, revolvers and lances. The Prince of Peace was with us, no doubt, but the manger was better accoutred than usual.

We need all the divine help we can summon, to get us through the worst winter of my life. At last, Canada has shown me her true hibernal face, sans nose, sans ears, sans pity. Blizzards, Ezra! To paraphrase Micawber: snow drift six feet deep, NWMP officer six foot four, result happiness; snow drift six feet deep, NWMP officer five foot six, result unhappiness. Fortunately for me we are not called upon often, in such sub-zero fury, to deal with violators of the law, as they, Indian and white alike, are "holed up" till the temperature moderates to merely intolerable.

In the circumstances, you may wonder that I persevere in this last-ditch endeavour to make the name Francis Jeffrey Dickens one to conjure with. I have my old drinking problem under control, thanks to the Montana Redeye that discourages over-indulgence in any but him whose throat is tiled with slate. My deafness, d—n it, fades and swells according to the stress of situation. I am thinking of asking our farrier to fashion me a buffalo-horn ear-trumpet. The possibilities for animistic magic with such an instrument should be boundless. Every Indian chief will want one, probably a pair. An ear-trumpet, wielded with a majestic flourish, may be just what I require to overtake officers like Macleod and Walsh in being held in awe by all and sundry. Yes, I shall stop at nothing to get *my* picture on the mess-room wall.

With very best wishes for the New Year.
Frank.

∽

Fort Walsh, NWT.
June 10th, 1879.

Dear Miss Butts:

I am very grieved indeed to learn of your father's death. It comes as a double shock to me, as I have been expecting, or rather hoping for, a letter from England these past months, and when it came at last it bore this sad news.

Ezra Butts has been a good, though rarely met, friend to me. May I offer you my most sincere condolences? I regret that we were never introduced – you were, I believe, a young lady (fourteen?) when I left Britain, and I had but glimpses of you during my few visits to your father's inn. I don't know what to say about your finding my letters to your father, in his office safe, as well as my brief correspondence with your mother. Your family solicitor is doubtless correct in suggesting to you, as the sole heiress, that your father considered the personal correspondence of Charles Dickens's son to be of value. But I am more grateful still that your interest in the letters, and in me, is that of learning more about Canada as a place to which you would one day like to emigrate. To answer your question: yes, so long as you and what remains of your family do not consider it improper for us to correspond, I shall be delighted to do so. Five years ago I should have said "No" – a hard-drinking wastrel like Frank Dickens has no business writing to a young lady under twenty. But the leopard has changed his spots – the Canadian mountain lion *has* none. I shall look forward to hearing from you, Miss Butts. For the moment, however, I observe a silence out of respect for your bereavement. Your father was a generous human being. We shall both miss him.

I have the honour to be, ma'am, your most obedient servant,

Frank Dickens.

∾

Fort Walsh, NWT.
September 17th, 1879.

My dear Miss Butts,

What a very great pleasure to hear from you again so soon! Your cheery account of your moving in with your Aunt Sarah in Shrewsbury, and your plucky resolution to take French lessons in order to prepare yourself for a life in Canada, could not have arrived at a more appropriate time.

We have had a stern summer here at HQ. Of which the most doleful circumstance has been that the Indians are starving. Every day, more of them stagger into the fort as mere skin and bone. The buffalo are disappearing from the plains even more rapidly than we feared. Until recent years, the Indians used to slaughter wastefully, cutting out the tongue and choice cuts but leaving most of the carcase to fatten the wolves and coyotes. No longer. They have adapted badly to farming, preferring to let the white settlers do the ranching, then stealing a cow, but only – we must be fair – in times of domestic distress. I spend much of my time doling out the daily ration of one pound of beef and a half-pound of flour. It is sickening to see these proud people scavenging in our refuse bins and swill buckets. I suppose that their fate is no different from that of hundreds, nay thousands, of other nomadic tribes that since biblical times have foolishly exhausted the resource upon which their lives depended. God grant that the NWMP may help to spare the Blackfoot and the Sioux the lot of the Lost Tribes who didn't manage to become the English!

Compounding this dismal side of the summer, Fort Walsh itself has become a place of pestilence. The illness – which they call typho-malaria – has struck down many of our officers and men, as well as townsfolk, settlers, and Indians. Even the indestructible Sam Steele has been forced to take to his bed. Our hospital has every bed occupied by sweating, fevered, debilitated victims of the plague, and even our doctor has been felled by the same scourge, necessitating the transfer here of the Fort Macleod physician. We have, however, at last discovered what we believe to be the source of the disease: these hills nurture a number of swamps and tributary creeks into which the Indians cast the remains of buffalo and ponies and other waste matter, to rot. In time of freshet, these miasmic waters overflow into the stream that supplies our drinking-water. Dr. Kittson, our surgeon, on his recovery from the illness pursued his theory that it was the contaminated water that produced the depleting dysentery. He also found cesspools under the floorboards of the barracks: a terrible blow to our reputation for clean living. How easy it is to look and feel like the noblest work of God, when all the while we are sinking invisibly into our own filth!

I can take none of the credit for this medical sleuthing, being fully occupied thanking my lucky stars for being spared the devastating illness. Any germ vicious enough to put Staff Sergeant Steele on his back (and he is still hobbling about on a cane, weeks after recovery) would have certainly transferred me to the celestial Troop whose mounts are fleecy clouds. My salvation, obviously, has been that I never drink water. In India I learned, painfully, the essential rule: the warmer the weather, the hotter the tea. Cold drinks – whose temptation can be excruciating in a hot prairie summer – are the ally of contagion. I was able to spurn the siren gurgle thanks to a gift from your father, with which I was able to keep myself awash in scalding char.

Please note that Ottawa has changed my rank. I am no longer Sub-Inspector but Inspector Dickens. Much as I'd like to impress you with promotion, the truth is that the Sub has been lopped off all Inspectors, while Inspectors are elevated to Superintendents. It is plain that the government wishes us to gain the sensation of being moved onward and upward, without increasing our pay. Inspector . . . Superintendent . . . Commissioner – who knows to what heights I may rise, and still earn but $1000 per annum?

Lest this sound cynical to your young ears, Miss Butts, I'll tell you that the same order from Ottawa reduced the pay of our men wishing to re-engage in the Force to 50 cents a day, at a time when new recruits now arriving are being paid 75 cents a day. Our veterans interpret this anomaly as a signal that, if they stay with the Force long enough, they will be paid nil, and may in fact be required to reimburse Ottawa for the privilege of risking life and limb.[19]

My men, have, of course, complained to me about this absurd injustice. I tell them that their best hope of redress is to attend services at the first permanent church (Anglican) in the town, and pray that the scales will fall from the eyes of the Minister of Justice. Until now we have had to depend on itinerant R.C. priests, such as Father Lacombe, who have been in this country long enough to know that it is harder to shoot a moving target. The Reverend Archdeacon George McKay also performs wedding ceremonies, a duty that previously fell to our Superintendent Walsh, who certainly did not need the additional burden on his conscience.

I apologize for the unconscionable length of this letter, Miss Butts. The pleasure of being permitted to write to you encourages excessive verbiage, I fear. And perhaps I ought to warn you that it is customary for a member of our Officers' Epistolary Club to read aloud any letter received from abroad (i.e. east of Winnipeg), as balm for the lonely heart that none of us confesses to.

I have the honour to be, ma'am, your obedient civil servant,

Frank.

19. FD omits mention of the additional good-conduct pay of 25 cents per diem.

PS To improve our drinking-water at the fort, we are to have a well. May I make a wish on your behalf? I shall be happy to provide the sacrificial penny.

F.

~

Fort Walsh, NWT.
November 3rd, 1879.

Dear Emily,

What an absolutely splendid letter! Twelve pages, in your own generous hand! I am the envy of the fort. I don't say that an NWMP officer's social worth is judged by the girth of the letters he receives, but do you know of a better way of weighing the regard in which the receiver is held, by someone, somewhere? I don't, and am therefore doubly rewarded for reading your account of your first trip to London. It was kind of you to visit my father's house in Tavistock Square. Yes, it is indeed a very large abode, bought to accommodate Pa's burgeoning brood and the faithful servants, who were out-numbered by the *un*faithful servants, all needed to keep the family clear of his study. Oddly enough I remember little of the house, probably because it served more as a base of operations for my father's efforts to find me an education somewhere else.

I do recall that the house had its own school-room, formerly the drawing-room, on the ground floor, so that the tears of our tutors would not stain the stair carpet. I remember that from the third floor (servants' quarters) I could look down into the genteel gorge of Tavistock Square, at the iron railing around the park and gardens, and wonder why the trees had been thus jailed. What offence had the geraniums committed to spend their life behind bars? And I remember what seems to me now, here, like a preposterous luxury: a basement. A place where a small boy could find cool, dark sanctuary from the hot summer's day, and listen to the coal singing wistful Welsh lays.

But all in all Tavistock House was like living in Euston Station, with my father as the Station Master. The main fear, for a child, was that of getting mixed up with the lost luggage. I felt very much like a travelling-case myself, what with the family holidays abroad and the boarding-school in Boulogne, and was at one point quite ready to leave home for Hamburg, to learn the German language and fulfil a dream of becoming a famous physician – Herr Doktor Frankenstein Dickens – performing medical marvels in that country. I don't doubt that this aspiration was seeded by my seeing the deference with which my father treated the doctors who were constantly stalking in and out of Tavistock House, attending to my mother in her multitude of difficult pregnancies. I coveted the status of the kind of demi-god who could order England's most famous novelist to pay attention to his kidneys. A career never realised, alas, thanks to my confounded stutter and the belated discovery – not really compatible with becoming a great surgeon – that I simply can't stand the sight of blood.

April 19th, 1880.

Mail delivery is halt and lamed by another fierce winter. I thus have ample opportunity to reply to a question in your last letter, namely how often am I called upon to pursue, on dogsled, "the mad trapper guilty of murdering a beautiful halfbreed girl". I regret to have to report, Emily, that the fur trappers around Fort Walsh are not only few but disappointingly sane. The only murder we have had this winter was that of one of our own men – Constable Marmaduke Graburn. Perhaps his sad (and unfinished) story will serve to allay your curiosity.

In November Graburn was on duty at our Horse Camp

(where we pasture ponies that are poorly), a few miles up Battle Creek. He and a scout had stopped off at a vegetable plot, to gather some greens for dinner, and on the way back to Horse Camp he found that he had left his axe at the vegetable garden. He went back for it, alone – and was never seen alive again.

When Graburn's horse turned up at Horse Camp, saddle empty, the others there reported his absence to Fort Walsh, and the Superintendent at once organized a search party, led by the intrepid Jerry Potts, who had just arrived from Fort Macleod. An overnight snowfall made tracking very difficult, but the searchers found three sets of hoof prints, one of a shod horse (Graburn's), and two made by unshod Indian ponies. We knew that a small band of Blood Indians were in the vicinity, and that one of the band – a rodent-faced, scurrilous individual inappropriately named Star Child – had been making a nuisance of himself begging for food from our people here and at Horse Camp. We were to learn that Constable Graburn, a lad with a lively temper, became so irritated with Star Child's pestering that he ordered him to make tracks, calling him a "miserable dog".

After several hours of backtracking, Potts discovered Graburn's forage cap. The searchers redoubled their efforts, and at last one of the other halfbreeds of the team found Graburn's body at the bottom of a gully – a gaping bullet hole in the back of his head. Murder, without a doubt.

The searchers also established that one set of Indian pony tracks took off, at a gallop, in the general direction of Montana. The Commissioner's report noted that the guilty party or parties probably fled south of the line, but that they are bound to blab to other Indians about their nefarious deed, and when they return to Canada we shall be waiting to nab them. Sure enough, a few weeks ago our men arrested a couple of young Bloods, residents of the camp near the fort, on suspicion of horse-stealing. Their wives, as is the custom, were allowed to visit them while they awaited trial. So it happened that I saw them, as I was passing the guardroom on inspection: the prisoners in animated conversation with their wives. I was, I admit, touched by the close rapport between the women and their menfolk. The Indian so often treats his wife as a mere chattel that it was good to see these young men whispering feelingly into the ears of their women.

A short time later, when the Bloods were being exercised in the yard, the pair broke away from their guard and bolted for their camp on the nearby hillside. At the same time, their wives rushed to meet them, carrying Winchester rifles and belts of ammunition. So much for the romantic savage!

To exacerbate the unscheduled departure of our guests, a third Indian prisoner, also out for exercise, took the escape as his cue to "hightail" off in the opposite direction, towards town. The prisoners' break occurred in full view of Superintendent Crozier, Inspector Cotton, and Surgeon Kennedy, who were playing tennis at the time, in the fore-fort. Not being a tennis player, I missed the initial excitement. But the hullabaloo did bring me from my quarters in time to see the officers toss aside their racquets and grab their rifles (a dramatic reversal of beating swords into ploughshares), and take off on foot after the fugitives. They were quickly passed by Inspector Steele and several mounted men giving chase. Confronted, the Bloods made a feeble show of resistance but quickly dropped their rifles and were marched back to the fort.

Later that night, apparently broken in spirit, the two Bloods asked for a private interview with Superintendent Crozier, and in a room whose windows were screened with blankets they gave a full description of Star Child as the murderer of Constable Graburn. As for the unfortunate third escaper, he was found the next morning behind a store in the village, quite dead from exposure, after a night of sudden sleet and plummeting temperature. I watched as a party bore his scrawny, almost naked body back to the Indian camp for burial. The Indians accused us of having hanged the poor devil without a trial, but were soon convinced when shown the ravaged corpse.

Thus, in this oddly circuitous fashion, we learn the identity of a murderer, at the cost of another life. Strange indeed are the ways of justice, in real life, and altogether less symmetrical than the stories you read about the NWMP in the press.

You may have noticed that our Sam Steele has been promoted to Inspector for his fearless exploits and repeated demonstrations of courage and leadership. I, in contrast, languish with the same rank I won six years ago on the strength of an unflinching exchange of letters.[20] No, Emily, I do not begrudge Sam his success. What I yearn for is his luck in finding opportunities to show his mettle. These continue to elude me, much more successfully than our suspects evade the long arm of the law. I am beginning to think of myself as the *short* arm of the law. Which will never do. My time *shall* come! And when it does, I swear that I shall seize my chance by the lapels and shake it for all I am worth.

Your letters help greatly to sustain me in this quest. More, please, more, more!

> Your greedy friend,
> Frank.

20.   FD wrote to Edward Jenkins, M.P., asking if Jenkins's brother (at Canada Government House) had succeeded in expediting Prime Minister Mackenzie's approval of FD's appointment to the Force.

Part Three
1880 ~ 1883

∾

Fort Macleod, NWT.
October 17th, 1880.

My dear Emily,

Not having received a letter from you for some months, I solace myself with the thought you missed my message of change of address: I am now back at dear old Fort Macleod. I am not clear as to why I was transferred to this relatively peaceful precinct near the Rocky Mountains. The fancy I favour is that my superiors were afraid that my reputation for forthright action was making Sitting Bull nervous, possibly enough so to precipitate a full-scale Sioux attack on Fort Walsh. Such an onslaught has in fact been threatened by the wily old rascal, after I decamped, but he has since abandoned the bellicose noises, doubtless because my departure robbed him of the chance to claim total victory.

For my part, I was – till my sudden posting here – fully prepared to sit on Sitting Bull. He has the notion that, as an American guest of the Great White Mother, hospitality extends to his stealing our horses. He needs to be taught the lesson that the Queen objects to visitors' pinching not only the silverware but also the royal steeds.

However, the laying on of hands-across-the-border has led me into a small adventure that may amuse you. When one of our scouts reported that a Blood resembling the description

of Star Child, our prime suspect in the murder of poor Marmaduke Graburn, had been seen in nearby Montana, I persuaded
the Superintendent to let me embark on a secret mission to
Fort Benton, to examine the spoor of our fugitive and –
though this was not explicit in the undertaking – to satisfy
my curiosity about this American wild-west town from which
is transported to us our mixed bag of things good and bad.

Accordingly, in September I set forth alone, disguised as a
civilian (one of my easier transformations). Jerry Potts, our
incomparable scout/interpreter/totem factotem [*sic*], advised
me to tag along with a returning ox-waggon train. However,
the 245-mile trail is now so clearly defined as to qualify as an
English country road, give or take an ambush. Wherefore it
was unaccompanied that I trotted into the main street of
Fort Benton, Montana, and took my first deep breath of
American frontier vice and violence.

We NWMP must ever feel grateful to Fort Benton, since it
was a pair of its dauntless traders – the immortal Joe Healy
and the equally imperishable Al Hamilton – who in the sixties
crossed the border into British territory to set up the trading-
post at the junction of the Belly and the St. Mary's rivers.
There they pioneered the lively trade with the Indians: buffalo robes for firewater. They named their emporium Fort
Hamilton and buttressed it with ramparts, stockade, and
gates worthy of Troy. When one of its employees returned
to Fort Benton for fresh supplies of liquid dynamite, and was
asked how trade was, he replied:

"We're whoopin' it up."

So was born the name Fort Whoop-up, which alarmed the
Canadian government into forming the Force and providing
employment for the pilgrim who addresses you now. So it
was with some emotion that I returned to the fount of this
benefaction. If I did not go at once to the town's church to
give thanks, it was because the way was blocked by a street
brawl between a couple of the parishioners.

You see, Emily, Fort Benton is geographically blessed by
being a font placed on the upper reaches of the Missouri

River, which creates the wonder of paddle-wheelers carrying all manner of human flotsam upstream, in defiance of known laws of hydraulics. The town itself has of course taken on a higher tone since the heyday of Fort Whoop-up. The sheriff, I had been told, was less tolerant of gunfights that occurred directly in front of his office, to the detriment of his window glass. But the old commercial spirit survives, even in that law officer, who has been known to demand $2000 for the return to Canada of a miscreant wanted by the Force.

Thus I entered the bar of the Montana Hotel on the qui vive for standards of free enterprise considerably more elastic than those of sleepy Fort Macleod. Unfortunately I had arrived in town late in the day and very thirsty, requiring me to sidle through a noisy conglomerate of cowboys, traders, and grizzled men whose black duster cloaks could conceal any number of decks of marked cards, with plenty of room left for a field piece. I was not armed. The NWMP service revolver is a purposely conspicuous object and is normally worn, in its equally forthright holster, positioned on the belt to assure that a quick draw will result in my shooting myself in the foot.

I had therefore left my armament in my hotel room, trusting that discretion would be the more livable part of valour. I bellied up to the bar at its relatively less crowded end. From previous encounters, in Illinois, I knew that in the American west speaking with an English accent can be like waving the Red Duster in front of a bull. I waited till the bartender had moved close enough for me to catch his eye and whisper, "Whisky and water, please. No ice."

To my horror the bartender cupped his ear and yelled "Come again, sonny?"

Despite my hearing problem, I had no trouble picking up his clarion call for an encore of my order. Nor did the half-dozen customers in the immediate vicinity, they turning to grin at my discomfort. I tried to mouth the words – "Whisky and water, please" – hoping that the bartender had learned to read lips. But he clearly didn't trust the unheard, as he yelled even louder: "Spit it out, man! Cat got your tongue?"

This evoked a guffaw from the onlookers. I decided that it was better to arouse anglophobia than get further into a mime act. I said loudly: "Whisky!"

Now, Emily, I doubt that you will ever have any practical application for this information, but for the purpose of this account you should know that we English, even when abroad, make the correct mistake of pronouncing the "h" in "whisky". This can be as pernicious as the "h" in "H––l", when one's listeners are accustomed to hearing the word as "wizzky".

"Hey, we got us a limey!" crowed a patron.

"One wi-hisky comin' up," mocked the barkeep.

Towards me weaved an inebriate, a small, elderly man wearing a battered bowler over a face that was a crock of prematurely-mashed potatoes. The owner was clearly hostile. He placed himself, swaying, to put the roiled spuds a few inches from my chin, and he hiccuped: "Oi hate the English."

Knowing that anything I might say (with a Home-counties accent) would only aggravate the Fenian's belligerence, I nodded and winked at the assembly to indicate that I was tolerating a drunk. The wink did not succeed, as the smirking onlookers were plainly on the side of Hibernia. But it did provoke my assailant, whose breath was making my eyes water, into prodding me hard in the chest with a stubby forefinger and snarling, "Oi spit on the grave of Queen Victoria!" With that, he spat on my boot, whose leather immediately turned to blarney stone.

Since the Fenian was even shorter and slighter than I am, allowing myself to be drawn into fisticuffs would have resulted in at best a Pyrrhic victory and at worst in total mortification. I therefore smiled broadly at him, as though discovering a long-lost brother, and while he was still nonplussed I seized his hand, clapped him warmly on the back, and frog-marched him out the swinging doors to the street. There I deposited him in the dust, a neat trick that elicited no applause whatever. To avoid further trouble, I unhitched my horse to seek a saloon free of the Irish Question. But before I could get my foot into the stirrup, I felt someone tap my shoulder, and I turned to find a gigantic man towering over me. He wore the leather harness of a dock navvy, and his maw was that of a person who wins bets by catching cannonballs with his teeth.

"You shouldna d-d-d-done that to D-d-d-dinty. He d-d-d-don't hurt nobody."

Since his friend was in the act of jerking a revolver from his pocket and staggering back into the saloon in search of me, I could have argued the point. But – and this is more advice on manners for you, Emily – when a large, menacing person with a stutter accosts one, it is a serious error to make a vocal reply if one is prone to stammer oneself. It is impossible to avoid the implication of deriding the primary stutterer. The only prudent course, therefore, is to remain as silent as the moon. Which I did, letting my eyes and ingratiating head gestures express an apology.

This did not satisfy my Gargantua, however, who seized my shirt in a mighty paw and demanded, "W-w-what's your name, stranger?"

"Ah," I said, pointing to my throat. "Ah." To be a mute seemed the height of eloquence, in the circumstances, but he shook his huge head. "You ain't d-d-d-dumb. I heard you in the b-b-b-bar."

Now, I had entered Montana mindful of the stories I had heard of the ritual duels to the death – called "shoot-outs" – held on the main street of the lawless towns, the duellists slowly approaching one another on foot till at last one of them feels compelled to draw his six-shooter, sudden death the price of being tardy. Being unarmed, I judged my only chance would be to challenge my opponent to a jousting-match, lances levelled at fifty yards. By the time he found a lance, tempers might have cooled. However, reality obtruded on heroic legend in the making, as I was nose to chest hair with a behemoth unschooled in settling affairs of honour without bloodshed, and probably unwilling to be taught.

So, I did what common sense seemed to demand – I gave him a very sharp kick in the shin.

For a moment, this had no effect. It took an awesome length of time for the message of pain to travel from his leg to his tiny brain. When it did register, his eyebrows rose slightly, and his grip on my shirt relaxed enough for me to break away, jump into my saddle, and spur my horse to rapid if undignified departure. As I did so, Dinty emerged from the saloon firing his pistol into the air, followed by other customers whose angry bellows made plain that my visit, though short, had not been found sweet by a considerable part of the populace of Fort Benton.

Fearing a posse bent on avenging the burning of Washington by British troops, I headed my pony straight out of town, choosing a by-way less likely to accommodate a large group of vigilantes in hot pursuit. Another error in judgment. My mount found a gopher hole with his foot and pulled up lame. I had to dismount and lead the limping beast to the nearest structure at trail-side: a small, whitewashed school steepled with a plain cross. It stood, stark and alone, in a field of brown stubble. The setting sun cast the school's shadow as a refuge into which I hastened my halt horse, hitching it to an incumbent buckboard. Not a moment too soon. The posse – consisting of Dinty sprawled over his nag's neck, his mammoth chum, and a third avenger – thundered past, viewing halloo and too bent on overtaking me to notice that they had done so.

But they would be back. I moved my horse out of sight of the trail and went to the rear door of the school, on which I knocked. Receiving no response, I pushed open the door and entered the single, diminutive classroom. Its cool darkness smelled like classrooms everywhere – the blend of powdered chalk and nervously-wetted underdrawers – but with something added: a faint scent of incense that gave this small room the dimension of Chartres cathedral. . . .

I heard a murmuring voice. It came from a room, even smaller than the classroom, that I deemed to be the teacher's living-quarters. I tiptoed to the door, which stood slightly ajar, and beheld a man on his knees, his back to me, his head bowed to the silver crucifix that was the only object on the white wall. I waited till he had completed his prayers – and these were protracted beyond belief – and was about to cough discreetly when he suddenly rose, deftly pocketed his Bible with one hand, and in the same movement turned to face me with a revolver in his other hand.

"Bonsoir, monsieur," he said. "Que voulez-vous?"

October 20th, 1880.

To continue my story, Emily:

The man holding the pistol on me was about my age, of medium height, with dark, wavy hair; a strong, oval face; the usual – should I say Dickensian? – moustache. But it was the eyes that held me mesmerised, eyes as black and threatening as the muzzle aimed at my middle. They were the eyes of a madman . . . or mystic . . . depending on which end of the gun one faced. Since I found myself on the end that called for tact, I replied in my school-boy French:

"Bonsoir." (For some reason, I don't stutter in French.) "Je suis chassé. Par des hommes de la ville, ivres." I jerked my thumb at my open mouth, the universal gesture for drinking spirits.

My host allowed a ghost of a smile to relieve his features. He returned the revolver to his belt and motioned me to sit on the one chair the room offered, the only other furniture being a monk's cot and a wardrobe in and on which were stacked books, in piles that reached to the ceiling. Beneath the bed, surrounding the chamber-pot like a multitude pressing upon the Pope, were heaps of papers and files. The room was a study in chaste disorder.

"You are English," he said. (For your information, Emily, and something to keep in mind when you come to Canada, the French-speaking North American prefers discourse in English when talking to un Anglais, or une Anglaise. This serves as both a rebuke to our execrable French and the unexpressed judgment that his English *must* be more tolerable than our mauling the language of Racine.)

I sat on the chair and admitted the undeniable. "Yes, sir, I am English," I said. "And I apologize for disturbing you in your school."

"It is not my school. I am borrowing this room for a short time to do paper work. I am a trader."

A trader whose face was vaguely familiar, I thought. But at that moment I was more interested in the bottle of wine he was fetching from the wardrobe. I'm afraid that I actually ran my tongue over crusted lips. He said:

"You appear to have come some distance. You must have thirst. May I offer you un petit coup, for the digestion?"

"G–d, yes, you may!" I blurted. "Will you join me?"

"For me, God says No." Odd, I thought, for a trader, a calling that normally demands a deal of social drinking. But I was too desperate to slake my parched gorge to be an immediate convert to temperance. The wine was warm and watery – sacramental, I'd wager – but it went down like mother's milk. Asked the trader: "What is your name?"

"Dickens. Frank Dickens, sir." I omitted rank and number, being the prisoner of none but my curiosity about this man.

"Dickens?" The dark eyes bored into mine. "That is a famous name."

"I am the famous name's son."

"Oo-là-là!" It was a sombre oo-là-là, the most pious oo-là-là I had ever heard. "I am a great admirer of Charles Dickens. I have read *Une Conte de Deux Villes*, several times." His face took on a rhapsodic expression, and his voice a vibrant timbre. "Magnifique!"

"You share my father's sentiments about the French Revolution?"

"Mais oui. About the glory of the martyr to revolution!" he replied. "Your father must have loved France, and the French, very much."

"That indeed he did, sir. And I dare to presume that you share that affection. May I know *your* name?"

He studied my face for a moment, then said: "You may call me David." He gave the name the French pronunciation – "Dah-veed".

The penny dropped. Landing in my stomach like a lead ingot. The words of an American Catholic missionary passing through Fort Walsh came back to me, his account of meeting a man who told him: "These people" (the Indians and half-breeds) "are just as were the children of Israel, a persecuted race deprived of their heritage. But I will redress their wrongs. I will wrest justice for them from the tyrant. I will be to them a second David."

Yes, I was looking at that man – Louis Riel.[1]

"Enchanté," I said, extending a hand whose palm was suddenly sweaty, "Monsieur David."

He smiled, and I braced myself for his having noticed the alarm in my eyes. He said: "Your father and I also have in common our love of puns. Synonyms – joyful play on words. Language can be an escape from the tyranny of convention, n'est-ce pas?"

"D'accord," I nodded, my mind too stunned to attempt a jeu de mots. So here he was before me, the man they call the Father of Manitoba. Who, though vastly outnumbered, took on the Fathers of Confederation and began a full-scale armed

1.   After his release from a Quebec mental institution, Riel had returned to his government-imposed exile in the United States, and after a futile effort to establish himself in the New York farming community he had come west to Montana in 1879 with the grand design of rallying all the Indian tribes and Métis into a revolt against the white man. His ultimate goal was to create a Catholic North America with Bishop Bourget of Montreal as Pope of the New World. FD apparently encountered him during a lull in his machinations.

revolt, seizing control of Manitoba while I was still in India.[2] To Quebec a saint, to Ontario a murderer. A free man for no other reason than that it was expedient politics for Ottawa to banish him. I felt a certain kinship with this fellow, despite his being patently mad as a hatter. I too was, in a sense, sent into exile for being naughty. For John A. Macdonald, read Aunt Georgina.

Truly, Emily, I couldn't help liking the bloke. I suppose that it is always comforting to meet another person who is even less integrated with polite society than oneself. I downed my drink and said: "What, sir, do you trade?"

"Not whisky," he said, and for a moment I feared that he had spotted the NWMP inspector under the grubby, red-check shirt and the grime of the Benton road. "Only the essentials that keep body and soul together."

"That also eliminates rifles." The attempt to be jocular died an unshriven death. His gaze merely tightened on me, as he asked: "And what is the son of Charles Dickens doing in the wilds of Montana?"

To tell him the truth, namely that I was trying to track down the murdering Star Child and return him for trial in Canada, seemed inappropriate in the circumstances. I was closeted with a mental patient known to be a fierce champion of Indian rights, who probably regarded the murder of a NWMP constable as the will of God, and who had a revolver tucked into his belt while my Winchester sat in its bucket on my horse in the yard.

"I travel," I said, and my averted eyes fell upon a framed portrait of the Blessed Virgin. Inspired, I added: "I am an artist. Painting scenes of the Far West." Plausible enough. God knows, the country crawls with painters and cartoonists, most of them reproducing Custer's Last Stand for an insatiable market in the eastern states. "I'm not very good, though, I'm afraid." This at least was true. As a lad I often watched

2. December 23, 1869, Riel became head of his self-proclaimed "provisional government" of Red River.

the innumerable artists who came to our house to sketch or paint my father's likeness. Whenever I tried to ape their strokes in my copybook, the result proved that, as Pa cordially apprised me, I "couldn't draw flies".

"Un artiste!" Louis "David" Riel's face was suddenly animated. "Perhaps I may commission you to make *my* portrait?" He plainly was not joking. The man was in real need of his own picture. While my brain scrambled for a reason to decline this papal commission, he elucidated: "I am active for the Republican party in this state.[3] I can use an agreeable likeness on posters, to promote our campaign. I have no money to pay for this, but will be pleased to provide you with dinner and shelter this night. As you see, it is too dark now to ride farther."

He was right. Dusk was mercifully masking the dismay I felt must be manifest on my countenance. As he lit a lamp, I gave him the only reply available: "I'll be glad to try, sir," I said.

"Bon! See to your horse. I shall put your supper on a chair in the classroom. You don't mind sleeping on the floor? Now you will excuse me – I have some letters to write."

Unsaddling my horse, I wriggled on the horns of a dilemma: should I take my rifle into the Catholic school and shoot the man who was giving me asylum? Or try to arrest him? Neither procedure looked inviting, on American soil, with a hobbled horse. I could see no other horse about, belonging to Riel. I decided to let the peace officer in me prevail. Re-entering the rapidly-darkening classroom, I found a tin plate of bread and cheese placed on a chair. Both were a bit mouldy, but an empty stomach has no sense of time – I wolfed them down. I lit the stub of a candle also provided, and using my saddle blanket as a pillow lay me down on the floor. I could hear the scratching of Riel's pen from the other room. Even as wordless sound the passion of his writing came through the door. As

3. Riel revived his interest in politics and delivered Métis and Indian votes to various Montana right-wing groups.

did a slit of light. Exhausted though I was, I responded to the vibration of energy gone awry emanating from the man's chamber. I couldn't sleep. Then at last the quill's rasping stopped. The slit of light widened. Riel was moving, on silent, moccasined feet, into the classroom. I braced myself for the abrupt and violent proof that he had not been gulled by my posturing as an itinerant Gainsborough.

However, he went only to the table on which he placed a square of paper and a pencil. My artist's tools! He then tiptoed out as quietly as he had come, leaving me to absorb the gently admonishing gaze of the Jesus whose faded picture hung on the wall of the classroom. We both knew that our fate was ineluctable, and this certitude shepherded me into slumber.

October 27th, 1880.

To continue: I was shocked awake to a hazy dawn by the rapid fire of a magpie on the school's roof. For a moment I slowly extended and retracted my limbs, to allay my fear that these were permanently petrified. No sound came from Riel's room. But I did seem to be receiving a message from the Messiah on the wall. I rose, and as if guided by a divine hand, I picked up the drawing-paper and pencil, stood before the portrait of God the Son, and, placing the paper over the picture, traced the face of Redemption. The facial contour I achieved was not a true resemblance, but I flattered myself that the nose and mouth were quite believable, and the upcast eyes shone with the same light that never was, on sea or land. I had to change the coiffure, of course, replacing the long, straight strands with curly locks. And I added the moustache. Altogether, a plausible similitude, unless viewed in outside light.

I placed the portrait on the teacher's table, like a pupil who has completed his assignment, and returned to my chair to await the arrival of the master. I had not long to wait before I heard stirrings in the other room, then a voice raised in prayer. (I translate, rather freely I suspect, from the French:)

"Jesus, author of life! Sustain us in all the battles of this life and in our last day give us life eternal!

"Jesus, grant me the grace to know how beautiful you are!

"Jesus, I beseech you, give me a precise idea, the most complete idea, of your physical beauty!"

Unconsciously, I bowed my head like a seminarian, during this morning Mass. There was no denying the compelling tone of Riel's voice, even through a closed door. In a surprisingly short time the man himself appeared, completely dressed in his severe suit and white shirt with stiffly starched sleeves. He carried a steaming mug and a slab of bread.

"Bonjour," he said, gravely. "In honour of Dickens père, I offer you a cup of English tea."

"Merci, monsieur." I took the scalding brew and sipped it. It tasted like pew varnish. I nodded and smiled approval, dreading his discovery of the homework lying on his desk. I was spared temporarily, as he said, "I must now pay a visit to the little chapel." He smiled thinly. "You are welcome to accompany me, if that is your wish. The school boasts what is called a two-holer."

"Thank you, no. I'll finish my breakfast first."

"I am taking with me these letters from my sainted sister, Sara.[4] I love to read them, over and over again. Do you hear from your family often?"

I gazed with frank envy at the wrinkled sheaf of correspondence in his hand, replying "Rarely." Close enough. "Never" would have been more accurate. I added defensively: "My main epistolary link with home is a young lady living in England."

"Ah, you have une petite amie. Excellent. Every man should have a mate. My believing so was why I left college,[5]

---

4. A professed nun, loyal to Riel to the end.
5. The Collège de Montréal. Riel liked to tell that he abandoned it

you see. God wants every man to have at least one wife, and preferably many wives. I expect to marry, myself, soon, and beget many, many children."

With that, he departed for the outhouse. I reflected briefly on his putting his imprimatur on polygamy. In Canada I had heard the stories that Riel's theology was a curious mix of ancient Hebrew and New Testament, but only now understood the appeal of such doctrine to the western Indians, who are as heartily polygamous as Solomon. Penurious indeed is the chief who is down to his last spouse. Being a bachelor, I, of course, am regarded as a real pauper.

I nipped outside and briefly contemplated the lee side of the school, asked its pardon, and was back in my seat, like a dutiful student, when Riel returned from *his* devotions. He at once discovered the portrait on the table, taking it to a window with "Ah, Dickens the artist has already been at work. Let us see if he has inherited his father's gift for le portrait."

Waiting, I tensed myself for the quick dash to my horse before he could go for his gun. But my patron turned to me, smiling, his eyebrows raised in approval. "Pas mal. Pas mal du tout. You are not a slave to form, I see. This is not his hair, but you capture the expression of the eyes very well. Très bien!"

He was regarding himself in the Third Person, like the Holy Ghost. I had traced just enough of Jesus for Riel to identify himself with the image. I said: "Thank you, sir. You are most generous in your judgment. And your hospitality. Now, if you will excuse me, I shall be on my way. . . ."

Before Riel could anoint me as his Artist By Appointment, a thunder of hooves broke into the school-yard. Was divine justice to be so swift? Were Dinty & Co. directed to their prey by a large finger projected from the sky's surly clouds?

"Attendez," said Riel. "It is my hunting party." He strode

---

for the love of a girl whose parents later forbade the marriage, because of Riel's mixed blood. In fact, he failed the course.

out the door to the half-dozen horsemen milling around in the dust. I followed, warily, to peek around the door jamb. The visitors – a mix of Indians and Métis – exchanged greetings with the Prophet, and after an animated discussion Riel returned to the classroom. I was already on my way out the back door when he hailed me:

"Monsieur Dickens! My trading associates go to hunt the buffalo. Perhaps you care to join them, to sketch the drama of the kill?"

"Merci, non," I declined quickly. "I do pictures only of people. Au revoir!"

With that I slung the saddle on my horse in record time, thanked Heaven that the animal seemed to have recovered from its lameness, and cantered into the yard. My way was blocked by the members of the hunting party, who were busy taking buffalo hides off their pack mule. As my pony picked its way through the crowd, one of the Indians glancing at me appeared to recognize me. I had no difficulty recognizing *him* – a renegade Sioux from Sitting Bull's camp. He let out a whoop that sounded to me like the Sioux for "Little Prairie Chicken"! My heels promptly clapped my pony's flanks, and we took off through the yard, scattering the other visitors in a manner contrary to the rules of prairie etiquette. I headed my horse north, at the gallop, fully expecting pursuit from Riel's regulars. But nothing followed me except – as I charged up the road – a burst of laughter.

Now that I am back in Fort Macleod, I am able to regret that a punitive "David" did not take after me, that I missed a golden opportunity, not only to rid Canada of a festering thorn in her side, but to settle the score for having to drink an American cup of tea. It was not to be. Yet. I trust that our paths will cross again.

A too-long letter, Emily. I promise to do better, in return for the great pleasure of hearing, however briefly, from your dear self.

> With much affection,
> Frank.

❧

Fort Macleod, NWT.
December 18th, 1880.

My dear Emily,

This Christmas in Macleod is made very special for me by
my having tucked into my stocking not one but *two* letters
from you. Double delight! It is also good news that your aunt
is encouraging you in your secretarial skills. Your excellent
penmanship – it shames my chicken tracks – bodes well for
your success, should you choose to be so employed. I wager
that one day most of England's clerks will be women, and
the Empire the better for it.

You inquire about the status of Canada's star boarder: Chief
Sitting Bull. The old warrior has fallen on hard times, with
many of his Sioux returning to the States to accept their fate
as American reservationists. But his wits have not lost their
edge. The American press recently reported that he an-
nounced to his kin on both sides of the border: "My people
are cold and hungry. My women are sick and my children
are freezing. My arrows are broken and I have thrown my
warpaint to the winds." As you can see, he has not lost his
flair for the dramatic. The Force must remain wary of turning
our back to the Bull in the belief that he is too weak to
muster one last charge.

Although I have not lately visited his camp at Wood Mountain, I am close enough to the Superintendent's vain efforts
to dislodge him to have a clear impression of a character out
of a pastoral *Bleak House*: a born lawyer, always suspecting the
worst and usually correct. As for the Americans, they are
unrelenting in their attempts to take advantage of the wily
chief's reduced circumstances. Several times they have
almost succeeded in luring him back across the border,
tempting him with the warmth and security of an agency
reservation. On one occasion he and his few remaining follow-

ers were actually making the return of the prodigal, and nearing the border, when Sitting Bull got word that he was to be greeted by General Miles and 3000 troops. About turn! A welcoming party too large by half. I doubt that Custer's countrymen will entice their favourite fugitive till he ceases to receive copies of American illustrated newspapers that depict Sitting Bull as having a pair of horns jutting from his head, and a ring in his nose. One day, perhaps, the carrot will prove irresistible, simply because it is edible.

The Indians, by the way, call the border "the Medicine Line". They have learned that they can cross the magic line and live a charmed life, stealing horses or raiding camps, while the policeman must stop at the line. We hope to arrange an extradition treaty with the Yanks, but in the meantime it keeps us busy minding the Queen's business. Our main ally in subduing the tribes is still the skeletal threat of death – by starvation. With the buffalo fast disappearing from the land, some bands are reduced to eating dogs . . . snakes . . . even the grasshoppers. It is a doleful sight, on patrol, to come upon one of these proud people squatted in rags beside a gopher hole, holding a looped cord in hopes of lassooing vermin.[6]

It is a mercy that the Indians do not celebrate Christmas, as it would only remind them of how bare their manger is, even of hay to feed their horses. This festive season can be trying for me, too. The barracks are inflicted with a fines fund, to which I have reluctantly contributed more than my share as a result of minor indiscretions, most of them at the behest of Bacchus. This Christmas the fines fund has been used to buy books. Need I tell you the name of the author best represented? No, indeed. I am fated to see even more

6. In his report for 1880 to the Governor General, Prime Minister John A. Macdonald, as Minister for the Interior, wrote: "The most amicable relations continue to exist between the police and the Indians, and manifestations increase of growing confidence and good feeling on the part of the latter."

of my comrades than formerly, sitting in the mess, or lying on their bunks, reading *The Old Curiosity Shop* or *David Copperfield*, and looking at me as though marvelling at how drastically genius diminishes with its offspring. To have helped to fund this odious comparison is enough to make me swear off drink altogether. I have taken a private oath to begin the new year of 1881 as dry as a rattlesnake's wit.

Lest you deem me deucedly dour, I'll tell you that the Commissioner has looked favourably upon my report on the desirability of employing heliography as a means of signalling by the Force. The idea was his, as he has studied sun telegraphy in England. But I have quite enjoyed estimating the percentage of Blackfoot who wear a small mirror strung around their neck, not only as an aid to personal toilet – here I refer to the males only – but also for the purpose of transmitting a message from hill to hill. The mirror is clearly superior to the smoke signal, in my opinion, since the sender is not required to build a fire, or to own a blanket with which to articulate the smoke. All he needs is sunshine, which this part of the world has in abundance, even in winter. Also, thanks to the flatness of the terrain, it is possible to heliograph for considerable distances – up to 30 miles, by my reckoning.

As I state in my report, it should be possible to improve on the Indians' sun telegraphy by teaching our men Morse Code, which, despite its North American origins, the redskins have yet to master. I shall not be surprised if a mirror became standard issue in the NWMP, and at last the name of Inspector Francis Dickens will be associated with a glass that informs.[7]

Before closing, let me thank you, with all my heart, for your avowal that you will never exploit our correspondence for your own monetary gain, as "Dickensiana". I am emboldened to write to you as intimately as I do with these words: you mean a great deal to me, my dear.

7. The project got no further than the Commissioner's recommendation to the Minister of Justice.

With warmest wishes for your happiness in the New Year,
Frank.

∽

Fort Macleod, NWT.
June 21st, 1881.[8]

Dear Emily,

At last, a letter from you! I feared that I had driven you off
with my ramblings. My joy in the renewal of your letters is
of course tempered by the circumstances of your unfortunate
liaison with your instructor at the secretarial school. It is
lamentable that a man should try to take advantage of his
protégée in this disgraceful manner. It is no family secret
that my father was such an offender, repeatedly engaging
in dalliances with actresses in his theatrical productions,
episodes that caused great distress to my mother, and to me.
Everything in Pa's life was so public, you see. When he bought
that bracelet for Ellen Ternan, and the jeweller mistakenly
sent it to Tavistock House, where my mother opened the
package, the resulting row was as much in the public domain
as any burlesque in his books. Indeed, my father took the
extraordinary – and for us children totally humiliating – step
of having a demurral published not only in his own *Household
Words* magazine but in all the newspapers of London.[9]

If I read you correctly, you too fell under the spell of an
older man of considerable charm. But at least you have been
spared the limelight. And I am sure that with your natural

8.   It appears that an indeterminable number of FD's letters earlier
in this year were lost.
9.   Headed "PERSONAL", the statement said in part ". . . this trouble
has been made the occasion of misrepresentations, most grossly false,
most monstrous, and most cruel – involving, not only me, but innocent
persons dear to my heart. . . ." FD was fourteen.

joie de vivre you will quickly recover from the episode. Life is so rich an adventure, we must never let the misfortunes of our youth overshadow the wonders to come. I, for instance, have, I believe, at last come to terms with my father. (I took his gold watch out of its case, the other day, and looked it straight in the face.) You will do the same, one day, with that affair of the heart which at the time blurred your vision with tears.

Think on this! – the newspapers that fight their way west tell us that the Canadian government has at last signed the contracts for the completion of the transcontinental railway from Winnipeg to the west coast. Before you are much older, you will be able to travel in comfort on this Canadian Pacific Railway, all the way to the Pacific Ocean near the village they call Granville,[10] on the inlet discovered by Captain Vancouver and said to be a feast for the eyes. Perhaps I may even join you there! After all the politicians (white *and* red) that I have escorted in this country, it will be a splendid change to stand guard while you dip a toe in that vast ocean that neither of us has yet seen.

The extension of the railway westward, and the venturing thither of settlers, have been facilitated by – finally! – the surrender of Sitting Bull to the American authorities. I wish I could report to you that I had a part in the repatriation of a legend. The fact is, however, that the delicate negotiations occurred eastward near our Wood Mountain post, with the Bull insisting that he was a British subject right up to the last bag of flour he could scrounge. In the end he had to choose which he wanted in his belly: American army beef or a Canadian rifle bullet. But I'm told that the chief of chiefs played his role to the hilt, even in submission. When he and his sorry train of Sioux arrived at Fort Buford, Dakota Territory, and the moment came to surrender to Major Brotherton of the U.S. Army, the old warrior deliberated in the

10. Later, Vancouver, British Columbia. The originally planned terminus, Port Moody, was less famed for its saloons.

council tent for some time before rising and putting his arm around one of his sons, an eight-year-old, who stood wide-eyed beside him as he spoke:

"I surrender this rifle to you through my son. I wish him to learn the habits of the whites. I wish it to be remembered that I was the last man of my tribe to surrender my rifle, and this day have given it to you."

The scene must have been a bit deflating for the Americans, who had a small army of soldiers ringing the fort, poised to avenge the Little Bighorn. But they appear to have been generous in victory, as is only right and proper, since they promised Sitting Bull amnesty, and we assured him that he could trust their word as Christian gentlemen. Sitting Bull has been transported in style to his reservation at Standing Rock, Missouri, and is said to be so favourably impressed by the appointments that he is thinking of bringing down all of his other families – wives, sons, and daughters – that he left north of the line. I suspect that we have not heard the last of our guest. When not making speeches on international topics, the chieftain has as little regard for the border as does a chicken-hawk. I shall not be surprised to hear that he has turned up again at Fort Walsh, to complain that the field glasses he appropriated from the trading post, as a farewell gift to himself, have developed a squint.

Of more immediate concern to us here at Fort Macleod are the waters of the Old Man's River, which became a *riparian deviate* last winter when it changed course to flow on *both* sides of the fort, torrentially at times. From being a castle with a placid slough for our moat, the fort has become marooned, with a swift stream eroding the foundation of the west stockade. There is a very real possibility that one night we shall have a cloudburst that snaps our anchor, so that we wake up floating downstream as royal marines, but without the advantage of helm or rudder. The Commissioner has petitioned the Powers That Be for the fort's removal to higher and dryer ground. If these letters end abruptly and without explanation, you may assume that H.M.S. *Macleod* went down with all hands. My aunt Georgina will be relieved to know that, in finding a watery grave, her wayward nephew has joined the heroes of England's victory at Trafalgar.

In the meantime, I have renewed my association with an old friend – Boz. The ancient mongrel recognized me at once, the first time I went into town, and bounded down the trail beside the river as if our rambles together had not been interrupted by two years devoted to giving the wild and woolly West a shearing. We are once again hiking these bonny braes. Sometimes, Emily, on a warm, spring day, the scent of the prickly wild rose is so affecting, that my heart cries out for a hand to hold, for someone with whom to share the incense of these hills. That a flower of such riotous custom, and barbed touch, can yet perfume the air as to make the very Elysian fields turn green with envy – what a comfort! To those of us, I mean, who are equally nondescript in form and fruit. Yes, yes, I know of the miracles wrought by rose-hip tea, and perhaps I too have some special virtues when boiled. But it is the sweet redolence of this rose that hallows all things errant. Waxing lyrical, I observed to one of our local ranchers:

"Truly, sir, these foothills may be called 'wild-rose country'."

He edged away from me, I regret to say, with a look suggesting that he doubted my red-bloodedness. How difficult it is, Emily, to speak the memorable!

Wishing you a quick and full recovery from the malodorous ways of my sex,

Your friend,
Frank.

❧

Fort Macleod, NWT.
August 31st, 1881.

My dear Emily,

Please, I entreat you, do not see this relentless surf of letters breaking upon you as a pressure to induce a reply. Such is of course the truth of the matter, but I should much prefer that you thought of my fertility in producing missives as a trait inherited from my father – deplorable, even heinous, but quite beyond my power to constrain.

Besides, I excuse this particular wave of words as being of special interest to a young lady whose compassion for affairs of the heart is in full bloom. Not, I hasten to add, that the romantic episode into which I was precipitated this spring is likely to take its place with Hero and Leander, Romeo and Juliet, or even Snodgrass and Emily Wardle. Indeed, nothing was further from my mind, that May morning when I took French leave from the post for a ride towards the greening foothills.

Although our regulations forbid us to venture forth alone from the post, for someone who values solitude as much as I do, the rule chafes like a burr under the saddle blanket. Before enlisting in the Force, I had envisaged myself as a sort of lonely ranger, silhouetted against the sunset in moments of repose, racing into action in splendid isolation or, when required for a parley with the foe, accompanied by a single, loyal redskin who never heard of Mrs. Gamp. However, the reality of service for me has, most regrettably, been one mob scene after another.

I had therefore waited impatiently for the chance to defy the commandment – thou shalt not kill unless properly accompanied – till that morning of May last. It was then that I heard that Four Finger Pete (the American gambler of whom I believe I spoke to your father during my earlier term

at Fort Macleod) had gone too far. The night before, Four
Finger Pete bet his Peigan wife against the pot in a game of
stud poker. He lost, but instead of turning over his unhappy,
abused woman to the winner, he knocked her unconscious
and, making off with her, headed westward into the hills.

Setting forth from the fort at dawn, I thought I had their
cart's tracks in my sights as my horse took me deeper into
the foothills, into thicker forest and lustier streams, but at
last I realized that I was hopelessly lost.[11] As a navigator I
have been spoiled by the plains where the trails run straight
and the sun is a compass. In the hills, on a winding path, the
sun mocks me. I spent a miserable night in my bed-roll, and
the next morning was relieved when I came upon a cairn of
rocks, at least ten feet high, that appeared to be a man-made
marker of some kind, the sort of thing a Scotch surveyor,
demented by "no-seeums" (black flies born of Hecate),
might build to mark the mileage between East Nowhere and
West Someplace.[12] While I sat on the ground studying the
cairn, and the river that swirled around the point of land on
which it stood, a group of Blackfoot youths, on foot, came
down the trail from the mountains, dragging lodge-poles they
had hewn in the woods. I have rarely been so happy to have
company. I approached them and tried to indicate to them
that the path of righteousness had led me astray. Bless me,
Emily, but it is hard to convey with sign language the information that one is lost! Try it some time, shielding your eyes
with your hand to peer to the four points of the compass,
then watching the blank faces grow more wary of being too
close to a person sidetracked from Bedlam.

At last I found a piece of paper in my pocket, and a stub

11.   The sort of impulsive foray that helped to earn FD his reputation
for "recklessness".
12.   FD appears to have blundered into "the Gap", the spot where
the Oldman River swirls out of the mountains. The Blackfoot, holding
the mountains in fear, tried to propitiate the evil spirit by reverently
placing a rock on the cairn whenever they needed to venture beyond
the friendly prairies. By 1930 the cairn measured 14 feet by 8 feet.

of pencil, and tried to draw a map for them on which to pinpoint us. Because of the breeze blowing down the trail, I took a rock from the cairn to hold the paper down, while I drew. This elicited a strange moan from the Blackfoot bucks, one of whom hastily took the rock and replaced it on the cairn. I took another rock, and it at once went back on the pile. Then my paper blew onto the pile, and the Blackfoot, growling, grabbed it, balling the paper and throwing it down the steep bank towards the river. Was this how they gave directions? Probably not, since they cast offended looks at me and then proceeded, muttering, to lug their lodge-poles towards their camp. I set off in the opposite direction into the mountains, letting my pony have his head till we entered a dry gulch that my steed – wily brute – knew afforded some shade from the nooning sun.

I breathed in the wolf-willow scent that must be one of the most agreeable of pungencies, and was about to abandon my quest, turning my mount for a reluctant home leg, when from somewhere farther along the twisting gully came the sound of a woman's scream, followed by a gun shot. I dug in my spurs and made for the source of the sounds, my horse's hooves clattering on the rocky trail. My approach being anything but stealthy, I held my carbine across my chest ready for action that did not wait upon formal introduction.

Rounding a bend in the gulch, I reined up at the sight that met my eyes: an Indian woman keening over the body of a man lying on the ground beside a horse-drawn cart. She ignored my approach, throwing herself across the inert male, who I could see now had been felled by a shotgun blast that had blown off the face, but for an ear and part of the jaw. These I did not recognize. But when the woman lifted her tearful face to look at me, yes, indeed, her I *had* seen before. She was Four Finger Pete's wife. And unless I was very much mistaken, the object bleeding on her moccasins was her gambler husband.

Also at her feet lay a shotgun, still smoking. My primary deduction was, of course, that Four Finger Pete's wife had killed him. Against this premise I had to weigh the fact that the woman was sobbing uncontrollably with what appeared to be grief. Could this not be a case of accident, or even suicide? When the woman turned her face to mine, I was startled by the dark beauty of that face, the eyes luminous, framed by strands of black hair silkier than one normally sees among native women. A fresh bruise marred her complexion, and I saw that she bore wicked welts where her dress was torn at the brown, gleaming shoulder. Since she was staring at me, in terror, I hastened to dignify my casual and in fact somewhat dishevelled dress.

"Do not be alarmed, madam. I am a police officer."

She didn't understand a word, of course, but my tone must have been reassuring, as she closed those wondrous eyes with a little sigh and fell into my arms, her head resting on my shoulder, that fine filament of hair caressing my chin. It had been a long time – I confide in you, Emily – since I held a woman so close to me. The scent of her warm person filled my nostrils like a souvenir of the earth in its beginning, and the tremors of her breast against mine made me suddenly weak in the legs, so that I nearly fell over backwards with this passionate parcel of woe atop me – a position from which a polite recovery would have been all but impossible.

However, having gingerly pried myself free of pure bliss, I busied myself in searching for a flat stone with which to dig a slight depression in among the wolf-willow bushes, and into this I rolled the body, while his wife rocked to and fro, head bowed. I covered the corpse with rocks to protect it, temporarily at least, from scavenging animals, and I fashioned a small cross of bleached cottonwood limbs, which I placed at the head of the grave. I then bowed my head and recited the Lord's Prayer, the woman holding my hand, her black hair hanging desolately over her face. Again, she had no comprehension of the words, so that I was able to end the prayer, in clear conscience, with ". . . and good riddance, you ugly brute!"

The woman gave my hand a gentle squeeze, and I determined right then: yes, Four Finger Pete's death was an accident. Moreover, it was an accident incurred by an American gambler, which made it even more of an Act of God.

I loaded the woman into the cart, with her gun, and she drove off with a burst of speed that rather diminished the sentiment of her taking leave of me, but then again the horse may have been unused to her hand on the reins. I returned at once to the fort and wrote a full report of the incident, which I promptly tore up. I could still feel those dark eyes pleading with mine. I therefore submitted a verbal report to Superintendent Crozier, who was not greatly elated by my solitary expedition.

"D—n me, Frank," says he, "whatever possessed you to go haring off into the hills like that?"

"I hoped to apprehend an American gambler who was raising hob with the native women, sir. But, confound it, he's holed up somewhere."

"Holed up?"

"Yes, sir." I told no lie. "I doubt that he'll trouble the Peigan women again, but I wish I could have got my man. The Mounted Police should always get their man."

The phrase seemed to mollify him. "Right!" says he, with a far-away look in his eyes, as though committing something to memory. "The Mounties get their man!"[13]

"The Mounties always get their man," I added helpfully, and he indicated that the interview was over.

You understand why, Emily, I ask you again to keep these letters for your eyes only, till I have completed my service in the Force.

Always faithfully yours,
Frank.

13.   Crozier's relishing the phrase may have influenced his refraining from mentioning FD's escapade in his reports.

PS   I am enraged to tell you that the Americans have broken their word to Sitting Bull. After being taken, as promised, to his reservation, he was arrested and thrown into prison at Fort Randolph. It's a d––––d shame, and we all feel jolly bitter about it, given the Force's role in persuading him that it was safe to go south of the Medicine Line.

~

Fort Macleod, NWT.
September 15th, 1881.

My dear Emily,

Your kind gift of a linen handkerchief, monogrammed with my initials, has been called into immediate service. All brows are being thoroughly mopped along with everything else at this post, as we perspire with the anxiety of anticipating the visit from His Excellency, the Governor General, the Marquis of Lorne. (Lord Dufferin, my benefactor, reached as far as Winnipeg, but has shown no desire to keep up with my progress westward.)

The viceregal party is already en route to Fort Macleod, approaching from the north, via Battleford and Red Deer. Besides His Excellency, the entourage includes a chaplain from Edinburgh versed in justifying the ways of God to man even when the ways kill his horse; a surgeon (in case the chaplain loses his touch); a military secretary and several aides-de-camp; an artist from the London *Graphic*; correspondents from the London *Times* and the Toronto *Globe*; a French chef, and six servants. The French chef has already gained an insight into *la cuisine du pays*. When the party paused for a buffalo hunt near Red Deer, and after three of the beasts had been felled by shot, Poundmaker entertained the distinguished visitors by sitting on one of the carcases, tearing out the tremulant liver and wolfing it down raw.

His Excellency is making this long, bumpy trek in a converted military ambulance waggon. Not quite as imposing as the Imperial elephant on which the Viceroy of India – where the Marquis was once private secretary to the secretary of state (his father) about the same time I gave up escorting the pachyderms – moves among his subjects. Our officers and men have been fully occupied setting up and tearing down a series of viceregal tents in which the G-G can give an audience to every Indian chief who can ride, walk, or crawl to the route of march. Our Indians here are absolutely agog at the prospect of beholding the Great White Mother's son-in-law.[14] Thus one of our paramount concerns as escort is to ensure that nothing happens to diminish the visitation by a demi-god. If, for example, the royal waggon were to submerge while crossing the South Saskatchewan, we are to maintain the aplomb to convey to the natives the impression that this is how the Great White Mother rules the waves.

Such a delicate role was apparently considered to be beyond me, as I have been assigned the less hazardous function of stage-managing the official welcome as the Governor General's cortege enters Fort Macleod. I now understand better why my father was so nervous before the opening of one of his plays, or the first appearance on a lecture tour. As I write this letter, the viceregal party and its escort are only two days' journey away. My lads have been issued with new white helmets and scarlet tunics, every mount has been brushed so that not a single hair goes against the grain, and the old barracks are spruced up as much as dry rot can stand without collapsing from sheer excitement.

Advance scouts report that the Unexpected struck our exalted guest less than a week ago, at Blackfoot Crossing, when Chief Crowfoot greeted him with a large and rambunctious gathering, tribal dignitaries in their finest raiment con-

14. Lorne's appointment to the governor-generalship is attributed to his having married Queen Victoria's fourth daughter, the Princess Louise.

fronting His Excellency, who was plumed and fully armed with protocol.[15] The Indian braves rode around wildly, discharging their rifles over the heads of the assembled. This moved the G-G's secretary to sidle up to Superintendent Herchmer to whisper hoarsely: "Are your men loaded?" Truly, *opéra-bouffe*.

Need I say that *I* am loaded, fore and aft? Already the environs of the fort are alive with Indians, halfbreeds, settlers, and Americans up from Montana to see for themselves how a member of the British Royal Family keeps his coronet on while riding in sneeze-producing dust. We are doing our best to avoid being anticlimactic, as the last stop on His Excellency's safari. I have put our pair of ancient cannon atop a ridge overlooking Willow Creek, and the plan is that these old darlings will be fired to salute the approach of the Crown made flesh. I pray nightly that the NCO in charge will remember to check the guns, before the flash in the pan or, worse, the evidence that some malcontent has dropped a ball into the muzzle. One state funeral in my family is quite enough.

Now I hasten to check the invitation list for the reception within the fort. The discharge of a loaded cannon will count as nothing compared to the roar and ravage wreaked by a local beldame left off this list. To be continued . . .

October 4th, 1881.

Victory is ours! We carried the day, Emily, as gloriously as any Roman triumph welcoming home a Caesar from the wars. The Governor General of Canada entered Fort Macleod as a conquering hero, to the cheers of the populace and the pounding of many tom-toms, echoing the frantic beat of my heart. The viceregal party has now departed southward,

15.   The scene captured by artist Sidney Hall became famous under the title "The Last Great Council of the West".

gracing American soil long enough to give the indigenes a taste of civilisation, before entraining for the journey homeward as the ward of the Utah Northern Railway.

The only crisis arising during His Excellency's stay at Fort Macleod was the discovery by dear Mary Macleod, wife of our former commissioner and latter-day magistrate, that her sole formal garment – a black-plush coat trimmed with silver fox – had been raided by moths that pillaged the sleeve, leaving a large hole. The resourceful lady – whom I love dearly, though from afar – did not hesitate to attack the salient elbow with stove blacking. The stratagem was every bit as successful as the war paint on the braves.

As for Colonel Macleod, he found at the last minute that he didn't own a top silk hat to go with his black frock coat, and his coat and his broad-brimmed felt made him look like an Orthodox Jew, off-course on a pilgrimage to Jerusalem. He greeted the G-G bare-headed, explaining that he never wore a hat in summer. Had the day been cold and wet, the Father of Our Fort would perhaps have had to borrow a section of stove-pipe from Mary's kitchen and hope for a mote in milord's eye.

As for me, the most tumultuous moment of the reception came when I was introduced. "And this, Your Excellency," said Commissioner Irvine, "is our Inspector Frank Dickens. Son of the great novelist, sir."

"Indeed!" The Marquis gazed at me with the special interest that people of all ranks show for a child of my father. "How novel – if you'll pardon the pun."

I laughed an absolution, and he added: "I should like to speak with you again before I leave, Inspector Dickens."

I had a reasonably good notion of what he wished to talk to me about. I went to my room, fetched my father's gold watch from the case hidden under my pallet, wound it alive, and set the time by the more utilitarian clock on my desk. I am thoroughly accustomed, you see, to being a sort of ambulant showcase in the literary hall of fame.

With the watch in my pocket I returned to the reception,

where I didn't have to wait long. The Governor General wended his way to where I stood, and drew me into a charmed circle of aides-de-camp where we would not be disturbed. But his first question outflanked me:

"I wonder, Inspector Dickens, whether you can recommend a good publisher back home?"

"A publisher, Your Excellency?"

"Yes. You see, I do a bit of writing myself. In fact, I am putting the finishing touches to a work entitled *Memories of Canada and Scotland*." For a second, I feared that he would produce a sheaf of manuscript, right there in the mess hall. He looked to be a man about my age, young enough still to dream dreams of one day waking up like Lord Byron, to find himself famous for something besides marrying the Queen's daughter. I have since learned that his enthusiasm for the arts and letters spurred him to found the Royal Canadian Academy.[16] However, he spared me the manuscript, saying:

"I hope you'll excuse my presumption, but I assume that as Charles Dickens's heir, you are familiar with the publishers that keep his work in print. I am particularly anxious to find a house that publishes verse, the writing of which is one of my printable vices."

O G—d, a poet.[17] Another one. What is it about this country that changes a normal person into a wilderness Wordsworth? I swear that the two books deemed essential to the traveller thrashing through this titanic terrain are his Bible and his rhyming dictionary. Yet – on my oath, Emily – beastly though some of my other habits have been in this land, I have resisted the temptation to pen an ode. When I feel a sonnet coming on, I dash cold water into my face till the urge subsides. As for letting Canada's heroic dimensions draw me into epic verse ("Paradise Stretched"?) – Heaven forbid!

"I shall be honoured, Your Excellency," says I, "to provide

16. In 1880. Two years later he founded the Royal Society of Canada.
17. For Lorne's poem inspired by sighting the Rockies, see Appendix C.

you with the name of the publisher handling my father's literary estate. The name escapes my mind at the moment, but I shall find it for you and pass it along to one of your equerries."

"You're so kind. And, forgive me, if I might trouble you for one more treat for a Dickens disciple – I'm told that you brought with you to Canada your father's gold watch . . ."

How precious is *your* interest in me, Emily! You help me to remember that I too have a pair of hands, and my own time to tell.

> From him who has much time for *you*.
> Frank.

PS   For the whole of the G-G's visit, I remained sober. Now *that* deserves a panegyric!

❧

> *Fort Macleod*, NWT.
> *October 10th, 1881.*

My dear Emily,

The recent months have afforded me the opportunity to become better acquainted with a Great Man of this region. No, not the Marquis of Lorne, bless him. I speak of Jerry Potts. I have, I believe, already mentioned the intrepid trailer-cum-scout-cum-interpreter who founded this fort by leading Colonel Macleod and his Troops to what must be the most pleasant desert isle this far from the South Pacific. Jerry Potts more recently escorted the viceregal party on its departure leg into Montana. Celebrating the successful completion of the transfer of milord to the care of the U.S. Army, Jerry partook too freely of the liquid refreshments so readily available south of the line, at Hazlett's trading store,

and in this uninhibited frame of mind and body he remembered an ancient grievance against a local Blackfoot. He was
rolling out of camp brandishing his rifle when, fortunately,
our police picquet recognized the adversarial aspect of our
masterful Métis, tackled him, and despite voluble protests
tied him up and placed him in a waggon to spend the night
in enforced meditation.

Now, if this had happened to Inspector Dickens, this lapse
from propriety, it would have been the subject of a formal
tut-tutting report, and Ottawa would have billed me for the
overnight accommodation in a government cart. But such is
the admiration and respect in which Jerry Potts is held, by
the Blackfoot and the Métis and the Force alike, that the
man can do no wrong. What is worse, he has initiated the
smoking of so many peace pipes in our councils with the
Indians that his breath alone is enough to stun a buffalo.
Heaven knows, my own briar has a bouquet readily distinguished from a rose bower, but I am convinced that the Force
owes much of its record of quick compliance by the Indian
to the effluvium radiated by our man in a tent where the air
circulates groggily.

"Jerry Potts!" I expostulated to the Commissioner one
evening in the mess. "Even his name is tautologous for a
commode. How do you explain his having a renown in the
West which – if I may say so, sir – rivals your own?"

"Exceeds it, Frank, exceeds it. Potts has won his credentials as a warrior. I have not had to . . . yet, thank God."

I assumed that Irvine was referring to Jerry's well-known
bloody role in the Peigan rout of Crees and Assiniboines, a
running battle that, because of his cunning in the field,
became a slaughter from which our prodigy returned triumphantly with 19 gory scalps, not to mention a severe head
wound of his own, and an arrow in his chest.[18] A trifle ostenta-
tious, in my view.

18. The battle occurred in the autumn of 1870. For years afterwards

"Potts," continued my superior, "is an object lesson in not judging a book by its cover."

I looked at him sharply, ever sensitive to criticism of my father's work. But his remark was guileless. He meant what everyone saw on meeting Jerry for the first time: the result of the mating of a Scots trader with a Peigan woman to produce the worst features of each race, like a spotless coach-dog with dachshund legs. Potts's underpinning is so bowed that he walks as a lurching of parentheses. Not till a pony is inserted between his legs do the man and the beast become a marvellous entity, a totally effective synthesis in motion.

Above the waist, Jerry in repose is not prepossessing. He is slouch-shouldered, his arms longer than his legs, and his squat torso announces nothing of its strength, which is Samsonian. His round face, equally taciturn, is trifurcated by his nose and his Mongolian moustaches into three equal segments. He tops off this ill-assembled visage with a brimmed hat worn jauntily to the right, to counterbalance the revolver slung on his left hip, butt forward.

"You know how we came by him?" asked the Commissioner. I did not. "Jerry's father, a Scot named John Potts, was a respected trader in the employ of the American Fur Company. His mother, a Peigan, died when he was a child. The lad helped with chores in the trading post in Fort Benton. One evening a renegade Indian who had had a quarrel with another employee returned, bent on revenge, at the moment when John Potts happened to be upstairs closing the shutters for the night. A single shot rang out, and Jerry, working at the counter below, saw the body of his father plummet past the window.

"The youngster jumped onto his pony and took off in pursuit of the murdering redskin. He tracked him day and night, for weeks, till he finally caught up with him well north

Potts wore the souvenir ear-ring of the shot pellet lodged in his left lobe.

of the line, in a Blackfoot camp, where he shot him dead. That is how we in Canada inherited this formidable orphan of the storm."

"Thanks to the savage blood in his veins," I said.

"Yes," smiled the Commissioner, "and his *Peigan* blood is quite savage, too."

Can you wonder that my curiosity about Jerry Potts is more than casual? That I crave to know more about a man who kills, ruthlessly, and kills again, yet enjoys the regard and trust of everyone in the Territories, while I, who have never killed anyone, am treated with no more respect than the Queen's uniform demands, regardless of what's in it?

My inquisitiveness overcame the normal bounds of conversation between an NWMP officer and a halfbreed guide. Encountering Jerry on the road to the village, I feigned a problem with my pony's hoof, and while he was examining the animal I asked him:

"Jerry, how does it feel to kill a man?"

He glanced at me with his accustomed impassiveness and said: "Feels good."

It was not the reply I had hoped for. I had to press him further: "It is told that in the famous victory over the Crees you took nineteen scalps. What, to you, was the meaning of that primitive act?"

Jerry's eyebrows rose slightly. He shrugged and said: "Same like when you English cut off de head." His hand made a violent chopping motion at his neck, and he grinned, grunted, "Don't see nudding wrong with your pony," and went on his way.

He was right, of course. Jerry's father had obviously told him about our beloved Good Queen Bess and her truncation of Mary Queen of Scots, which was indeed a sort of scalping in depth. Moreover, the heads on English pikes were struck from the living, not the dead. That ritual decapitation occurred in a time when English culture was never more vigorous or splendid. Perhaps this kind of barbarism is a token of a people's vitality, and I, in my revulsion at such trophies, represent something effete in our aging Empire.

No. I find it more reasonable to blame the circumstance that my father was not killed before my very eyes. He died without giving me a chance to show how much I loved him. Not that it would have mattered much to him, should his ghost have been informed that I had pursued his murderer to the end of the earth, to destroy him. My father's worst enemy was ever himself, and he destroyed that implacable foe by working him to death. Truly wert thou favoured, Jerry Potts!

Yours of the bloodless coup, affectionately,
Frank.

∽

Fort Macleod, NWT.
November 4th, 1881.

My dear Emily,

I am taking to heart your question (asked in your delightful letter of October 2nd): "Have you ever been surrounded by a horde of hostile Indians?" It has taken exactly seven years of service, but at last I think I can honestly reply that, yes, I have been in a situation that promised a quick cure for dandruff and other scalp problems.

The story begins at the aptly-named Blackfoot Crossing.[19] A white man employed by the Cochrane Ranch Company – one of the new "ranching outfits" that are spreading across the foothills area – tries to retrieve a stolen horse from a

---

19. What follows is the first officially (RCMP Archives) recorded critical situation in which FD plays a central role. The official account confirms the accuracy of this letter.

brace of young Blackfoot, who respond by pointing loaded rifles at him. Naturally upset, he reports the incident to me, and I have an opportunity to swing into action before my superiors can order the usual – and tedious – drill of letting cooler heads prevail.

With a corporal's guard of men I proceed at full bore to the Blackfoot camp and have no difficulty identifying the pair of offenders, whom I immediately place under arrest "in the name of the Queen!" The Q in "Queen" always alerts my stammer, unfortunately, giving the Indians time to consider the due process of law. Before I can complete the consonant, I and my men are surrounded by a depressingly large number of Blackfoot. From their scowling mien I deduce that they are not merely volunteering as an escort back to the fort. Most of them, in fact, have their rifles levelled at us.

"I think, sir," says one of my men, "that they want us to release the prisoners."

I wish he hadn't made this observation. It is an accurate but gratuitous comment that doesn't solve our predicament. My choices of action are clearly two: surrender our prisoners to the Indians, or die in a fusillade of bullets. I therefore do the only thing that recommends itself: nothing. I remain straight and motionless on my mount. My men do the same. I pick out the ugliest of the Blackfoot glaring at me, and I look him steadily in the eye, straining every fibre of my being not to blink. Indians are nonplussed by this kind of optic attack. They may, like other primitive peoples, fear the Evil Eye. I put all the evil I can muster into my stare. We remain locked in ocular combat for several minutes. Then, deliverance! From nowhere appears dear old Chief Crowfoot. He speaks to his bellicose kin, breaking up the convocation, and he nods to me to take my two prisoners to their fate.

Am I relieved? Yes, indeed. But vaguely let down, too. When one has braced oneself for death with honour, mentally saying goodbye to this mortal coil and rehearsing a disarming greeting for St. Peter, it is deflating to find oneself still of the flesh. I have missed my chance to be the first officer of the North-West Mounted Police to be killed in a massacre. Sic transit gloria mundi, and Canadian history is cheated of Dickens's Last Stand.

One of my men is said to have described my performance as "iron-willed determination". It was nothing of the sort. I merely waited out a debacle. Commissioner Irvine, who took over the prisoners at Fort Calgary and committed them for trial here at Macleod, did so without awarding me a medal for gallantry, let alone kissing me on both cheeks. In fact he has said nothing to me. I know why. This "outfit" is so badly undermanned that it can't afford a hero, dead or alive. Because they don't conform to the Minister of Justice's annual budget for law enforcement, feats of bravery are viewed as d––n foolishness. If General Custer had been a Canadian, the government would have sued his widow.

We in the Force must depend entirely on bluffing, in order to win, as we have been given too few chips to play for higher stakes. One day these people – the Indians, the halfbreeds – are going to call our bluff, and old Crowfoot won't be there to slip me an ace.

The episode has left me with the same feeling – one of derring-don't – that I had after what my father wryly referred to as The Night of the Woolly Ghost. I was living at home at the time, which was eerie enough, but even more bizarre to a young lad were the rumours in our neighbourhood that the nearby cemetery was haunted by a ghost that wheezed. A white, spectral form had been seen among the tombstones, particularly one called Larkin's Monument. The theory was that Larkin, for reasons unknown, had returned from the dead to complain about the memorial stone, which was indeed in rather bad taste.

"Let's hunt the haunter down!" said my father, one evening when I and a young chum were discussing the phenomenon. I suppose that he was seizing a rare chance to be a father to me, initiating his puny son to the rigours of the chase. Anyway, he fetched his double-barrelled shotgun, and off the three of us went, tiptoeing through the shadows of a smuggler's moon till within earshot of Larkin's Monument. Almost at once my blood ran cold as we heard a heavy breathing, a fearful gasp, repeated again and again.

"Did you hear that, Pa?" I whispered.

"That I did, Frankey." My father cocked the gun. To my alarm, he motioned us forward. I crept along in his wake. We circled slowly around Larkin's Monument, and there it stood, in a shaft of moonlight – the ghost!

Actually, a sheep.

My father hooted with laughter. "We almost killed an asthmatic sheep!" he chortled. "God rest ye, Mr. Larkin!"[20]

The deflation left me with a life-long aversion to sheep, just as the incident at Blackfoot Crossing has soured me on stolen horses. But I comfort myself with the hope that you, at least, Emily, have faith that inside this Dogberry's body is a Lancelot screaming to be let out.

May I wish you the happiest of Christmases.

Your devoted friend,
Frank.

∾

Fort Macleod, NWT.
February 20th, 1882.

My dear Emily,

Having received no letter from you since my last effusion, I fear that my accounts of the Perils of Dickens of the Mounted have put you into a deep slumber, from which you may be wakened only by the recounting of my latest imbroglio.

The saga begins with Inspector Dickens stationed at the small post of Blackfoot Crossing. Twelve men under his

20. For Charles Dickens's account of this adventure, see the Nonesuch Letters, vol. 3, pp. 188-9.

command. A clear, chilly day in the first week of a new year for which Inspector Dickens has resolved to earn his spurs.

The provocation: Charles Daly, who works for the Indian Department, had a row with Bull Elk, a minor Blackfoot chief, during distribution of beef offal. Bull Elk attempted to take a certain beef head for which he had bid without success, and Mr. Daly wrestled it away from him. In high dudgeon, Bull Elk rode off, but paused to discharge his rifle in the general direction of Mr. Daly. Mr. Daly, taking exception to this form of envoi, registered a formal complaint with Inspector Dickens. Inspector Dickens took off at once, with Sgt. Joseph Howe and two men, galloping to the scene of the trouble. Bull Elk (with friends) was waiting, rifle raised in what Inspector Dickens was beginning to recognize as a traditional form of greeting. Undaunted, Sgt. Howe strode forward to put Bull Elk under arrest, ignoring the shout of one Eagle Shoe: "Stop, he will shoot you!"

Yes, it *does* sound like a revival of a Dickens farce. But the comedic element was lost on me as we faced about 700 yelling warriors brandishing guns. At last Bull Elk agreed to dismount, and the intrepid Sgt. Howe and Cpl. Wilson each took an arm. Meanwhile I, having unaccountably fallen off my horse, brought up the rear with revolver drawn.

Perhaps emboldened by my horsemanship, the resistance of the braves quickly expanded from minor jostling to loading of carbines. Shots were fired over our heads. My men looked to me to decide whether we should all die here, the four horsemen of a petty apocalypse, or release the prisoner. At this point Chief Crowfoot, responding to the brou-ha-ha, arrived with other dignitaries and proceeded to berate me for the Indian Departments's unfair treatment of his people. This was the first time that Crowfoot has sided with justice at the expense of the law, and unluckily he chose me for the historical precedent.

In the end, the chief took personal responsibility for Bull Elk's eventual appearance, as required, in Magistrate Macleod's court, whereupon the whole rout of Indians rode off, jeering and firing rifles into the air. Left in place were four ashen-faced whites, including a C.O. envying Don Quixote because he at least bagged a couple of windmills.[21]

Inspector Dickens dispatched Sgt. Howe to Fort Macleod to inform Superintendent Crozier of the circumstances of the rapid turnover in custody of one Bull Elk. Inspector Dickens dearly hoped that the Superintendent would treat the affair as one of life's little contretemps. The Superintendent did not. Instead, he fired off an urgent letter to Ottawa demanding additional personnel,[22] and rode north with 20 men to the Blackfoot camp, seized Bull Elk, and brought him to the Blackfoot Crossing post for preliminary examination. Meanwhile, Inspector Dickens and his doughty dozen had been stacking sacks of flour and oats as a breastwork in the post and making extra loopholes in the walls for which they had no rifles. The Superintendent had also called for reinforcements from Pincher Creek and ordered that the field guns at Fort Macleod be readied for action.

When Crowfoot and his 700 arrived at the Blackfoot Crossing post to demand the release of Bull Elk, Inspector Dickens made a point of being present at the parley conducted by the Superintendent, in order to learn how it is done.

Asked Crowfoot: "Do you intend to fight us?"

Replied Crozier: "Certainly not – unless you commence."

They gazed at each other for a moment. Then Crowfoot nodded and withdrew. He had obviously been informed about the Force's preparations for a long and bloody battle. Without the element of surprise, the Indian is uncomfortable about shooting first. The lesson *I* learned: never try to face down the foe in *his* place of business.

21. Some historians blame this fiasco, and FD, for the deterioration of relations between the Indians and the whites that primed the North-West Rebellion, three years later. Certainly, the abortive arrest, marred by FD's falling off his horse, did confirm FD's reputation for having the managerial acumen of a bull in a china shop.
22. To Commissioner Irvine, who was in Ottawa, Crozier wrote: "Unless the Force in this district is largely increased, I cannot answer

"My apologies, Lief," said F. Dickens. "I nearly precipitated a tragedy."

"No, Frank, you did us a favour. It was only a matter of time till the Blackfoot put us to the test. You have reinforced our request for more men in this region. Now I'll lose no time in moving our prisoner to Macleod and a quick trial by Jim. You hold the fort here, Frank."

The upshot, Emily, was that Magistrate Macleod found Bull Elk guilty of attempted murder, and sentenced him to a durance not only vile but at a safe distance from our powder keg. Although I have received no overt criticism for my role in the apprehension of that nondescript villain, neither have I received a promotion. I try to do my duty, but inevitably it is my duty that does me.

Sometimes, Emily, I try to ferret out the factor in my childhood that precluded me as a Leader of Men. If it be true that the battle of Waterloo was won on the playing-fields of Eton, there's my excuse. The Reverend Gibson's school in Boulogne was not renowned for being the cradle of great cricketers, or for the moulding of Old Boys who prepare themselves for executive powers by clutching one another around the waist and butting heads till an oblong ball squirts out of the scrimmage. I have never been able to kick anything, except myself for being such a clod on the pitch. Result: I don't even own an Old School Tie. All I wear about my neck is the dead albatross of my disappointing service record.

No, I am not despondent. But at the height of the drama at Blackfoot Crossing, my old nemesis – deafness – made it difficult for me to communicate with my own men. I much wish that the Force were permitted to use sign language, at which I am becoming quite adept. Indeed, I have more than once startled Indians who thought they were having a private conversation. When I can *see* what people are saying, I'm able to respond quickly. But when protocol requires the

for the consequences." No historian has hitherto credited FD with being instrumental in bolstering the Force in time for the rebellion.

intervention of an interpreter – especially one with a French patois accent – I often have to lip-read. If I overdo it in letting actions speak louder than words, often it's because I haven't heard the words in the first place.

The experiment with the ear trumpet, by the way, was not a success. A chief wearing a headdress of buffalo bull horns thought I was mocking him. How much more sensible in choosing a career was Herr Beethoven! Riding a piano stool into the sunset. And how fortunate I am to be able to hear *your* sweet voice, across the thousands of miles, through the miracle of pen applied to paper!

Ever greedy, I attend with avidity the repeating of that gracious phenomenon.

Affectionately yours,
Frank.

❧

Fort Macleod, NWT.
May 12th, 1882.

My dear Emily,

Rereading your letters I am reminded that I have never replied to your question "Have you ever taken part in a buffalo hunt?" The hunt is an activity which I have prided myself in avoiding, though this is a distinction difficult to achieve. Even the halt and the lame are somehow transported to the killing-fields, so that they may tell their children that they witnessed the death throes of a species. I had rather hoped to be the only Englishman to return to his homeland without having personally shot, speared, or otherwise discommoded a buffalo.

However, my luck ran out earlier on at Fort Walsh. The Commissioner ordered me to accompany a halfbreed buffalo hunter named Larousse as a surveillance team, to observe a band of Cree on a foray against an unsuspecting herd. Objective: to determine the extent to which this type of hunt is wasteful and therefore contributing to the disastrous diminution of the numbers of buffalo on the plains. You see, my dear, there are at least three conventional methods of slaughtering the beasts. One is to project the herd over a cliff, such as Head-Smashed-In in the nearby Porcupine Hills. Another is to seduce the herd into a pound, or corral, the most eminent practitioner being, of course, Chief Poundmaker. Thirdly, the hunters may put the herd to rout and pursue it on horseback, shooting as many animals as possible before running out of ammunition. The first two techniques presume in the hunter a degree of intelligence superior to that of the buffalo, which is not noted for its guile. The third kind of hunt relieves the hunter of the need to outwit the buffalo, so long as he is riding a horse that can distinguish between "giddap!" and "whoa!".

It was to this third type of hunt that I was assigned as an observer. If I were of a suspicious nature, I might have viewed the assignment as retribution for my repeated complaints to my superiors that the white man's providing the Indian with both the horse and the rifle spells doom for the buffalo, and indeed for virtually anything else that moves and can be eaten. Specifically, I believe that the Commissioner may have been trying to discourage another written memorandum such as the one I presented to him, suggesting ways in which the natives may be persuaded to return to hunting on foot, with spear and bow-and-arrow. He treated as facetious my recommendation that Canada withdraw the Christian missionaries (who devour buffalo steaks with a gusto that is hardly exemplary), and instead foster Hinduism. The natives of India – and I speak from first-hand experience – venerate all forms of life except Muslims. A few Hindu temples, from Winnipeg west, could spell relief for the buffalo.

However, my carefully-documented submission was ignored, and I was required to mount up and follow Larousse on the ridiculous mission of assessing to what degree the

Indians' traditional husbandry of the buffalo has given way to wasteful carnage, under the tutelage of the paleface.

Our first day out on the trail I found very rewarding: we sighted neither Cree nor buffalo. I learned again why they call them the Sweet Grass Hills. The grasses are indeed sweet, less to the palate than to the eye. The Indians deliberately burn the wild fields, knowing that the next year the grass will spring up taller and greener than ever – Green Pastures born of Hell. And I make you a confession, dear lady, that I have made to not another living soul, which is that when I am riding alone it is my secret vice to take off my boots and socks and let my legs hang loose so that the tall grasses tickle my bare feet. It is, I fancy, rather like being caressed by an angel's wing.

Needless to say, I kept my boots on, riding behind my halfbreed cicerone, who on the second morning brought us out on the plain where a vast herd of buffalo was moving slowly, like the earth made undulant, towards the horizon and beyond. The same fires that renew the grass and bring the buffalo have, of course, destroyed every tree on such a prairie. In India, despite the harshness of sun and soil, one finds the occasional tree – gasping, perhaps, and with buzzards for fruit – punctuating the monotony of the unbroken sentence. Here, no shade, no shelter, no place to hide. And here we caught up with the hunting band of Cree, who acknowledged the completion of our rendezvous by digging their heels into their ponies' flanks and taking off down the hill towards the shaggy mass of moving animals. The buffalo were too numerous for effective stampede, those at the rear and centre pushing and rearing frantically to escape the whooping redskins, while those in the van grazed on. The Indians soon had them milling madly, bellowing and stumbling to the ground in the fusillade of lead.

"Allons-y!" shouted Larousse, and unfortunately I had enough French to understand him. My optimum strategy had been to remain at the crest of the rise, like one of Boney's generals, and obtain an overview of the battle. Thundering hoofs have never been my favourite auditory experience, possibly because my hearing problem makes it difficult for me to hear a stampede, *any* kind of stampede – buffalo, elephants, Ottawa civil servants leaving their stools and ledgers – till it is almost upon me. But with Larousse careering in the wake of the Cree, I was obliged to join the rout, praying that my horse would have sense enough to maintain a margin of separation, anything less than a quarter of a mile being a severe disappointment to me. Instead, the animal got caught up in the excitement of the chase, closing in on the dark brown sea of bodies whose currents veered unpredictably, so that at one point I was consternated to find that I was galloping immersed in buffalo, with bawling, berserk behemoths to both port and starboard and no safe anchorage fore *or* aft.

By wrenching my pony away from the main torrent I was able to limit the contest to a race between my horse and a big old bull that was labouring gamely to keep up with the herd, but was falling behind with every heave of his great frame. Suddenly, and to my horror, the bull collapsed, virtually at my horse's feet. I reined up and dismounted. The main pack was already scattering, along with the hunters, into the near distance. I was left alone with this huge wild creature whose magnificent heart had clearly given out, but whose breath of life had not been quite extinguished, so that the brown eyes found mine and seemed to beseech me, as a courtesy to his pride as a former chief of his multitudinous tribe, to put him out of his misery.

In that moment, Emily, I had the totally inadvertent vision of my father's death, of those last hours after his fatal seizure when he lay helpless yet conscious, the hours of which I, being hopelessly distant by ten thousand miles, would learn far too late to be there to grasp his hand, say some word of comfort, of love. . . .

I took my carbine, placed the muzzle behind the dying buffalo's ear, and pulled the trigger. The light faded from the wide-open eye, and the shaggy head – quite like Pa's in its majesty – lay still.

Soon the Cree hunters returned, to claim and butcher their kills.

"You shot your first buffalo," said Larousse. "Félicitations!"

"Pure luck," I said.

I received further congratulation from the fellows at Fort Walsh on my return. "Brought him down with a single shot behind the ear, eh, Dickens?" But I fear that my written report of the buffalo hunt was a bit garbled, and I of course omitted the matter of the Dickens family resemblance. There are times, my dear, when I find it singularly easy to be modest.

Ever your friend,
Frank.

∿

Fort Macleod, NWT.
July 3rd, 1882.

Dear Emily,

I have received your letter of April 27th, informing me that you will be unable to correspond with me any more because you are engaged to Mr. Thompson, your former instructor at the secretarial school. I am of course happy for you in your reconciliation, and I entirely understand the difficulty of continuing to write to another man, avuncular though he may be.

I cannot let you go, however, with the impression that you have befriended one of life's unfortunates. A final report, ma'am:

Situation: Peigans from south of the line have been sidling into the Queen's realm in order to "ring in" (as we say) on treaty payments to our own Peigans. A South Peigan looks very much like a North Peigan, when standing with his hand out. So, our local agent for the Indian Department, J. J. McHugh, summoned police assistance in sorting out the bona-fides from the bogus. He was given an escort of 12 Mounted Policemen under Inspr. Francis Dickens, who made a solemn promise to himself that, this time, if he fell off his horse, he would feign a heart attack and just lie there.

At the Peigan camp I was shocked to find how quickly our Canadian Peigans had reproduced since the last time I saw them en masse. Moreover, they appeared to have given birth almost exclusively to full-grown males, some of them armed with American Winchester repeating rifles. With the indestructible Jerry Potts as interpreter, Mr. McHugh informed the assembled Peigan chiefs that there would be no treaty money forthcoming till the American Indians went home. He offered to supply them with beef, flour, tea, and tobacco as provisions for the homeward journey, as well as a formal escort of police (us) to the boundary line.

The chiefs declined his generosity, sitting on their haunches and awaiting further developments. Mr. McHugh promptly cut off all rations, to indigenes and freebooters alike. This did not go down well with any of the Peigans, who had been looking forward to their usual orgy after payment of treaty cash. The intruders among them tried every kind of bluff, including threats, to shake the McHugh hand off the locked-up treats. But Mr. McHugh is a man after my own heart: ready to die rather than have the Queen's larder violated by interlopers. Again, my role was to do nothing, as impressively as possible. I think I am getting better at this. In the end, to our great relief, about 200 Peigans fell into a disgruntled line, and with six of my men riding as honour guard straggled back to the Land of the Free and the Home of the Brave.

Our own Peigans lost no time in celebrating, the head chief receiving $25, the headmen $15 apiece, and every other man, woman, and child $5. I remained in their camp long enough to make sure that the place of the republican Peigans was not taken by whisky smugglers, who in the past have been the ultimate beneficiaries of Her Majesty's largesse. When drunk, Indians act like irresponsible children. I was glad to see that our Peigans, when I left, were acting like irresponsible adults.

So, you see, dear Emily, your moral support has not been wasted after all. I shall severely miss your (literally) fragrant letters. Perhaps your fiancé will come to share your enthusiasm for emigrating to the New World. Canada is an acquired taste, God knows, but I find that the country grows on one, like a wart that gradually refines to a beauty spot. The transcontinental railway moves westward apace, with the Indians so far intervening only to the extent of burning a few surveyors' stakes. Unlike what you may have read about railway travel in the western United States, the C.P.R.'s *dessert flambé* is not ignited by flaming arrows shot through the windows of the dining-car.

I believe that even my father could have come to tolerate this land, had he given it time enough to overcome his need to be loved by larger numbers of people than these plains afford at present. For one thing, we are totally free of lawyers. On the one occasion when the accused presumed to hire a lawyer imported from the States, to argue a point of law, our Magistrate Macleod silenced him summarily, saying: "We want justice in this country, not law." That remark would have endeared him to the author of *Bleak House*, don't you think? Not that Charles Dickens would have lacked social ills here to impale on his pen. But how can you condemn human suffering in a place where the strongest dentist is Mrs. Morden, at Pincher Creek, who cures the toothache with one standard treatment: extraction? Frivolous complaints are thereby discouraged, both in court and in the dentist's chair. Life is lived too close to the quick for malingerers and malcontents. Moreover, the soil is so rich in most parts of these plains that only the faint of heart can fail to respond to the challenge.

"What convinced me," said to me one of our ranchers, a

chap named Russell[23] who came west as member of a survey crew, "was when I came back and saw that a stake I'd driven had taken root, sprung branches, and produced a nice crop of cottonwood seed." (Canadians talk in this outré manner, Emily, but I'm sure that you will be able to communicate with them without an interpreter.)

This pioneer spirit weakens, however, as Fort Macleod is now readily reached, and left, by new Force recruits, many of whom do not stay around long enough to unpack their bags. Such is the mixed blessing of the Canadian Pacific Railway, which now makes travel preposterously effete almost half-way across the plains.[24] I see that I am now a grizzled veteran. Which means that I arrived in the Far West in the days when retreating home was a more harrowing prospect than remaining to face hardships that at least had the virtue of novelty.

For example, I am not elated by the rumour that the NWMP headquarters is to be at a place called Pile-of-Bones.[25] As the name indicates, the site's distinguishing feature – aside from the Wascana Creek, home to the world's most voracious mosquitoes – is a widespread heap six feet high of buffalo bones, left there by the Indians in the belief that herds inhabiting the area would not leave if the skeletons of their deceased were manifest. A pretty conceit, but in point of fact the buffalo bones have exerted a mystic attraction only to those who decide where to ensconce the Force.

Another ossuary destined to be a railway "depot" – and I trust that some day you will watch for it, Emily, as you rattle westward – is what the Indians call "the-place-where-the-

23. The Russells became a well-known family of the region, begetting the author Andy Russell.
24. The first train rolled into Wascana Creek (the future Regina) August 23, 1882.
25. Later renamed Regina, "Queen City of the Plains" – the name having been suggested by Princess Louise, wife of Governor General, the Marquis of Lorne.

white-man-mended-the-cart-with-the-jawbone-of-a-moose".
Surely the most dramatic use of a ruminant's jawbone since
Samson smote a thousand Philistines. Do not be put off by
the prospect of a progress from one charnel-house to another.
The settlers from Ontario, who encrust the railway's extending terminal like barnacles on a ship's mooring, bring with
them trees. By the time you arrive, the bone meal will have
nourished young, sturdy oaks and elms of Olde England, or
at least stout groves of poplar and birch. On these plains,
Eden must perforce be a man-made garden. But the gardens
that our men have planted around all our forts yield vegetables of fabulous size, such that promoters of the Canadian
Pacific Railway advise prospective settlers that some prairie
farmers have been injured because they ignored the warning
to step back smartly after planting their maize, and took an
uppercut from a burgeoning cob.

Fear not, however. We of the Mounted will shield you from
all harm – animal, vegetable, or mineral (the gold can be
deadly). It is a duty that I look forward to, with all my heart.

Until then, let me remain your good friend and well-wisher,

Frank.

Part Four
1883 – 1886

∾

Fort Pitt, NWT.
October 9th, 1883

Dear Emily,

After more than a year, a letter from you! I am doubly fortunate that it has found its way to me here at Fort Pitt, forwarded from Fort Macleod by some orderly-room clerk
exemplary enough to have remembered my name. So, you
are married! No wonder there was a pause in the post. I am
happy for you, my dear, though envious of the chap lucky
enough to have won your hand.

I count myself fortunate that Mr. Thompson does not
object to your maintaining your correspondence with "an old
friend of the family." I do indeed feel old for my years, having
found the trek here to Fort Pitt considerably more exhausting
than my first journey to this post, almost ten years ago.
Enclosed herewith is a sketch map on which I have tried to
show you the location of Fort Pitt, in relation to the other
great metropolises of the world. It is the fly speck that doesn't
move when you blow on it. It lies on the Saskatchewan, that
riverine territory which sounds like a sneeze, before you have
even inhaled the dust. Our "fort" is a venerable Hudson's
Bay Company trading post, still frequented by fur traders,
freighters, and other folk in transit from trap-line to town.
The town is either Battleford (to the east) or Edmonton (to

the west), making us a kind of oasis on the caravan route of the mighty North Saskatchewan, which is at least as high-spirited as its nether effluent. We fetch our water from the river – a matter of a few hundred yards – and are thus assured of a more salubrious supply than the well-dependent, such as our new capital of Regina, where the residents complained of an odd taste in the water till it was discovered that at the bottom of the Canadian Pacific Railway well lay a dead squaw.

I have in fact been posted north just in time to avoid the morally debilitating inroads of civilisation in the south, namely the building of the new and more spacious Fort Macleod (with latrines less aloof and – O Roman decadence! – a tailor's shop), and the flourishing of towns along the railway line: Calgary, Medicine Hat, Regina (in whose *Leader* the editor, Nicholas Flood Davin, broke into a paean of couplets:

> *"A pleasant city on a boundless plain,*
> *Around rich land, where peace and plenty reign,*
> *A teeming mart, wide streets, broad squares, bright flowers."*)

How have I come to be spared being trampled in a teeming mart? Because – and I say it with a puffer-pigeon strut – the Commissioner chose me to take charge of a NWMP presence at Fort Pitt, which is needed to tamp down the fractious Crees. My old friend Big Bear and his followers have been jostled by us into their northern reservation, not far from this post, but not without his customary balking at the wishes of the white man. Big Bear had been loitering along the C.P.R. line to the south, cannily seeking the optimum location for extracting tid-bits from the droppings of the "iron horse", as they have named our steam-driven machines. Another chief, Lucky Man, has actually moved his entire camp from the north, with carts supplied by the Indian Department, his avowed purpose being to set up agricultural pursuits along the railway right-of-way. He was summarily told, by Commissioner Irvine himself, to about-turn and make the earth fruitful far enough north not to make the railway passengers palpitant.

Big Bear has resigned himself to re-location with bad grace. Indian agents have reported rumblings from both the Crees and the halfbreeds in this region. Hence the bugle call summoning Inspector Dickens, and 25 men good and true, to Fort Pitt. Purpose: to put a damper on these smouldering fires of resentment. Which, if I do say so myself, we have duly accomplished. The rumours of revolt have faded on the wind, and I for the moment can bask in the glory (somewhat pale this close to the Pole) of at last being the Commanding Officer of a post large enough not to be readily mistaken for a necessary house, if you will excuse the expression.

This northern country is charming at this fall season, a land of pastels, so very different from the shades of England, let alone India's cardinal colours. The wild poplar is a miser's fantasy: a gold-coin-bearing tree. When the breeze rustles that hoard against the sky's blue arras, it seems to matter less how much one has in one's pocket.

I share the administration of Fort Pitt with the H.B.C., in the person of Mr. W. J. McLean, the chief factor. Mr. McLean has been engaged in commerce with the Indians and halfbreeds longer than I have served with the Force and, being a Scot, is doubly a force to be reckoned with. Also, he is supported by a civilian coterie of Company servants and their families – most of them highly transient in the manner of traders everywhere – so that my command has many of the elements of being in charge of an Arab bazaar. Though, of course, without the hubble-bubble.

This is the second Fort Pitt in my life. The first Fort Pitt lay between Chatham and Rochester, and my father once took me to see that ancient stronghold that he and *his* father, Grandpa John Dickens, often visited in their rambles around his home in Chatham. It was on one of these garrulous strolls that my father first glimpsed Gad's Hill "mansion",[1] and was struck to wonder by what to his impoverished eye was

1. Gad's Hill Place, not far from London, was bought by Charles Dickens in 1857, and became his favourite retreat.

magnificence. The Dickens family would appear to have come full circle in three generations. Here I am playing soldier in an indefensible Fort Pitt, through which wander all manner of tourists. Little wonder then that I am inclined to surrender to the informality of the milieu, and just hope to G–d that no Spanish Armada makes a belated attack up the North Saskatchewan.

The fleet would be likely to find me lounging on the river bank, in baggy pants and flannel shirt, with a Collie dog I've named Wilkie, after Pa's good friend and fellow novelist, Mr. Collins,[2] both of us keeping a sharp eye out for marauding ducks. Even duckless, it is an engaging prospect. The fort lies on the north side of the river, which here makes a graceful curve that assures any attacking foe the advantage of surprise. Across the river to the south the land is terraced by nature, like East Indian rice paddies but without their productive muck, before spreading out to the plains. Behind the fort's buildings the ground rises gradually through groves of ever-green and poplar – ideal approach for the enemy if he doesn't care to get his feet wet raiding us from the river side. All in all, Fort Pitt is a jewel waiting to be ravished. And, as the castellan, I intend to enjoy myself within the natural limitations.

My quarters, like those of my men, are part of the H.B.C. post, this bringing me into more intimate contact with civil-ians than I might wish. Because of my deafness – which has worsened somewhat – I try to avoid pleasantries, with the result that I have (I fear) acquired a reputation for being withdrawn and aloof. It hurts, to be seen as the snobby son of a popular writer famous for his lusty sociability, when in fact I am merely defending myself against that demeaning look that people give the hard of hearing. If I must choose, I'll be the C.O. whose aural activity consists of keeping an ear to the ground.

2. Wilkie Collins, author of the first detective novel in English (*The Moonstone*, 1868), wrote for Charles Dickens's magazine *Household*

I'm sure that your hearing is excellent, Emily, but let me repeat this anyway: I wish you all happiness in your marriage.

Your friend,
Frank.

❧

Fort Pitt, NWT.
December 29th, 1884.

Dear Emily,

I could have wished for no better Christmas present than your letter of October 8th. How very thoughtful of you to send me the print of one of your wedding photographs! You have no need to apologise because it was one of the less successful plates. Your husband makes a handsome blur. The only criticism I would make is that he is far too tall for you. At least six feet – no? The predilection of beautiful women for tall men is something that has troubled me all my life, or at least since I stopped measuring my own height.

I am putting your photo among the few personal belongings I permit myself, in order to travel lightly. Before I left Fort Macleod I gave my batman much of my clothing and my father's gold-watch chain and seal, keeping only the watch itself. (Forgive me, Pa, but unless a watch chain is being worn, across a prosperous midriff, it really is one of the most useless links with the past.) You, however, now that I see you for the first time, and may observe that you are every bit as fair and forthright as I had imagined – you in your portrait now rest, framed in chaste Canadian maple, on my bed-side table. I swear I now need less lamp to light up the room. Your smile shames the candle.

Words and collaborated with him on two stage plays. They were close friends.

You may be mildly astonished to learn that I am no stranger here to the photographer's camera, though distant from his London salon. Indeed, I should say that I have seen more powder exploded by the photographer's hand than by Indian rifles. The itinerant jockeys of the three-legged mount deem the Mounted son of Charles Dickens to be an exotic touch to any tableau of the Force, on parade or at play. One of my favourites of this genre catches me with three fellow officers in full parade dress, one sitting at a table purportedly reading aloud a letter from home, while the rest of us listen captivated by second-hand gossip. To convey the realism of this scene, none of us is looking at the camera. I myself appear to be lost in contemplation of something well out of range of the lens, a pose that I have watched my father assume countless times, as our house was a Mecca for photographers. Pa was, of course, a marvellous subject. Whether he was sitting for the camera or the painter's brush, he always managed to look incredibly handsome, leonine in beard and posture. He could be the consummate actor without moving a muscle – a talent (among many) that he failed to pass on to the son who photographs as a figure on whose back (not visible) is a key, which when wound up will make him beat a little drum till depleted.

Ottawa encourages us to allow photographers unlimited opportunities to line up officers and men in the parade square, on mornings that would freeze the horns off a musk-ox, and stand very still until the photographer has satisfied his lust. Ottawa believes that the resulting pictures appearing in eastern newspapers and periodicals will help to appease the taxpayer, being visual proof that we are standing on guard for Canada amid spartan quarters that would be begrudged by only the most resolute Scrooge.

There was – thank the Lord! – no photographer present for this Christmas's dinner, where I was guest of honour at the table of Chief Trader McLean. This may sound to you like a merry setting: me amidst the McLean family (mother, three daughters – eldest 16 – and myriad small sons), reliving the riotous festivities in the Dickens household of yesteryear. But lack of practice has reduced my capacity for merriment, when sober. Nor was the table readily set a-roar by the presence of the McLean women, who, through no fault of their own, epitomise the implacable aspect of the Canadian female pioneer. Chief Trader McLean has had an organ brought to the fort, for Mrs. McLean's *divertissement*. After dinner, as on many another evening after purgatorial evening, daughters Elizabeth and Amelia led the singing around that baleful wind instrument, translating the old, familiar songs into Cree or Saulteaux. Until you have heard "The Lost Chord" played and sung by the McLeans in Cree, you have no concept of how mislaid a chord can be. Being deaf does have its advantages.

After dinner I took part in a shooting competition in which I did better than usual, by imagining that the target was the man who built the McLeans' organ. I have little time to savour that triumph, however, as the police are host to the civilians for the imminent New Year's ball, in which yours truly is fated to walk with Mrs. McLean to lead the Grand March, which will be followed by the hand-to-hand combat of the Lancers. If you don't hear from me again, you will know that I fell on this foreign field, and was buried with full military honours, accompanied by the organ and "Rock of Ages" sung in Cree.

Assuming survival, I hope soon to be able to send to you a photo of me lounging, in mufti, with a gaggle of other local hoi polloi who have been told by the photographer, "Relax, gentlemen," and who have rather overdone it.[3] The tall bloke against whom I am busy relaxing (arms looped) is Tom Quinn, the Indian agent for the region. I don't usually hit it off with Indian agents, most of whom appear to have been chosen for the job because of a demonstrated aversion to the native people. But Tom is a Manitoban, a long drink of water of good education and amiable disposition, though a tartar

3. The resulting photo is to be found in the Saskatchewan Archives.

when aroused. Sioux blood courses through his veins, his father having been a halfbreed agency interpreter killed by Indians in the Minnesota massacres of '62. Tom's Pa was one of the couple of dozen volunteers who took on hundreds of redskins who had slaughtered 700 settlers and almost a hundred soldiers, before the U.S. Army stemmed the tide of spilled blood. With a pedigree like that, Tom Quinn is, you may believe, a proud and resolute chap and a friend well worth having.

Here at the "Little Fort" – as the Company people like to call it – and at the trading posts at Frog Lake and Duck Lake that lie within our imperial sphere of influence, Tom has brilliantly demonstrated, to Indian and white alike, that putting people into the ground takes less gumption than getting vegetables out of it. In the past year alone he rounded up 200 head of cabbage. (I adore cabbage, though not to eat; I simply am inspired by its overcoming being a Brussels sprout.) Tom has also introduced our local tribes to the wonders of lettuce, radishes, and peas. Almost single-handed, he has replaced the laurels of war with the green salad.

"Frank," says Tom to me one day this fall, "I think that as Commanding Officer you oughta inspect our rows of cauliflower."

"Very well, Mr. Quinn," says I. "Have them fall in."

And inspect them them I did, in the fort's field flanking the river, walking slowly through the leafy ranks with Tom solemn at my heels. I stopped at a particularly robust specimen of cauliflower and said: "Have this veg report at once for kitchen duty."

"Yessir. Him and a couple of turnip that are A.W.O.L."

A friend. I am hesitant to put such a fragile word on paper. Who dares to call a man, let alone a woman, a friend out here where there are no tiny hedgerows between our heartlands? The Map of Tenderness, cartographed by the French *précieux*,[4] cannot be superimposed on this country, whose horizon

4. The seventeenth-century exquisites mocked by Molière.

ever recedes from amity that endures. But Tom has endeared himself to me, temporarily at least, by treating me as though my father were a common mortal, and probably not my father at all.

"That barley-top head of yourn," he says, "there's a touch of the wild Celt there. I think your mommy was had by an Irish fishmonger."

Our camaraderie is, I know, partly that of two lonely men whistling in the dark. Tom is an Irish Métis in this territory where most of the halfbreeds are French. And, at this instant, furious. Ottawa in its ineffable wisdom has sent out surveyors who are cutting property lines along the Saskatchewan into neat squares that look tidy on a map but have no meaning, other than fatal meddling, to the 'breeds trying to eke out a living in the lanky tracts they have long since squatted on along the river. These people are desperately poor and hungry, especially so since the centre of government has been moved from Battleford to Regina. The plums went south; the pits remain to be chewed on.

Sitting together on the river bank, taking the late rays of the dying year's sun, Tom and I studiously avoid discussing what is most on both our minds: that Louis Riel – yes, my former schoolmaster – is once again manufacturing mischief north of the line. He and his military lieutenant, Gabriel Dumont, are buzzing around Batoche – which is not far enough away from here to be ignored – preparing petitions and ultimatums on behalf of the Métis. In fomenting revolt he is supported by the Canadian government, which has chosen this season to reduce by half the rations allotted to our Indians. M. Riel thus has an abundance of tinder with which to set the plains afire.[5] The reason why I don't debate this possibility with Tom is that he has enough Indian in him to trust the common sense of the native people, who he

5.   Riel had arrived back in Canada June 27, 1884. He and his Métis committee drew up the Bill of Rights that was submitted to the Dominion government in December.

believes will reject the mad messiah. He does not share my faith in the unlimited capacity of the government to exacerbate an already grim situation. With the backing of the redskins, Riel can easily overwhelm us paltry policemen, then sell western Canada to the Americans for enough dollars to keep him and his followers in clover for the rest of their lives. Only then will Ottawa forcefully strike a royal commission, to find out why Canada has been reduced by half.

To Tom, when we sit by the river tossing pebbles into the slow current, the body of a starved rat bobbing by is just a target. To me, it is an omen. And I feel uneasy that Tom is to be posted to Frog Lake, a day's ride from Fort Pitt, to take charge of that settlement where we have only a man or two from the Force. The H.B.C. store there stands as the bull's-eye of radiating reservations of Plains Crees that I must watch closely. Big Bear comes and goes on his shifty travels, along with some very volatile visitors named Wandering Spirit and Little Bad Man. With the muttering Métis, the Indians far outnumber the whites at Frog Lake. I shall note here that they have taken badly to cutting firewood for a living. I keep pleading with HQ for extra rations for the Crees, but Tom is the one who has orders to tell those famished folk, face to face: "No work, no food."

The western sky is darkening, Emily, with prairie chickens coming home to roost.

Another too-long letter. Forgive me. Next time I shall strive for brevity, perhaps strike the soul of wit.

Your friend,
Frank.

❦

Fort Pitt, NWT.
February 28th, 1885.

Dear Emily,

You, and the gentle hills of home, never seemed farther away
from me than at this moment. Shortly after I wrote my last
letter to you (end of December), I toured the nearby Indian
reserves to supervise treaty payments. To grasp the doleful-
ness of that excursion, you should understand that this past
growing season has been a monsoon. Unlike the parched
south, rain does not suit these parts, even in the best of
times. What to us in England is friendly patter on the pane,
here, on the northern plain, becomes an ominous drumming
on the tent cover. The Indians, those that have made a
sincere effort to become farmers instead of hunters, have
watched their crops melt away under grey skies, and they
stare accusingly at me as responsible for bringing upon them
the curse of an English summer.

It is apparent to these poor wretches that the Great White
Mother, though she rules much of the world's land and seas,
has no dominion over mud. The mud of northern Canada is
the most glutinous muck in creation. If I could establish as
durable an affinity for people as do my boots for Canadian
"gumbo", I should be a very popular person indeed. But the
Indians and halfbreeds who have watched their attempts at
cattle-raising wallow in mud instead of meadow become more
and more restive and resentful at the passing of the buffalo.
That beast shed the wet with equanimity. It was a rain of
bullets that spelled its doom. G–d only knows how the six-
legged creature that has replaced it – the Mountie – can
survive the torrent. *Après le déluge, nous?*

The one crop that has flourished in this climate has been
the trouble-maker. Amid rumours that the peripatetic Riel
is rousing *les misérables* to mayhem, I have had a visitation

from another malcontent, a Cree named Little Poplar, who has spent some years south of the line and returns as proof that travel is not necessarily broadening. Little Poplar hangs around the fort and keeps demanding to see me, as senior officer. I did grant him an audience, and he addressed me in my office with an unbecoming sneer, waiving his right to an interpreter and launching into broken English with the shamelessness of those who have been frequenting Americans.

"Little Poplar, Big Bear, our people, need more food," declaimed my informant. "Tom Quinn no give us food. He tell us work, work, work. Bad medicine."

Here was my chance to explain directly, man to man, how the Canadian government is trying to accomplish, in a few years, something – namely the conversion of primitive man from hunters and gatherers to agrarians – that in the Old World took millennia. But it is not easy to inform a savage with an empty belly that he is privileged to be part of a grand experiment in accelerated Progress. Besides, it is not my job. My task is to "maintain the right", even when it is wrong. So, all I could say to Little Poplar, who was stinking up my office, was:

"Tom Quinn is a good man. He will give you more food as soon as he receives it from the Great White Mother."

"Ha!" Little Poplar spat on my floor. "Great White Mother is only fat queen of England!" Before I could recover from this grossly American description of Her Majesty, the impudent wretch stalked out.

Tom Quinn would have dealt with him better. Tom is convinced (as I am not) that, by example, he can show the Indian how to grow his own provisions. Sometimes I wish that I too were Catholic. That faith seems to be more supportive of miracles than my personal belief that the dead go either to Heaven or to Ottawa.

March 29th, 1885.

I must leave off this letter, dear Emily, as events crowd in upon me, and I have little time for writing. We at Fort Pitt have just received word that Riel's rebels have ambushed my old colleague Superintendent Crozier and his men, plus volunteers, near Duck Lake. Our people suffered severe casualties,[6] and were forced to retreat. The halfbreeds and Indians are in full cry, from Batoche to Battleford. I must do what I can to prepare for the wildfire to spread to the Fort Pitt region, as Big Bear is reported to be having difficulty restraining the hot bloods among his headmen, and may be unable to stem the insurrection.

We are busy trying to fortify this utterly porous post. I have known since I arrived here that the gods were enjoying a private joke, putting me in command of a fort whose stockade is low enough for an enemy on the surrounding slopes to pour fire into us, but is high enough to prevent us from shooting back. I have pleaded with Tom Quinn to abandon Frog Lake, along with the settlers there, but he stubbornly refuses to budge. Instead, he insisted that I withdraw the small detachment of police there, lest they provoke the restive Crees. Which I have done. I hope to God his judgment is sound.

Pray for us, please, Emily.
Frank.

6.   Nine Prince Albert Volunteers and three NWMP died in the furious skirmish amid the snowdrifts, while the Métis and Indians lost five. At the height of the battle, Riel, unarmed but for the cross he carried, rode up and down the line exhorting his troops, and somehow escaped unscathed. Duck Lake not only destroyed the myth of the Force as invincible but convinced Métis and Indian alike that Louis Riel was the elect of God. Commissioner Irvine abandoned Fort Carlton (which burned during the evacuation) and retreated to make his stand at Prince Albert.

*(Ed. note: the tumultuous and bloody events of the next three weeks –
the critical period of the North-West Rebellion that opened such an
ugly wound in the Canadian West – are reported tersely in what has
been identified as "Inspector Dickens's Fort Pitt diary".[7] It is probably
a wrong attribution. An educated man, Dickens would never have
committed a misspelling such as "Secatary", nor would he have
referred to himself, in the post journal, as "Inspector Dickens". It
appears more likely that FD delegated the keeping of the log to a
subordinate. Comparison of handwriting is inconclusive, but it is safe
to assume that FD's personal records of the siege of Fort Pitt are his
official report[8] to the Commissioner, June 8, 1885, and this post-
bellum letter to Emily.)*

∾

Battleford, NWT.
May 27th, 1885.

Dear Emily,

No doubt you will have read in the English newspapers of
the rough time we have had here – what they are calling The
North-West Rebellion. You may even have found my name
mentioned – rather ingloriously, I'm afraid. When Canada's
West had its first Great Moment In History, and with it my
chance to inscribe my name forever in the term examination
to torment small boys, Fate once more gave me a bit part,
with no exit line.

I write these rueful words from my room in the Battleford
barracks. For the past month I have been too weak and
exhausted to do more than crawl in and out of bed.[9] I don't
even remember too clearly when I last wrote to you. It seems

7. See Appendix D.
8. Public Archives Canada.
9. His ordeal left Dickens almost totally deaf.

like a very long time ago, when these were peaceful plains
and General Middleton[10] had not yet cast his portly shadow
across the land. What a sad, sad shame, that after so many
years of managing to avoid the American Solution, the government was finally required to send in the army! What we in
the Force thought was a triumph for law and order turned
out to be merely a delaying action. Late, in this case, was *not*
better than never.

For us at Fort Pitt, all the tragedy began, as I had feared,
at Frog Lake. The Crees massacred all the white men – all
save William Cameron, the H.B.C. agent – and took the
women prisoner. I have since learned that Tom Quinn was
one of the first to fall. The stubborn fellow was being rounded
up with the rest when he balked at walking through a puddle.
"I'll get my boots dirty," he said. Those were his last words,
Emily. Wandering Spirit raised his rifle and shot Tom in the
back. Later, when Tom's body was still lying in the mud in
front of Pritchard's house, a bunch of revelling Indians rolled
him over and one of them drove a sharpened willow stick
into his heart. That was how much they hated Tom, whom
I loved. Loved, because the man was the kind who was
prepared to die with his boots on, but was d––ned if he'd go
to Judgment with them muddy.

Of what happened in the days immediately following, I
cannot remember times, only scenes. I remember that I tried
to follow the book, in preparing our pitiful post against attack.
My only information about the enemy came from an Indian
Department farm instructor who, with his family, sought
refuge in the fort and told us that he had met Wood Crees
who told him of the slaughter at Frog Lake. Third-hand
intelligence! There is nothing more daunting to a commander
than not knowing what he faces, or when.

10.   Commander of the Canadian Militia mustered to quell the revolt,
Middleton almost botched the Battle of Batoche despite superior
numbers and his Gatling gun. He ended his career as keeper of the
crown jewels, Tower of London.

However, I ordered double guards and had the stables burned, since they lay outside the stockade and would have provided cover for an attacking foe. We tried to surmount our stunted stockade with makeshift bastions, in full knowledge that the ramparts would deter none but a company of dwarfs. We also set up a rude barricade between the fort's buildings, using waggons and piles of cordwood, to deny the Indians freedom to circle each building in turn and pick us off. In my heart I knew these measures to be virtually empty gestures, intended to stave off despair among both my men and the Company employees. All the buildings were well within range of flaming arrows, and the water we needed to fight a fire lay in the river, across four hundred yards of open ground.

We still might have won a bit of the glory associated with defiant defence had I not been obliged to share my command with Chief Trader McLean and his formidable family. As soon as we got word of the Frog Lake massacre, McLean, who was also a justice of the peace, swore in every civilian in the fort as a special constable. This muster included his seven children. Thus our total force was split between regular NWMP, nominally led by me, and the McLean special constables, of whom the most fearsome answered to Daddy.

This, of course, should have been our best line of defence against the Indians: the McLeans, organ-ized and in full throat for "I Stood on the Bridge at Midnight". Horatius would have paled in comparison.[11] To their credit, however, the McLean womenfolk did help to barricade the windows with sacks of flour, leaving loopholes, and they stood sentry duty with rifles at the ready. From our competitions I knew that they were all excellent shots, and I solaced myself with the thought that any Cree warrior, seeing those implacable Scots faces at the barricades and facing the mortifying pros-

---

11. When the Crees, pillaging the fort, later discovered the organ, they were consternated by the unearthly sounds it uttered. Suspecting the presence of the Devil, they hacked it to pieces with axes.

pect of being killed by an adolescent female, would be deterred, at least momentarily.[12]

As we waited in our state of siege I remembered that when I was a lad one of my favourite stories that Pa wrote – I forget the title now[13] – was an adventure-filled yarn about a group of white folk trapped in a stockade on a Caribbean isle (a depot for the silver trade, I think it was) and waiting, soldiers and civilians alike, for the inevitable attack by swarthy pirates. How rousing and almost jolly a carnage my father made it sound! Even the children found it exhilarating. And how different from the reality of that situation, the cold clutch of fear, when one is caught in the talons of the Unknown!

My first act on hearing about the massacre at Frog Lake was to dispatch three scouts to confirm or refute the story that Big Bear had completely lost control of his firebrands. I sent forth Constables Cowan and Loasby, along with Special Constable Henry Quinn (Tom's nephew), who had escaped the slaughter by crawling through the bush on hands and knees to reach the fort. The McLeans muttered at this sortie, fearful that my men would be captured and their weapons used against us. O ye of little faith! For me, ignorance is not bliss. Particularly during the long night, when I am standing staring at that hill rising behind the fort, and the moon shuttles through clouds whose shadows move through the scrub, and the faithful Wilkie barks wildly at something . . . but what? Although dates are now fuzzy in my mind, I shall never forget what month it was, as a line of verse coursed through my thoughts like the ice-choked river: "Oh, to be in England, now that April's there!"

In a matter of hours after I sent out the scouts to find Big

---

12. Naturally at variance with FD's account is Elizabeth McLean's memoir, "The Siege of Fort Pitt . . .", reprinted in *The Frog Lake "Massacre"*, Stuart Hughes, ed. (Toronto, 1976).
13. "The Perils of Certain English Prisoners", one of the Charles Dickens's Christmas stories.

Bear, that worthy made the expedition look eminently futile by appearing on the ridge north of the fort, with about 250 of his friends, all mounted, war-painted, and armed, surveying us in the thin spring sunlight as a cat gazes upon a caged bird. To give us a foretaste of our fate, they killed a couple of Company cattle that had strayed up the slope. They lit fires and had a beef dinner, then sent down an old Indian, a former H.B.C. employee, hobbling to the fort under the flag of parley. He bore a message, written for Big Bear by one of the white prisoners he had seized at Cold Lake.

The message was not addressed to me. It was handed to my senior NCO, Sgt. John Martin, with whom Big Bear was on friendlier terms than with the senior officer who had known him long enough to trust him about as far as he could throw the Albert Memorial. Sgt. Martin was kind enough to show me the letter. In it Big Bear did mention me, not unfavourably,[14] but the gist of the letter was that we should all decamp at once, before his young men took matters into their own, blood-stained hands.

"What do we do, sir?" Martin asked me.

"We stay and fight, of course," I told him. "Here at least we have a chance. In open country, it will be open season for them."

"You don't believe that Big Bear can hold them long enough for us to escape?" From the pained look on Sgt. Martin's face I could tell that such a thought had occurred to him. Several times. I suspected that Sgt. Martin was "sweet on" one of the McLean girls, and I saluted Big Bear for craftily splitting the resolve of an already badly-mixed bag of besieged.

I overruled my sergeant, however, sending Big Bear's envoy packing with as firm, if polite, a negative as I could write with fingers that trembled on the pen. While the Indians pondered their next move, however, I ordered the Company

14. "... I do not forget, the last time I visited Pitt he gave me a good blanket...."

carpenters to check the readiness of the scow we had built to provide an escape via the river for the fort's civilians, while we two-dozen NWMP covered their retreat with all the gallantry entailed in fighting a battle that cannot be won. Unless, that is, reinforcements arrived from Battleford – a slim chance that soon became totally emaciated.

The situation began to slip out of my hands when the Indians later sent us word that they wished to parley with Chief Trader McLean, at a spot between the fort and the Indian camp. I grasped what their cunning was up to: they sought to extract from the fort their friends, the employees of the Company, while leaving us policemen to suffer the wrath of the young braves seething with lust for plunder and revenge for their brothers killed at Duck Lake.

I told Mr. McLean that he must not go to that meeting. "Divide and conquer, sir," I told him, "that is the rather clichéd strategy that you would be making available to Big Bear. As the C.O. of this fort, I absolutely forbid this rendezvous."

"Ye're no' *ma* senior officer, Inspector," says he, cool as a Highlander's knee-cap. "I believe that I can mak' reason prevail with Big Bear and his councillors. Aye, I'm goin' immediately."

I toyed briefly with the notion of putting the Chief Trader under arrest, but could think of nothing to charge him with. And because I refused to give his departure my blessing, I was shelled with a barrage of baleful glances from his family and friends, as I stood livid but impotent, watching McLean stride forth from our gate, to the hosannahs of inaudible trumpets and the applause of the Company's shareholders.

McLean and the halfbreed employee he took with him to interpret spent the night in the Indians' camp, while I tried to guess what kind of accommodation he was making over my dead body. The next morning, Blind Chance struck me a crushing blow. My three scouts – Cowan, Loasby, and Quinn – returned from their reconnoitring. The first I knew of it was when a cry went up from the Indian sentries, and

Cowan and Loasby galloped into view, making a desperate run for the fort amid a hail of bullets. I knew at once what had happened:[15] they had blundered into the Indian camp and scared the redskins into thinking I was attacking them from the rear. Utter havoc!

Constable Cowan was the first to fall. He survived the initial volleys, but when his horse started to buck, poor Cowan jumped to the ground and tried to race for the fort on foot. A sharpshooter in the bush brought him down, agonizingly close to our open gate – a dead man. Meanwhile Constable Loasby was urging his mount to the fort pursued by Lone Man, Big Bear's son-in-law. Lone Man's bullets caught Loasby in the thigh, his horse in the neck, and both man and beast pitched heavily to the ground. Another Indian tried to finish Loasby off with a shot in the back, and despite the fusillade we were furiously pouring from the stockade the b———d coolly took Loasby's cartridge belt and arms and rode away. So much for the efficacy of our target practice! Fear and anger do strange things to the trigger finger of men unaccustomed to the heat of battle.

Miraculously, Loasby struggled to his feet. To shouts of "He's still alive!" one of the Company men ran out and carried the badly-wounded constable into the fort. The skirmish – unsought by either side – was over. I was left to wonder what had happened to McLean while all of H—l was breaking loose around the Indian camp.[16] I did not have long to wait. Big Bear ordered McLean to write to his wife the message that his family and the other civilians were to leave

15. The third scout, Henry Quinn, turned tail and escaped with Indians in hot pursuit. FD was correct in assuming that the scouts had been careless – they broadcast their arrival by arguing in loud voices as their horses clattered over a wooden bridge about a mile from the fort.

16. At the first shots, McLean grasped what had happened and tried to make a run for the fort. He found himself staring down the barrel of Wandering Spirit's rifle. For the first time, he realized that he was Big Bear's prisoner, and not his guest.

the fort and join the Chief Trader in the Indian camp, and that the police should then evacuate the fort, with safe passage guaranteed.

Once again, I received a crucial communiqué at second hand. But I insist that it was not wounded pride that made me reject Big Bear's proposition summarily. Indeed, if History judges me harshly, it will be because it fails to understand the futility of trying to overcome a recklessly determined adversary – Mrs. McLean. Backed by all the little McLeans.

"It's a trap, ma'am," I told her. "Your husband is the bait. I beg you to spurn Big Bear's snare and help us make our stand in the fort."

Unavailing. By now the entire fort knew that the Crees had brought coal oil from their looting at Frog Lake, for the specific purpose of incinerating Fort Pitt and all us contents. Said Mrs. McLean:

"I'm goin' tae ma husband, Inspector. If ye'll be guid enough tae tell your men tae help us load the carts."

End of discussion. I watched in misery as my strategically-placed barricades were wheeled out the gate loaded with favourite dresses and prized lamp-shades and, of course, all the civilians. I cannot do justice, with mere words, to the silence that fell upon the fort as the last cart crawled slowly up the slope to Big Bear's camp. My 23 men, and the wounded Loasby, looked to me as the hungry schoolboys looked at Mrs. Squeers. Not a man of them tossed his cap into the air and cried, "Now we can fight the good fight, sir!" No, Emily. The silence was quite deafening – literally. I decided that there was nothing for it but to make a strategic withdrawal down the river.

Unfortunately, Constable Loasby chose this moment – our preparing to desert Fort Pitt – to display an unwelcome streak of heroism. "You'll never make it to the scow carryin' me, sir," he said, as we fashioned a litter from stakes and sacking. "Best leave me behind . . . with a loaded revolver."

"Jolly good idea, Loasby," I snarled. "I suggest we lash you to a horse and send it hurtling into Big Bear's camp to create a diversion, while we sneak off to the scow. Bl——dy decent of you."

I forget who first said that the better part of valour is discretion,[17] but if it be true, then the better part of a chicken is the parson's nose. Desperate and dismal: that was all I felt, as I crowded my men on to the already leaking scow, along with tents, ammunition, blankets, and enough grub to feed us, I estimated, for the 100 miles of bone-chilling voyage down-river to Battleford. There was of course no room for Wilkie. I sent my four-legged aide-de-camp off towards the Indians, and his was the only hurt look I got from any of the defectors.

I chose the coming on of dusk to make the first leg of the odyssey, a rough, rough crossing to the south shore of the river, where I made camp rather than risk a night-time passage of the current bristling with young icebergs quite capable of cleaving our scow from bow to stern. We were now totally at the mercy of the Indians, if they chose to attack. I had to trust the first and only direct word I had received from Big Bear, before we left the fort: "You asked me to keep my men in camp last night and I did so, so I want you to get away today." I had indeed asked for safe passage for the civilians, but – and I read and reread that scrawl as the sharp wind knifed through my tent – could find no excuse that the ultimatum suffered in translation. What a maddeningly moderate imperative to have to yield to! How dispiriting, to be forced into a retreat that could well see us all drowned like rats or frozen to death at our punt poles! Because a wretched savage was co-operating to the full!

"What time do we embark in the morning, sir?"

It was not till Sgt. Martin stuck his head into my tent that I realized that I had left my father's gold watch behind in the fort. I felt sick, having taken such care to hide the watch in my room to foil the light-fingered, only to forget it in the

17. Shakespeare. *Henry IV, Part I*. Act V, Sc. 4, Line 120.

turmoil of evacuating the fort. I shudder to think what has become of Pa's watch.[18]

"We leave as soon as you're ready, Sergeant."

As Sgt. Martin herded the men into the scow at dawn, I had one last look back towards the fort, which was lost in the snowstorm that the morning had favoured us with, making conditions so vile that not even the most vengeful Indian would consider it worthwhile to harass our departure. Through the thick, descending flakes dancing into oblivion, I saw my father standing in the open front door of our house at Gad's Hill, on New Year's eve, while we all crowded in behind him, we children intoxicated with being allowed to stay up until midnight, and when the church bells in the valley rang out, Pa would snap shut his watch and sing out in that wonderful, melodic voice: "A Happy New Year! God bless you all!" . . .

God's blessing is badly blurred, Emily, when one's clothes have frozen stiff on one's back, when one must order men to bail with frost-bitten fingers, when one must stand at the bow of a careering raft, peering for ice-rimmed sandbars in the river and Indian sharpshooters on its banks. As the inter-minable days went by, I became quite giddy with fatigue, and at one point shouted at my haggard, drooping crew:

"Should your Admiral be fatally felled by enemy fire, let no man heed my request that I be kissed! His lips would freeze to my nose!" No one smiled. I doubt that anyone heard me, over the creak of our splayed timbers and the wind's cold whistle. But I was very, very near the end of my wits' tether when, on what I'm told was April 20th, we were hailed from the shore by a small party of police sent out from Battleford to look for us. Battleford, then, was still in our

18. The watch was found by one of the pillaging Indians, who banged it against his rifle butt because it had ceased to tick, then traded the watch to a halfbreed, who in turn sold it for $15. The watch eventually found its way back to FD, who used it as collateral for a loan while waiting for his retirement pay. It is now in private Canadian hands.

hands. That knowledge gave us the strength to wallow and weave our way down-river for the last two days to reach the post that, to us, shone forth like the New Jerusalem.

We were expected. Every citizen and Mounted Policeman at the post was waiting at the dock as our craft sagged to a stop. They greeted us as heroes, even if they had to help us ashore. The police band had struck up a lively march – this for a straggle of men whose feet were numb as a fishmonger's block – and escorted us up to the barracks. Itself braced for siege, Battleford saw us not as vanquished but as reinforcements. The women had prepared a feast for us, and everyone shook my hand for having successfully completed one of the most ignominious retreats in the annals of warfare. In my mouth the food turned to ashes – the spoils of defeat. I wanted nothing so much as to be led to a warm bed, to pull the cover over my head, and close my already profitless ears against my father's voice asking me – his disappointment masked with heartiness – if I had any idea what I wanted to do with my life. . . .

May 29th.

Word has reached us here at Battleford that Sam Steele's Scouts, who are working with the Militia to quell the rebellion, reached what remains of Fort Pitt. They found the buildings destroyed, some still smoking. They also found Constable Cowan's body, before the fort. He had been scalped and his heart cut out, partly eaten, and impaled on a stake. Part of my heart, too, feels the thrust of that stake.

> Your very, very humble servant, and friend,
> Frank.

❧

Battleford, NWT.
August 12th, 1885.

Dear Emily,

If you have written to me during recent months it is unlikely
that a letter would reach me in the hurly-burly of the macabre
war that has wound down, with victory for the forces of right
and superior numbers. The Militia under General Middleton
have fought a series of battles against the ragtag 'breeds and
Indians led by the intrepid Gabriel Dumont, engagements
that make me feel much better about my own performance.
One of the Volunteers wounded at Batoche passed through
our sick bay here and told me of that epochal contest, how
in their last stand the Métis desperately supplemented their
ammunition with small pebbles and iron bolts, for guns held
by an inferior (numerically) force that included men in their
seventies and one ninety-three-year-old. In the end, of
course, Middleton triumphed. I am persuaded that I too
might have attained the heady heights of supreme commander had I joined the regular army, instead of a force whose
stated purpose is to keep the peace.

La famille McLean – those formidable females – survived
weeks of bush-whacking as prisoners of Big Bear on the run,
living charmed lives till the old rogue gave himself up. After
weeks of leading the combined forces of General Middleton
and Sam Steele a wild Canada goose chase through the brush
and muskeg of this northland, the chief and his young son
Horsechild were discovered, by three of our scouts, while
sheltering in a halfbreed's cabin across the river from Fort
Carlton. Big Bear convinced our chaps that he was so
exhausted by his trek that he was happy to surrender –
then tried to sneak out the door while the Redcoats were
conferring on whether it would be impolite to handcuff the
old rascal. The chief's followers had long since split into

smaller parties to elude the pursuing Militia and NWMP, and the only member of his council with him at the time of his arrest was a gentleman named All-And-A-Half. One wonders how, with a name like that, this worthy could come a cropper against any but impossible odds.

The deucedly astonishing thing is that, even though his retreating band was fired upon repeatedly by Steele's Scouts, and suffered casualties before withdrawing deeper into the marshes, Big Bear's prisoners – including the prickly McLean family – continued to be treated well, given food when the Indians themselves had none, with the smaller McLeans being carried across streams on brown shoulders, till at last the prisoners were freed to escape back to Fort Pitt. How do we hang a man whose respect for the rules of war would startle instructors at the Royal Military College?

Big Bear now languishes, with Louis Riel, in the Regina gaol. "David" too surrendered with confounded grace.[19] Altogether, a quite unsatisfactory war. The Americans do this sort of thing so much better than Canadians do that I doubt that bloodshed and violence will ever catch on in this country.

Among the Cree captives brought to Battleford, and presented to me as a belated trophy: Big Bear's tempestuous war chief, Wandering Spirit. The big brute, to show his defiance of the inevitability of surrender, stabbed himself with his sheath knife, piercing his lung and barely missing the heart. It says something about the vigour and hardiness of these natives, that a Wandering Spirit can survive both near-starvation and what for me would have been a mortal wound. I could not resist, but went to see him in his cell here in the fort. He still lay on the litter on which they had carried him off the steamer from Fort Pitt.

"Do you," I asked him, as he lay in the gloom of his cell, "feel badly that you killed Tom Quinn, shot him like a dog?"

19. Riel, and his ally Poundmaker, declined several opportunities in the course of the campaign to punish Middleton's men for their leader's bungling.

We had no need of an interpreter. Wandering Spirit knew the name Tom Quinn, and knew that I was Tom's friend. He may also have known that I was too deaf to hear his answer, unless he shouted. He lay silent on his cot, his dark eyes glittering like a snake. He had no apology to make, and I knew, somewhere inside my head, that I had no right to expect one.

Wandering Spirit is to go to Regina,[20] to be sentenced for murder. Unrepentant. One might as well hang a wounded wolf. I could only shake my head, sadly and angrily, and leave our prisoner to his last journey in his land.

October 24th, 1885.

Good news, Emily! I shall not be receiving the North-West Rebellion Medal. Only Canadian Militia who participated in the momentous campaign qualify for the medal, plus a grant of land or scrip worth $80. We policemen receive a warm vote of thanks. I do not resent being deprived of the medal.[21] Or very little. I don't really have the chest for a row of ribbons, not even a short row, of one. At this season of the year

20.   In the event, Wandering Spirit and several other perpetrators of the Frog Lake massacre went to the scaffold on the morning of November 27, 1885, at Battleford. His last statement may be of interest: "Four years ago we were camped on the Missouri River . . . [Riel] gave us liquor and told us he would make war on this country. He wanted us to join him in wiping out all Canadians. He said he had been treated badly and would demand money from the government. If he did not get it he would spill plenty of Canadian blood. Last fall he sent word to us that when the leaves came out the halfbreeds would rise and kill the whites. The Americans would come and buy the land; they would pay the Indians lots of money for it. . . . I was chosen by Ahyimissees to do this thing. It had to be." Ahyimissees (Little Bad Man) was Big Bear's elder son.

21.   FD was eventually awarded the North-West Rebellion Medal – posthumously. Now on view at the RCMP Museum, Regina.

and of my life, what I should welcome more from Father Christmas is a return to something resembling good health.

During the past few months I have been assigned the duties of the feeble: paper work, documenting the apprehension of the rebellion's ringleaders, if indeed one can imagine a ring of such large circumference, and their dispatch to seats of justice. I am, shame to say, grateful to those varlets who, like Gabriel Dumont, made good their escape to the States.[22] The Canadian government is even more thankful than I am. The brilliant field tactics of Dumont have, of course, been duly reported by the press in Quebec, whose French Canadians relish his exploits as proof that General Wolfe was simply lucky, in defeating Montcalm on the Fields of Abraham, the French general having an off day because he knew how to enjoy himself the night before.

Ottawa, I'm told, remains on tenterhooks because of the need to try Riel for murder and treason. The fragile unity of Confederation hangs by a thread with a noose on the end. You see, Emily, M. Riel is the darling of French Quebec, so that Prime Minister Macdonald must view St. Louis of Manitoba as a person too politically ticklish to be hanged as a common traitor. The hemp could simultaneously strangle the Conservative party. Ottawa fervently prays that Riel will plead guilty but insane, so that the rebel may be quietly sequestered in a comfortable asylum for distinguished lunatics.

The worst that can happen is that the jury condemns the Tories to a fatal loss of Quebec votes, a condition that may last for, who knows, a hundred years. Although I harbour no pretensions as a political seer, the Riel case suggests to me

22. After Batoche, Dumont and Riel's other lieutenant, Michel Dumas, sought refuge in Montana and in time joined Buffalo Bill's Wild West Show as sharpshooters, displaying their skills before the traditional crowned heads of Europe. When amnesty was granted, Dumont returned to Canada (1888) and to Batoche, as hunter and trader. He dictated two oral memoirs before dying of heart failure (1906) at the age of 69.

that Canadian unity must ever teeter on a tightrope strung, rather loosely, between the poles of French and English.

All of which helps to explain why – as I hear – at the Militia camp his guards have given the Métis messiah plenty of room outside his tent to stretch his legs, or better yet his wings, ascending straight to Heaven. However, the prisoner confounded Ottawa by remaining totally tractable, refusing to oblige by getting shot while attempting to escape.

As for me, the nearest I come to completing a divine mission is to attend church parade. In my parlous physical state I should find more solace in this ritual than I do. This despite my father's pressing into my hand – as he did with all of us departing sons – a copy of the New Testament with the admonition to say our prayers each night and morning. I lost my copy of the Scripture soon after I arrived in India to find that my brother had died suddenly and rather grotesquely.[23] What comes to my mind, while I'm lying in my bed waiting for restoration of my tiny strength, is the Gospel According to Pa. No one knows that my father wrote a little book called *The Life of Our Lord*.[24] He wrote it exclusively for us children, to be read to us when we were very young and susceptible to Christian thought. I remember Aunt Georgie sitting beside my cot, holding that sacred manuscript and reading me a chapter at bedtime. The story that impressed me was that of the loaves and fishes, because I did love going on a picnic.

Now, remembering the total impact of our Lord's life on mine, the greater revelation is that it was always my aunt, or my mother, or a servant, who read those glowing words aloud

23. Walter Dickens, weakened by a wastrel career in the Bengal Mounted Police, was about to return home on sick leave when, while talking to some friends in the Calcutta hospital, "he became excited, had a rush of blood from the mouth, and was dead." (As reported by his father.)

24. Charles forbade publication so long as one of his children lived. The last of these (Sir Henry) died in 1933, and the book appeared in 1934.

to me. I have no recollection of my father ministering in person. It was as though he had written the book, and forbidden its publication or even the removal of the manuscript from our house, as his personal penance for being Our Father who art in Absentia.

> May that other God bless you.
> Frank.

∼

> *Regina, Saskatchewan.*
> *November 10th, 1885.*

Dear Emily,

Both Louis Riel and I were brought here (Regina) under escort. His escort was measurably larger than mine, which consisted of Hospital Sergeant E. A. Braithwaite. Yes, I needed a nanny, after my journey from Battleford to reach Canada's steel stays – the railway. But I am determined to regain my form – such as it was – with proper rest and creature comforts that I believe I have earned. Whom the gods love die young, but I'm sure the gods find me too comical to ring down the curtain after Act One.

Let it be noted that I attained Swift Current without my instigating another North-West Rebellion.[25] The journey south from Battleford afforded me the opportunity to see – through admittedly bleary eyes – some of the less attractive parts of the West. When one has dined on snow-crested

25. It is difficult to determine exactly when FD left Battleford. A letter dated December 1, 1885, from the Battleford C.O. Morris to Force Comptroller White in Ottawa, enclosed a pay cheque for FD's October pay, suggesting that FD had transferred to Regina during that month.

mountains and crystal streams, one loses one's taste for bald humps and mud holes. Therefore Swift Current, whose name is the English for "Saskatchewan", and whose resident creek almost lives up to both, burst upon my senses like a vision of the future. I speak not only of the gleaming rails themselves, beckoning me eastward to the sybaritic delights of Canada's Orient, but also – behold! – my first sighting of a C.P.R. dining-room.[26]

Whether from the excitement of this manifestation of *haute cuisine*, or exhaustion from my journey south, I collapsed on my arrival. Sergeant Braithwaite was delegated to hold my hand for the bouncy leg of rail to Regina. Braithwaite also made me feel better by saying – respect glowing in his eyes – "Sir, I heard that when you ran out of ammo trying to drive off the redskins at Fort Pitt, you threw your father's watch at 'em."

"Apocryphal, Sergeant, apocryphal," I said, choosing a word not likely to enlighten him.

Regina is such a lively dot on the map that I regret that I must partake of it as a convalescent. The town lies a couple of miles east of the barracks, to distance us from the temptations that beset the thousand or so residents. (The main temptation is an old squaw who stands glumly near the railway station, waiting, with the patience of a degraded Job, for a customer whose vision is so impaired by engine soot that he will accompany her to her lonely tepee of ill fame.)

The Force has a corporal and one constable quartered at the railway station to handle telegraph messages for us. This has proved to be a convenience for me, since I am engaged in relentless pursuit of pay cheques owing from Battleford. I rarely go into the town, not only because I am still weak in the withers but because the vistas afforded by Regina – endless expanse of bald prairie in every direction, punctuated by clay-bottom puddles to which Narcissus himself would

26. As of 1883, Swift Current also boasted a dam, a roadhouse, and freight sheds.

hesitate to trust his reflection – are enough to make a fatal relapse look good. Were it not for the telegraph poles, the place would have no distant spires whatever, let alone antique towers.

Our HQ barracks are little better favoured by nature. Indeed, the sole eminence, and that visible only on clear days, is the evocatively-named Dirt Hills, on which grows a species of tree whose odour is so offensive that even the Indians have an obscene name for it. Near by, the Wascana Creek must win the admiration of the connoisseur who prefers his streams dry. As with fresh peaches at home, the Wascana appears in season. Usually this happens in the springtime (hence my missing it), but I am told that occasionally a summer cloudburst will bring it to sudden life, and everything in its path to sudden death. Obviously not your standard Avon.

The good thing about having such bleak environs is that they greatly enhance the quality of life under the cheery red roofs of our barracks. These are sumptuous by hinterland standards, and contain the last word in heating-stoves. What a luxury, not to have to keep one's ink bottle atop the stove to prevent it from freezing! More than once, in other posts, I have hurled my ink at the wall in Lutheran frustration. No need for that in this palatial Pile of Bones, which I am glad to report has already imported a European tree or two to put the wind straight up the Champs Elysées . . . one day.

On days when weather invites, I wander out of my room to watch the latest recruits brought hither by rail from the East. Selection is plainly more stringent, now that these strapping young fellows can see the West as both less distant and more domesticated. I don't impress them, as a battle-scarred veteran ought to, having no visible wounds to put on parade, not even an ear lost to frostbite. Deafness is not a demonstrable badge of courage. Admiral Nelson could put the telescope to his blind eye, and win the plaudits of history, but he who has to cup his ear is a figure of fun.

November 12th, 1885.

Before I close this letter, Emily, I must tell you about the bizarre incident that has enlivened my sojourn here at Regina barracks. One evening this week there swaggered into the mess an extraordinary figure of a man, dressed in the full, red-coated regimentals of an officer in the Canadian Militia. I judged him to be in his fifties, a tall but portly person wearing a girdle to try to reduce his years by a decade or two. The face, jaunty if somewhat jaundiced of eye, was puffy but ruddied, the black, waxed moustache tailored to a T. So help me, Emily, he was wearing a monocle! The only other officer I have seen in the West who wore a monocle gave it up shortly after the Indians started calling him "Eye-Fall-Out".

To my considerable surprise, this officer no sooner spotted me at the table than he strode over with his hand extended and his teeth exposed in a very wide smile.

"Inspector Dickens, I declare!" says he, seizing my hand in his hot, somewhat sweaty paw and shaking it energetically.

For a moment I was too dazzled to reply, staring at the rows of ribbons on the man's breast – Victoria Cross, Chevalier, Légion d'Honneur, U.S. Medal of Honour, and a half-dozen more medals marching row on row towards his belly. I noticed the rest of the mess turning to gaze at him in some awe, and replied politely: "Sir, I am he."

He sat himself down heavily, beaming in a bluff, manly way that reeked of insincerity, and leaned towards me. "Allow me to introduce myself. Name's Flashman. Major Harry Flashman. Perhaps you have heard of me?"[27]

Well, I very nearly tumbled off my chair. I had, of course, heard of Harry Flashman. The hero of the First Afghan War, and the Indian Mutiny, not to mention the charge of the Light Brigade. The one-man army outwitting American slave

27. There is no record of a Major H. Flashman in the Canadian Militia sent to subdue Riel's rebellion. It may be that, under the stress of his recent ordeal, FD's memory is playing him false.

traders . . . headhunters in Borneo . . . the mad black queen of Mozambique . . . the wildest Indians that the United States have to offer. Flashman! Truly a name to conjure with. My confounded stutter came back.

"Indeed, yes, I have heard of you, Major Flashman. I –"

"Call me 'Flashy'," says he, winking broadly. "All my friends do."

"What may I do for you, er, Flashy?"

He put his face even closer to mine, and the blast of whisky breath shrivelled my eyebrows. Nor did I care for the closer look at the chancre suppurating on his fat lower lip. "They tell me you've had a dozen years of service in the Far West, Dickie, my lad. I'll wager a bottle of good port – name your brand – that you had some lively adventures, eh? Lots of scrapes involving gunplay and nerves of steel and damned daring escapes, I'll be bound! Been captured by bloodthirsty savages a few times, no doubt? Been dragged, naked and cursing, before some gorgeous halfbreed hellion with a shape to make a rock randy? Rogered her, did you, only to have her turn on you like a tigress?" He was breathing heavily now. "Tortured you, did she, the voluptuous vixen, ordering her big brown buck bodyguards to shoot arrows at your feet, while she screams 'Sun dance, d––n you, sun dance!' "

I stared at him, incredulous. "Sir, I have never met anyone like that in my entire life," says I.

His face fell like a shot duck. "*No* one?" he says. "D––n me, man, no violent females, no grizzly-hunting mountain women, queens of the gold-mine towns . . . ?" He worried his monocle.

"Terribly sorry. But why do you ask? Surely you have had your own extraordinary exploits during our rebellion?"

He gave a loud, hearty laugh and his eyes took on a guarded look. "Of course. But a fellow doesn't like to . . . you know. But did you happen to be in the thick of the fierce battle at Cut Knife Creek?"

"No, I was not."

"Ah," says Flashy, squaring his shoulders. "I *was* there.

And a d––n dicey show it was, too. Must have been a thousand howling redskins charging us handful of Militia. So few of us it was a d––ned near rum thing."

"Then you must have met Corporal Sleigh, of my D Troop."[28]

"Sleigh? No, I don't remember a Sleigh. Don't normally chum around with the other ranks, don'cha know. Friend of yours, is he?"

"Was. He was the first man killed at Cut Knife Creek. Shot in the mouth, poor devil. Your force took him back to Battleford for burial, if you remember."

"Hate funerals," Flashman says, scowling, and with that he gets up and waddles out of the mess. Never came back, so far as I know. I hate to speculate about such a renowned hero, Emily – and I trust that you will keep my suspicions private – but I do believe that the man was trying to pick my brains, for some private purpose, and found them very lean fare. Yes, Emily, I will say it: the man's a humbug!

November 20th, 1885.

What does God say, one wonders, about the people who paraphrased His commandment by killing Louis Riel? No, my dear, I did not witness the hanging.[29] Nor did I attempt to visit him in his cell, to repay the courtesy of his Montana hospitality. Besides, Riel did not want for attention. The eyes of the entire Canadian nation – of *both* nations, French and English – were upon the man about to walk to the gallows.

The morning of the execution was so gentle, a thing of

28.   Cpl. R. B. Sleigh was one of the five men stationed in the village of Frog Lake just prior to the massacre and withdrawn at the behest of Tom Quinn, who died in the massacre.
29.   At the Regina barracks jail, November 16, 1885.

mist and hoar frost, that it was as if the Almighty were denying anyone an excuse to absent himself from the scene. Morbid curiosity is not paramount among my failings, yet I too was drawn forth by the sparkling pageant, into the compound where a rather self-conscious crowd had gathered. Outside, on the road, shuffled those latecomers who were disgruntled because limited space had denied them their wish to observe the hanging in the barracks yard. I stayed well beyond the flagged cordon, desirous to be only in the vicinity, should an angel of the Lord appear, with silver sword to slash the black flag atop the staff, and pluck the prisoner from the noose, to bear him off to higher ground and prove that, yes, indeed, God is Catholic.

Unlike the doomed Sydney Carton, Louis Riel in his last moments was not subjected to a cicada chorus of knitting-needles. I'm told that the only sound was the occasional nervous laugh from the troopers on guard, at the kind of joke that men use to buffer a situation that is larger than life. At last even I heard the thud, the thrum of a rope suddenly taking the full weight of a sturdy, pinioned man. Someone said:

"The son of a b——h is gone for sure now."

It was an accolade of a sort, quite in keeping with the respect shown by the compatriots of Madame Defarge. The French execute an Englishman, the English execute a (mostly) Frenchman, and the story is sad in both tongues. Perhaps my father's hero had the better of the quietus, but I'm told that Riel, too, died bravely, stoutly refusing the legal defence of insanity, to the end. On the scaffold, he prayed for so long that the sheriff had to set a time limit, and when Riel reached the part of the Lord's Prayer "deliver us from . . ." the sheriff signalled for the trap to be sprung. Such brusque delivery! The noose knot slipped from beneath Riel's ear during the drop, so that the fiery champion of the oppressed was strangled to death – a process which took two minutes. Carton's guillotine was more charitable.

Riel is on his way home, to St. Boniface, for burial as a

saint *manqué*. I envy him his final departure from Regina, because he knew where he was going – au Ciel. I, on the other hand, am going to Ottawa, and to what reward I know not. What a curse it is to be entirely rational!

For all of my life I have felt as though I was being groomed for obscurity. Now, at last, I have it within my grasp. I have asked the Commissioner to find me a less strenuous posting,[30] where I may be useful to the Force, but in my heart of hearts I know that there is no place in the NWMP for a creation of Charles Dickens who is too old to be pitied and too young to be "a character". This winter, for the first time since my first in this land, I see it as too vast and unfeeling for the human dimension, or at least *my* human dimension. To be comfortable in Canada a person must have at least the *delusion* of grandeur. As a transient English journalist told me: "The Mounted Policeman has put the nag in this Brobdingnag." Being tailored for Lilliput, I am chilled not only in body but in spirit to see the winter's sun hugging the horizon for warmth, and casting across the frozen snow a spear too bright to contemplate. Here in Regina the sky intimidates the land, browbeats the billiard-table plain around us. I long to see the sky once more through the window of a London flat. Suitably framed. Moderated by chimney-pots and kites that circle out of whim, not predation.

"Invalided out": that is the official term for the fate I am seeking to avoid. The words alone are enough to shiver a man's timbers.

I wish you a better Christmas, Emily.

Your friend,
Frank.

---

30. FD repeatedly applied to Commissioner Irvine for extension of his sick leave (see Appendix E). Irvine's assessment: "Since writing the above I am pleased to ascertain that Inspector Dickens has become much more steady in his habits. He is very deaf."

~

The Russell Hotel, Ottawa, Ont.
February 27th, 1886.

My dear Emily,

Your Christmas letter raised my spirits at a time when such dredging seemed altogether fanciful. Thank you, thank you. Your happiness in your marriage is infectious, and I welcome the contagion. If I have been tardy in replying, it is because I have been fully occupied at the escritoire of my hotel room here in Ottawa, firing off letters to all and sundry in the stultifying endeavour to leave the Force with something in my pocket besides the hole.

I find it humiliating that I must call upon persons of influence to secure me employment as I am leaving the Force, as I did when trying to enter it.[31] I am promised a gratuity,[32] by no less than the prime minister, but the management of this hotel does not accept promises as legal tender. Meanwhile, I have formally resigned from the Force, effective March 1st. This is my birthday present to myself – a bit late, but that is fashionable in the nation's capital. In '74 I sat here waiting for my nomination as an officer of the NWMP to be confirmed. Now, 12 years later, I sit in the same place and wait for the coins to be placed on my eyes. Sometimes I feel as though I have been caught in the web of history and, sucked of my juices, am about to be cast out as debris.

I have had ample time, in these past two months, to renew my love affair with Ottawa. Perhaps "love affair" is too strong an expression for what we feel for each other. In my private

31.   F. W. Chesson, in London, wrote to Sir Charles Tupper, pleading FD's case for a better settlement and asking for his intervention with Sir John A. Macdonald to find FD a new appointment.

32.   On January 28, FD wrote to NWMP Comptroller F. White accepting the settlement of $1000 (having originally asked for $2000).

version of Genesis, the Creator spent six days to make the world, and on the seventh day He rested, and where He sat down made the Ottawa valley. Not that the depression is totally without charm. The town itself perches on a bluff above a confluence of rivers that burble through rapids and falls with a certain Gallic verve. In terms of human life, however, this centres in Hull, Quebec, across the Ottawa River, where the logging industry keeps the inhabitants on their toes, and where, when the frozen river "breaks up", vast rafts made of logs float past on their way to Quebec City and thence to the sawmills of Europe. In contrast, the production of paper by Ottawa's civil servants never seems to go anywhere and, possibly, accounts for the rather odd smell. This paper industry is responsible for the circumstance of my sitting here waiting for my cheque, only a few hundred yards from the mills of the legislative gods – the Parliament buildings – which grind slow to the point of inertia.

The pace of life in the capital is more congealed than usual in this winter season, with the steamers unable to freight passengers and produce on the Rideau Canal, a man-made artery of commerce that saves the town from having no discernible pulse whatever. Now frozen into what the locals call "the world's longest ice rink", the Canal has tempted me to learn to skate. Although my physical resources seem better restored lately, I have so far managed to resist the opportunity to mimic *les patineurs* of Holland. I have stoutly refused even to partake of the curious sport of curling, which was introduced by Scots militia as a method of subduing the populace. My benefactor of '74, Lord Dufferin, built a curling-rink at the official viceregal residence, Rideau Hall, and I'm told that the facility counts among its patrons Sir John A. Himself, curling being one of the few sports in the world that depend on the consumption of large quantities of alcohol in order to preserve what passes for mobility.

I have passed the Prime Minister once or twice on the street, but one hesitates to offer an informal introduction to the Father of Canada in the middle of a blizzard. In my gloomier moments I wonder whether the delay in processing my gratuity may not be the way by which the Conservative leader shows his disapproval of my father's work. Pa was, after all, a fierce social reformer. That may have been of advantage in gaining the imprimatur of Prime Minister Mackenzie, a Liberal who refused to be knighted – in short, a man after my father's heart. Now, having been engaged by a Grit (for such is the term presently employed by what pass for Liberals here), I'm at the mercy of a Tory prime minister.

You know I was conceived during Pa's euphoria at being returned home from frightful America. At the moment I wish that he could have enjoyed his stay more. However, my dear Emily, I refuse to let myself become prey to the periods of depression that, after Pa's death, indentured me to the bottle. Please, please admire me for my abstinence *though sorely tried.*[33]

It is very hard to say "No" to the hotel waiter when in winter the bar is the only sociable place in the town accessible without snowshoes.

I have had the good fortune – an isolated instance, I regret to say – to meet at this hotel an American gentleman who has encouraged me to discuss my fledgling plan of a leisurely lecture tour of the United States. A fatherly, middle-aged gentleman, Dr. A. W. Jamieson not only is a devout votary of Pa's works but has enough tact not to remind me, more than is necessary, that as the god's son I have not distinguished myself in redeeming mankind.

"The American public, Captain," said Dr. Jamieson over a demure pot of tea, "has an insatiable appetite for Dickensiana. Never mind that your father gave our performance as a nation an unfavourable review. As his son, you will attract throngs of gentlemen, and particularly ladies, eager to hear your personal account of life in the Dickens family. As well

---

33. This resolution may have been eroded by the frustration of waiting for the supplementary estimates, as FD's bar bill at the Russell was exactly half that for food.

as of your military career, of course. And if you can add some comic relief, so much the better. But what can be more diverting than young Frank Dickens's observation of that lively household – the uproarious parties, the domestic rows, the medical crises? Nothing is so enthralling as to hear of the physical and moral frailties of the great, you know. It makes them a little more human, sir, to us mere mortals."

"I can start with my own deafness," I said. "Unless you think this unsound." Ignoring my attempt at humour, the doctor had the grace to shout into my better ear:

"Deafness is no handicap to the public speaker. On the contrary, he is spared hearing not only whatever he is saying but also the response of the audience. In our literary club in Moline, several of our most regular patrons of visiting lecturers are totally deaf. They simply enjoy an animated silence."

Dr. Jamieson also discounted my demurral that public speaking is not the most obvious avocation for a person afflicted with a bad stammer. "Down in Illinois our medical people are having good success curing people who stutter. There's more to speech impairment than being born with a silver spoon in your mouth."

I let the laugh die in my throat. Dr. Jamieson is plainly a good sort, the kind of American that, single-handed, can change one's opinion of an entire nation. "Stress is the main factor in stuttering," he continued. "I'll bet you don't stutter when you're good and drunk." True. "Tension will also explain your biting your nails, blinking your eyes, and grimacing." (My grimacing helped me in India, because the Hindus thought I was possessed by the Christian god and liable to have a fit that could result in an order to demolish a village.) "Have no fear, Captain, we'll put you at ease so fast down in the States – without liquor – that you'll never stammer again."

Although not totally reassured, my mind has since been mulling over the possibilities of an anecdotal account of life in the mounted police of both Bengal and British America, using such *bon mots* as those of our illustrious guide Jerry

Potts, who, when asked on a long trail by an officer, "Potts, what's beyond that hill?" replied, " 'Nudder hill."

When I look at myself in my hotel-room mirror I am forced to concede that I shall never dominate the stage as Pa did – a dynamic, vibrant figure. Wearing shoes soled and heeled to elevate me behind the podium and avoid the hazards of standing on a greengrocer's box, I must come on as Puck.

I expect to see Dr. Jamieson again in Montreal, a little junket that I believe to be absolutely necessary if I am not to be permanently crippled in the reasons for living, by these months of marking time in Ottawa.[34]

> Your obedient and almost cheerful servant,
> *François*!

PS Should you be writing to me in the near future, my mailing address in Montreal: The Windsor Hotel, 13 St. Catherine Street, Montreal, Province de Québec, Canada. En pleine ville – *formidable*!

∾

> *Windsor Hotel, Montreal, P.Q.*
> *April 6th, 1886.*

My dear Emily,

Now, this is more to my taste. Montreal is a *city*. An ebullient metropolis where a person who happens to be in a filthy mood can permit himself a temper tantrum in the street and cause no more sensation than a Quebecker paying his cab fare. The reasons for my simmering spleen are (1) that I must continue

---

34.   In a letter dated March 17 to Dr. Jamieson, FD wrote: "My claim would be a mere fleabite to Washington 'lobbyists' but it is something to me . . ." adding wryly: "Truly this is a great Country."

to importune the government for my gratuity, the bureau-
cracy moving with the glacial grinding of the nearby St.
Lawrence River (visible from my hotel room), and (2) the
need to dun a fellow officer for a bad debt,[35] a demeaning
exercise that has availed me nought but the bills for telegrams
and postage stamps.

However, my business with Dr. Jamieson shows promise
of relieving me of my dependence on the wages of virtue,
which are poor pay indeed. Despite the abundance of Montreal's churches, I am not ready to take a vow of poverty,
having been reliably informed that it is not the way to make
money. I should prefer to be able to afford an evening of
theatre. That would be the Théâtre Royale, on Côte Street,
where Pa held forth during his first conquest of North
America in '42. As I heard him tell it – before he and Ma
separated – it was a special theatrical triumph, because it
was the first time my mother took part in one of my father's
stage productions. I don't remember the names of the other
two playlets that my father stage-managed and in which he
played parts,[36] but the title that stuck in my mind was *Deaf
as a Post*. In which Pa played Gallop. In short, he summarized
my career in Canada, though I was yet to be conceived.

I leave it to the priests who study omens, the question of
whether my mother – by then a plump and red-faced matron –
who had an otherwise wretched time of it trying to keep up
with Pa's hectic itinerary through America, falling out of every
stage-coach or train carriage as though ejected by diabolical
powers, was grateful to Montreal for this fleeting moment of
sought laughter. So much so, that her next-born (me) was
predestined to come to Canada, like the returning salmon,
to spawn as many debts as my sire.[37]

35.   FD had lent the officer $120.

36.   Arranged by officers of the Montreal garrison as a charity benefit,
the May 25, 1842, program comprised Morton's *A Roland for an Oliver*,
Mathews's *Past Two O'Clock in the Morning*, and Poole's farce.

37.   In the playbill that CD sent to his friend Forster, the author

I walked over to the Théâtre Royale the other day and stood admiring its façade. The theatre smelled bad. Floods, I'm told, have seasoned it with sewage (which must confuse the critics). Outside looking in, I heard the echo of my father's robust laughter when he remembered how richly he enjoyed his own antics that night when, he said, "everything went with a roar."

April 16th, 1886.

I have been favoured with a pageant for which I needed to pay no admission charge: Montreal is in full flood. The St. Lawrence ice has risen up like children's blocks abused by naughty giants. Much of the river front has flooded dramatically, producing a curious, faintly Venetian procession of citizens getting about in all manner of improvised craft – shop doors, street planks, any furniture that floats. From my hotel window I watched a grim merchant paddling towards the older part of town aboard a chaise longue, carried away in a sense never intended for that love-seat. An urban voyageur!

The trains too are waterlogged, further delaying my interminable correspondence to extract my financial settlement from the coffers of the Treasury.[38] If the flood has also impeded delivery of a letter from *you*, I shall join Samuel Butler in moaning "O God! O Montreal!" – an expression for which he has not been forgiven locally.

Your faithful friend,
Frank.

inserted "Mrs. Charles Dickens!!!!!!!" as playing Amy Templeton in *Deaf as a Post*.
38. For FD's letter to Comptroller White, pleading for the expediting of his gratuity, see Appendix F.

PS I delayed the mailing of this letter till I had in fact heard from you. What joyful news, that you are expecting your first baby! I wish it were mine. An outrageous sentiment, but you invite excess when you tell me that you intend to name your son (if such the child is) William Francis, after Mr. Gladstone and myself. It is warming to think that two new lives are about to make their entrance – your child's, and this travelling lecturer's. Perhaps I have been infected by American enthusiasm, but Dr. Jamieson's projections of the money to be made on a lecture tour of the United States make my eyes large with wonder.

So determined am I that I have dared to mortgage Pa's watch. I'm told that Big Bear yielded the watch to his captors after the Fort Pitt fiasco, in an effort to placate the forces of law and order,[39] and like the proverbial bad penny the watch found its way back to me. I have asked a chap[40] I met in Toronto to keep the watch and cherish it with more heed than I have been able to summon. I'm confident that, if I am able to redeem it, the Canadians will take better care of my father's watch than they have of me. And one day, when I am very rich and very famous, I shall pay the ransom for the hallowed timepiece, and bring it home to England, to let your young son or daughter fondle what once lay, literally, close to the heart of Charles Dickens.

F.

39. Big Bear was sentenced to three years in Stony Mountain penitentiary, where he was baptized and broken for life.
40. F. W. Midford. The watch was collateral for a loan of $25.

～

Moline, Illinois.
June 10th, 1886.

My dear Emily,

I write to you from Richmond Farm. I sit in my room here in Dr. Jamieson's generous house, this June evening, beside the open window whose curtains are still as death, and my palm sticks to the paper as I move these words across it. Hot, hot, hot. American Mid-West hot. The very earth pullulates in heat, which makes for tall maize and short sentences.

Please excuse my addressing you in my underdr––s. This is not an epistolary perversion but a concession to the new suit that I bought in Montreal before I entrained with Dr. Jamieson for the journey to this hotbed of honeysuckle and homilies spoke by Honest Abe. The point is, in this clime I need merely to *think* of sitting in the suit to wrinkle it into a topographical map of Mexico. Mrs. Jamieson has been gracious about ironing the trousers, far beyond the hostess's call of duty, but I choose to risk being surprised in my lingerie rather than exploit her ironing-board.

The Jamieson family, all of it, is charming. The doctor himself *had* to be, to persuade me that my fortune lies here in the land of the free and the home of the brave lecturer. In his boundless optimism he reminds me of Pa. This disposition to believe that all things are possible is something I rarely encountered in Canada. Like my father, the Americans mine enormous amounts of energy from their rock-set faith that the wrongs of the world *must* yield to an exuberant whoop from the just and the good. Not being the sanguine type myself, I welcome the positive charge of electricity. Canadian diffidence may be more prudent, but a person's soul can wither from an excess of phlegm.

The Jamieson farm lies hard by the Mississippi, which is already a sturdy river this far north. Mr. Mark Twain – my father's American counterpart as a spinner of yarns about young folk caught in a pickle – has anticipated me in fishing this river for tales. The farm flourishes four miles out from Moline town, and Dr. Jamieson has treated me to several rides in the buggy to the thriving centre of industry, whose main claim to fame has been as home to John Deere, inventor of the steel plough that is turning America upside down.

The doctor's two small sons are, I fear, somewhat disappointed that I decline to regale them with my harrowing accounts of Mounties wreaking justice in the frozen North.[41] This is not modesty. Truth to tell, Emily, I cannot remember a single episode of my 12 years that I can parade with pride, or indeed with anything but chagrin. If I am to make personal experience a theme of my lectures, it must perforce be as humorous monologue, in the manner of Twain's account of his giving up smoking ("It's easy – I've done it a thousand times"). If I change the name of Big Bear to Sitting Bull I may generate a few chuckles, though I must take care not to libel the old Sioux chief, who is still a force to be reckoned with down here,[42] and quite capable of piercing me with a flaming lawyer.

I believe I can do it, Emily. I shall, naturally, be playing upon my father's name and fame, at first. But surely from so much genius there must have been sifted down to me enough grains of wit to sustain an hour's lecture. I shall try to turn the joke upon myself. The questions I shall have to endure after the lecture – "Oh, Captain Dickens, how do you feel about your grandma being Mrs. Nickleby?" – will be purgatory, but perhaps I can contrive to conclude my address by disappearing down a trapdoor. A quick and merciful exit.

41. In her memoirs, Louise Jamieson Alsterland describes how FD read to her and her young brothers from his father's novels, pausing to look up and say: "I'm glad that my father never wrote anything that was harmful for young or old to read."

42. Sitting Bull, who continued to agitate against white settlement, was arrested (Dec. 15, 1890) and, during an attempted rescue, shot and killed by his captors.

My confidence is boosted by having a little money to jingle in my pocket. The Comptroller was able to advance me $200 on my gratuity, with which I paid back my loan from Dr. Jamieson and forgave Dame Fortune for habitually dealing me cards from a marked deck. The remainder of my gratuity ($800) should shortly expand the cloud's silver lining into a full garment. Like Micawber,[43] I don't need my sky to be totally blue for me to find it blissful.

Until now, I have seen myself as one of the few unsuccessful characters that my father created. His life was one huge exclamation mark; mine, one small query. Heretofore I have been a failed eminence, the moon seen pale in a winter's-day sky. My career in the NWMP saw me reach the foothills of a new life, but somehow I failed to cross the Rockies. I have had to retreat, step by step, post by post, to the Ottawa, where this career began.

But! No more! No more a backwater born of the maelstrom of Pa's creative juices! Tomorrow I start anew, Emily. A good friend of Dr. Jamieson's, Mr. Sam Kennedy, Editor of Moline's *The Republican*, has invited me to address a meeting of the local Literary Association, the Friday Club. Preceded by dinner chez Kennedy. I have already set my face to repel any attempt to re-create the Pickwick Club. Undoubtedly I shall be shaking hands with an American version of Mr. Snodgrass and Mr. Winkle, but the social rites of the clubbable are something to which I must adapt myself, like a cat in a room full of rocking-chairs.

Of fame and fortune, I seek only a little of the latter. Celebrity I leave to my progenitor, since this globe, capacious though it is, cannot accommodate more than one Dickens with the stature of a Colossus. I shall be content to walk a trail less well blazed than the paths of glory, so long as I have

43. Who said: "Annual income twenty pounds, annual expenditure nineteen six, result happiness. Annual income twenty pounds, annual expenditure twenty pounds ought and six, result misery." (*David Copperfield*)

a dollar or two in my poke, and a letter from you in my hopes.

In my next, I shall give you a full report on the debut of Demosthenes Minor. Wish me luck, Emily!

Your friend ever – Frank.

(Ed. note: the following extract is from the letter written by Dr. Jamieson, on The Republican *stationery, June 11, 1886, to* NWMP *Comptroller White:)*

. . . [We] drove down this evening [to Kennedy's house], reaching his house at about 6 p.m. – where we remained some little time before being called in to dinner. Having sat down the Cpt. [Dickens] was helped, and after a little I noticed that he was rather slow in beginning – he then placed his hand to his breast and indicating some distress said he would retire into an adjoining room for a few minutes. We all arose from the table and went with him and left him seated by the open window (as it was very warm) and he implored us to go on with our own dinner as he would be *all right* again in a few moments, and we did so, but had hardly been again seated before Mr. Kennedy's daughter called us quickly in, as he seemed to have fainted, and as we reached him, he gave only a few labored gasps and expired. To our grief and consternation. Please be *kind enough* to inform his family, and also to let *me* know what they wish to have done. We shall place him in casket and place *temporarily* in cool vault *pending* instructions. He was in such good spirits all day and pleased at being invited to attend the meeting tonight – I am so overcome that I cannot a [*sic*] present *realize* it, and I fear my letter will not be very clear, but will write fully when I hear from you which I hope to do *soon*. I shall trust you to inform his freinds [*sic*] at once – believe me yours most sorrowfully

A.W. Jamieson M.D.

Even in the manner of his death, Frank Dickens could not escape the example of his father. Charles Dickens, too, was stricken while sitting at dinner on a warm June evening (the 8th, 1870). On this June 11, almost exactly sixteen years later, his son succumbed to the same type of stroke. The more constitutionally sturdy man lay unconscious for twenty-four hours before giving up the ghost, while Frank left the stage at once – as a good bit player should.

In her account of Frank's last dinner at the Kennedys', Mrs. Jamieson says that he complained of dizziness immediately after drinking a glass of iced water. It is idle to speculate whether it was the ice or the water that was too great a shock to his system. But it is irony compounded that a tumbler of ice water should have been Nemesis for a former alcoholic who had survived the deadly floes besetting the dreadful trip down the North Saskatchewan.

The bulk of FD's records consists of the posthumous correspondence, some between the harried Dr. Jamieson and Canadian officials or Frank's older brother Charles, in England. In a subsequent letter to Comptroller White, Dr. Jamieson reports the amount of Dickens's wealth at the time of his death: "I was sure that what money he had here was in his pocket, and at my request Mr. Kennedy, in my presence and that of another, took charge of it, exactly $43 and 25 cents, all of which was in Canadian money." "Poor Dickens" – the doctor's favourite locution – had the remainder of his gratuity ($800) delivered to Moline a few days after his death.

Among the buzzards attracted to the corpse with unpaid bills was a Toronto tailor with an account for "a fancy pair trousers – $11". Frank was probably buried in them.

Charles (Junior) Dickens and the rest of the family in England showed a polite interest in Frank's death, but declined to substantiate Dr. Jamieson's assumption that they would bear the cost of returning the body to Britain. They did, however, volunteer to pay for a small headstone. It was not till a year later that Charles, on other business in America, made the side trip to Moline to pay the family's respects to the wayward brother. (Frank's brother Alfred, on a lecture tour of the United States in 1911 with a stop in Cicero, Illinois, had a fatal cerebral embolism while staying at the Astor House, New York City, and was buried in that city.)

Thus, it was up to the people of Moline, among whom FD had lived for all of two weeks, to take up the slack of memorial. They did so with a generosity of spirit that was a tribute to them and to Frank's father. As reported in the Rock Island Argus*:*

"The secretary of the cemetery board has offered any lot they may choose for temporary or permanent use. It is hoped the body may be allowed to remain here and a suitable monument will be erected by subscription, which as a well-known gentleman said, would take about eight hours to raise a sufficient amount. It is not expected, however, that the relations will allow the brother to lie so far from home and kindred."

The pallbearers comprised the town's first citizens, including the mayor, and among the twenty-five carriages making up the funeral procession rode representatives of the exalted Deere family. The Sunday funeral service at the Moline Congregational Church coincided with Children's Day, and the minister, the Reverend C. L. Morgan, in his sermon noted the appropriateness of the occasion for the son of the author whose work was an extended eulogy for the rights of children. The coffin, too, Frank had to share with his father's shade.

The engraver of the headstone had asked for a photograph of the deceased. As the Jamiesons had none, Mrs. Jamieson drew Frank's likeness in profile, which the stonemason copied as a medallion for the stone. The lonely little grave in Rock Island Cemetery remains a curio come upon by the stroller along the rocky bluff jutting into the Mississippi. The inscription on the headstone:

In Memory of

FRANCIS J. DICKENS

*Third Son of the Distinguished
Author*

Born Jan. 15, 1844

Died June 11, 1886

Take Ye heed. Watch and Pray. For Ye know
Not When the Time Is.

Perhaps it was fitting that Frank Dickens, NWMP, *did not know when the time is, as he was able to die at a rare moment of expectancy in his life, among new-found friends, and with some hope of one day not only recovering his father's timepiece, but also having his own hour in the sun.*

APPENDIX A

~

Statement showing extra expense incurred by the Agent of the Minister of Justice in providing transport for Sub:Inspector Dickens.

November 2   Account of John R. Benson for services rendered in connection with the above

Horse & Man to Lower Fort for Horse for
Sub:Inspector Dickens $5.00

Team and Driver to White Mud & return
with Sub:Inspector Dickens & load $40.00

Feeding Sub:Inspector Dickens' Horse
13 days $13.00
                                        _____
                                        $58.00

The above account was paid Mr. Benson the 7th December by

Thomas Nixon
Agent

APPENDIX B

In a letter from Winnipeg dated November 19, 1874, FD gave to the Minister of Justice the demanded explanation for his failing to report for duty on time. The details jibe with the account in his personal letter, and his official report was forwarded with the annotation by the Commissioner:

> This explanation appears to be satisfactory. As matters have turned out it is well that Mr. Dickens returned, as otherwise E Division would have had three officers in excess of strength and D Division would have been an officer short.
>
> G. A. French, Comr.

The why and wherefore failed to satisfy the Department of Justice, however, whose Minister wrote a December 15 memorandum to Lt.-Col. French:

> The Minister of Justice considers that Sub Inspector Dickens' explanation of his delay in Toronto after receiving explicit directions to proceed on from Ottawa without any loss of time in order to arrive at Fort Garry in time to accompany Mr. Frechette to Pelly is insufficient.
>
> The time wasted in Toronto in disobedience of such positive instructions caused clearly the loss of connection. The Minister of Justice directs that the extra expense incurred in the abortive attempt to overtake

Mr. Frechette be borne by Mr. Dickens personally. Mr. Nixon has been requested to send to the Commissioner an a/c of the extra expense thus incurred.

An advance of $200 was made to Sub Inspr. Dickens before he left Ottawa to meet travelling expenses to Manitoba and the Commissioner will be good enough to direct the Paymaster to charge Sub Inspr. Dickens when he accounts for this $200 with the extra expense which Mr. Nixon reports as having been incurred.

In the event, FD had to account for his $200 advance, from which was docked $58 for the "extra expense".

(Public Archives Canada)

APPENDIX C

∽

(Penned by the Governor General, the Marquis of Lorne,
after sighting the Rockies, September 1881)

Among white peaks a rock, hewn altar-wise,
   Marks the long frontier of our lonely lands.
Apart its dark tremendous sculpture stands,
   Too steep for snow, and square against the skies.
In other shape its buttressed masses rise
   When seen from north or south; but eastward set,
God carved it where two sovereignties met,
   An altar to His peace, before men's eyes.

      (J. P. Turner, *The North-West Mounted Police.*
      King's Printer, Ottawa, 1950, vol. I, p. 599)

APPENDIX D

❧

(Extract from the alleged FD diary of events at Fort Pitt, April 1885)

Sunday April 5th.

Le Cotau Indian, arrived from Onion Lake with barrels reports Big Bear due at Bighills today, also that some of the Indians are inclined to leave him.
Stable levelled in the afternoon.
False alarm during the night.

Monday April 6th.

Sever snowstorm during night and morning
General system adopted for general use
9 special constables sworn in
Flying sentries taken off and sentries posted in each post through port holes/. Nothing unusual

Tuesday April 7th.

Fine weath. Everything quiet last night
Magazine torn down
Little Poplar and 9 teepees arrived from B'frd he asked for beef and provisions, proposed talking it over in the morning

Everything quiet during night

Wednesday April 8th.

Fine weather
Grub taken over to Little Poplar
Stockage [*sic*] and Bastion built during day (Bastion to command back of Fort.
Little Poplar reports that Indians have burnt houses at Onion Lake.
Nothing unusual last night.

Thursday April 9th.

Fine weather
Rev Chas Quinney left to scout across the river, returning in morning.
Indian Le Cotau persuaded Little Poplar to bring his camp to the bank of river.
Extra Bastion built behind Orderly Room
Everything quiet during the night

Friday April 10th.

Fine weather
Francois Dufresne and Le Cotau left to scout, they went as far as Onion Lake, and report no Indians there, Indians burnt down Farm House and priest'd house before leaving taking all provisions with exception of some 50 Bgs of Flour.
Mr Quinney scouted across the river, reports 3 teepees of Little Poplar's band missing
Nothing unusual during night.

Saturday April 11th

Fine weather

Sentries posted outside during day
Started to build scow in day, Horses excercised
Nothing unusual during night

Sunday April 12th.

Fine weather but windy, large quantity ice drifted down river
Divine service in morning
Horses excercised in morning
Dogs very uneasy during night.
Fire signals supposed to have been seen by No 1 Sentry
  (behind Mission House) during night.

Monday April 13th.

Fine weather.
Consts Loasby, Cowan & Quinn left on a scouting expedition
  to Frog Lake
A number of Indians arrived from Frog Lake, sent a letter
  demanding that Police lay down their arms and leave the
  place, they report prisoners safe. Mr Halpin accompanied
  them acting as Secretary.
Mr McLean parleyed with them and gave them grub. By
  contents of letter it appears 250 armed men are around
  Fort.
Chief Little Poplar crossed over to help McLean in pacifying
  Indians
Everything quiet during night

Tuesday April 14th.

Very windy weather.
Mr McLean still parleying with Indians, during parley the
  three scouts out yesterday rode through the camp, Const
  Cowan shot dead, and Loasby wounded in two places.
  Quinn got away. Indians there fired upon.
McLean & Dufresne taken prisoner

Indians threatened to burn fort tonight unless police left
after a great deal of danger got the other side of river all
the white people & half breeds in Pitt went to the Indian
camp as prisoners

Wednesday April 15th.

Very cold weather
travelled

APPENDIX E

❧

When his effort to extend his leave failed, FD wrote to Comptroller F. White (February 16, 1886) accepting the inevitable:

> . . . I cannot deny, however, that the disability which you point out exists, and that it has been aggravated by the breaking down of my system in consequence of the exposure and fatigue to which I have been subjected from time to time since 1874.
>
> Under these circumstances, I have no other alternative than to place my resignation at the disposal of the Minister, wishing that, in the event of the same being accepted, I may be allowed a retiring gratuity of one year's pay. . . .
>
> I would also respectfully beg that the Minister will endeavour to give me some other employment in the public service where the disability under which I labour will not be so seriously felt.
>
> I have the honour to be, sir . . .

(Public Archives Canada)

APPENDIX F

෴

On April 24, 1886, FD was writing from Montreal to Comptroller White:

> I have written you two letters since I have been here, but having received no answer think that they must have miscarried.
>
> Will you kindly let me know whether you have received my letters or not. If you have, an answer will oblige. If not, I will let you have the substance of my former communications.
>
> Yours faithfully, Francis J. Dickens.

A couple of weeks later (May 13) FD finally drew a drop of blood from the Ministry's stone, informing White:

> I received your letter of the 11th enclosing a P.O.O. for fifty dollars, this evening.
>
> I did not telegraph you as I thought I could explain matters better in a letter. I wrote to you Tuesday that I had a good opportunity of going to Rock Island County Illinois and asking for $150 to go down there. If this could be advanced I should be very glad, but the sum sent is quite sufficient for me here.
>
> Yours sincerely . . .
>
> (Public Archives Canada)

NEW AND RECENT BOOKS FROM
⟦DOUGLAS GIBSON BOOKS⟧
PUBLISHED BY McCLELLAND & STEWART INC.

ON THE SKY Zen and the Art of International Freeloading *by* Robert Hunter
"*On the Sky* is the funniest travel book written here or anywhere else in a long
time." *Vancouver Sun*   *Travel/Humour, 6 x 9, 256 pages, hardcover*

ALL IN THE SAME BOAT Family Cruising Around the Atlantic *by* Fiona McCall and
Paul Howard
"A lovely adventure that is a modern-day Swiss Family Robinson story ... a winner."
Toronto Sun   *Travel/Adventure, 6 x 9, 256 pages, maps, hardcover*

WELCOME TO FLANDERS FIELDS The First Canadian Battle of the Great War:
Ypres, 1915 *by* Daniel G. Dancocks
"A magnificent chronicle of a terrible battle ... Daniel Dancocks is spellbinding through-
out." *Globe and Mail*
                     Military/History, 6 x 9, 304 pages, photos, maps, hardcover

NEXT-YEAR COUNTRY Voices of Prairie People *by* Barry Broadfoot
"There's something mesmerizing about these authentic Canadian voices ... a three-
generation rural history of the prairie provinces, with a brief glimpse of the bleak
future." *Globe and Mail*   *Oral history, 6 x 9, 400 pages, hardcover*

UNDERCOVER AGENT How One Honest Man Took On the Drub Mob ... And Then
the Mounties *by* Leonard Mitchell and Peter Rehak
"It's the stuff of spy novels – only for real ... how a family man in a tiny fishing community
helped make what at the time was North America's biggest drug bust." Saint John
Telegraph-Journal   *Non-fiction/Criminology, 6 x 9, 176 pages, hardcover*

THE PRIVATE VOICE A Journal of Reflections *by* Peter Gzowski
"A fascinating book that is cheerfully anecdotal, painfully honest, agonizingly self-
doubting and compulsively readable." *Toronto Sun*
                     Autobiography, 6 x 9, 320 pages, photos, hardcover

LADYBUG, LADYBUG ... *by* W. O. Mitchell
"Mitchell slowly and subtly threads together the elements of this richly detailed and
wonderful tale ... the outcome is spectacular ... *Ladybug, Ladybug* is certainly among
the great ones!" *Windsor Star*   *Fiction, 6 x 9, 288 pages, hardcover*

AT THE COTTAGE A Fearless Look at Canada's Summer Obsession *by* Charles Gordon
"A delightful reminder of why none of us addicted to cottage life will ever give it
up." *Hamilton Spectator*   *Humour, 6 x 9, 224 pages, hardcover*

ACCORDING TO JAKE AND THE KID A New Collection of Stories *by* W. O. Mitchell
Jake, the Kid and his ma, and the folks of Crocus, Saskatchewan are back, in a collection of never before published stories by the author of *Who Has Seen the Wind.*
                     Fiction, 6 x 9, 280 pages, hardcover

OTHER TITLES FROM
⟦DOUGLAS GIBSON BOOKS⟧
PUBLISHED BY McCLELLAND & STEWART INC.

THE PROGRESS OF LOVE *by* Alice Munro
"Probably the best collection of stories – the most confident and, at the same time, the most adventurous – ever written by a Canadian." *Saturday Night*
Fiction, 6 x 9, 320 pages, hardcover

FOUR DAYS OF COURAGE The Untold Story of the Fall of Marcos *by* Bryan Johnson
"What may well be the best book on the Marcos-Aquino election campaign and on the 'People Power' that toppled a tyrant ...." *New York Times*
Politics/Journalism, 6 x 9, 288 pages, map and photographs, hardcover

THE RADIANT WAY *by* Margaret Drabble
"*The Radiant Way* does for Thatcher's England what *Middlemarch* did for Victorian England ... Essential reading!" *Margaret Atwood*
Fiction, 6 x 9, 400 pages, hardcover

DANCING ON THE SHORE A Celebration of Life at Annapolis Basin
by Harold Horwood, *Foreword by* Farley Mowat
"A Canadian *Walden*" (*Windsor Star*) that "will reward, provoke, challenge and enchant its readers." (*Books in Canada*)
Nature/Ecology, 5 1/2 x 8 1/2, 224 pages, 16 wood engravings, hardcover

NO KIDDING Inside the World of Teenage Girls *by* Myrna Kostash
This frank, informative look at teenage girls today "should join Dr. Spock on every parent's bookshelf." *Maclean's*
Women/Journalism, 6 x 9, 320 pages, notes, hardcover

THE HONORARY PATRON A Novel *by* Jack Hodgins
The Governor General's Award-winner's thoughtful and satisfying third novel mixes comedy and wisdom, "and it's magic". *Ottawa Citizen*
Fiction, 6 x 9, 336 pages, hardcover

RITTER IN RESIDENCE A Comic Collection *by* Erika Ritter
This collection by the noted playwright, broadcaster, and humorist reveals "a wonderfully funny view of our world". *Globe and Mail*
Humour, 5 1/2 x 8 1/2, 200 pages, hardcover

THE LIFE OF A RIVER *by* Andy Russell
This yarning history of the Oldman river area shows "a sensitivity towards the earth ... that is universally applicable." *Kingston Whig-Standard*
History/Ecology, 6 x 9, 184 pages, hardcover

THE INSIDERS Government, Business, and the Lobbyists *by* John Sawatsky
Investigative journalism at its best, this Ottawa exposé is "packed with insider information about the political process". *Globe and Mail*
Politics/Business, 6 x 9, 368 pages, photos, hardcover

PADDLE TO THE AMAZON The Ultimate 12,000-Mile Canoe Adventure
by Don Starkell, *edited by* Charles Wilkins
"This real-life adventure book ... must be ranked among the classics of the literature of survival." *Montreal Gazette*
Adventure, 6 x 9, 320 pages, maps, photos, hardcover